# Vines

# Vines

by
RICHARD H. CRAVENS
and
the Editors of TIME-LIFE BOOKS

TIME-LIFE BOOKS, ALEXANDRIA, VIRGINIA

Time-Life Books Inc.,
is a wholly owned subsidiary of
TIME INCORPORATED

FOUNDER: Henry R. Luce 1898-1967

Editor-in-Chief: Henry Anatole Grunwald
President: J. Richard Munro
Chairman of the Board: Ralph P. Davidson
Executive Vice President: Clifford J. Grum
Chairman, Executive Committee: James R. Shepley
Editorial Director: Ralph Graves
Vice Chairman: Arthur Temple

TIME-LIFE BOOKS INC.

MANAGING EDITOR: Jerry Korn
Executive Editor: David Maness
Assistant Managing Editors: Dale M. Brown (planning),
George Constable, Thomas H. Flaherty Jr. (acting),
Martin Mann, John Paul Porter
Art Director: Tom Suzuki
Chief of Research: David L. Harrison
Director of Photography: Robert G. Mason
Assistant Art Director: Arnold C. Holeywell
Assistant Chief of Research: Carolyn L. Sackett
Assistant Director of Photography: Dolores A. Littles

CHAIRMAN: Joan D. Manley
President: John D. McSweeney
Executive Vice Presidents: Carl G. Jaeger,
John Steven Maxwell, David J. Walsh
Vice Presidents: George Artandi (comptroller);
Stephen L. Bair (legal counsel); Peter G. Barnes;
Nicholas Benton (public relations); John L. Canova;
Beatrice T. Dobie (personnel); Carol Flaumenhaft (consumer
affairs); James L. Mercer (Europe/South Pacific);
Herbert Sorkin (production); Paul R. Stewart (marketing)

THE TIME-LIFE ENCYCLOPEDIA OF GARDENING

EDITORIAL STAFF FOR VINES:
EDITOR: Robert M. Jones
Assistant Editor: Sarah Bennett Brash
Text Editors: Bobbie Conlan-Moore, Margaret Fogarty,
Bonnie Bohling Kreitler
Picture Editor: Jane Jordan
Designers: Edward Frank, Albert Sherman
Staff Writers: Paul Clancy, Susan Perry
Researchers: Diane Bohrer, Marilyn Murphy,
Susan F. Schneider
Art Assistant: Santi José Acosta
Editorial Assistant: Maria Zacharias

EDITORIAL PRODUCTION
Production Editor: Douglas B. Graham
Operations Manager: Gennaro C. Esposito, Gordon E. Buck
(assistant)
Assistant Production Editor: Feliciano Madrid
Quality Control: Robert L. Young (director), James J. Cox
(assistant), Daniel J. McSweeney, Michael G. Wight (associates)
Art Coordinator: Anne B. Landry
Copy Staff: Susan B. Galloway (chief), Elizabeth Graham,
Celia Beattie
Picture Department: Barbara S. Simon
Traffic: Jeanne Potter

CORRESPONDENTS: Elisabeth Kraemer (Bonn); Margot
Hapgood, Dorothy Bacon, Lesley Coleman (London); Susan
Jonas, Lucy T. Voulgaris (New York); Maria Vincenza
Aloisi, Josephine du Brusle (Paris); Ann Natanson (Rome).
Valuable assistance was also provided by: Loral Dean
(Atlanta); Judy Aspinall, Karin B. Pearce (London); Diana
Asselin (Los Angeles); Carolyn T. Chubet, Miriam Hsia,
Christina Lieberman (New York); Mimi Murphy (Rome);
Carol Barnard (Seattle). The editors are indebted to
Margaret M. Carter, Angela Goodman, Michael McTwigan,
Rona Mendelsohn, Jane Opper and Maggie Oster, writers,
for their help with this book.

THE AUTHOR: Richard H. Cravens is a former staff member of the Associated Press and of TIME-LIFE BOOKS. Now a freelance writer whose interests range from anthropology to gardening, Mr. Cravens also wrote *Pests and Diseases* for The TIME-LIFE Encyclopedia of Gardening.

CONSULTANTS: The late James Underwood Crockett, author of 13 of the volumes in the Encyclopedia, co-author of two additional volumes and consultant on other books in the series, was a lover of the earth and its good things from his boyhood on a Massachusetts fruit farm. He graduated from the Stockbridge School of Agriculture of the University of Massachusetts and worked all his life in horticulture. A perennial contributor to leading gardening magazines, he also wrote a monthly bulletin, "Flowery Talks," distributed through retail florists. His television program, *Crockett's Victory Garden,* shown all over the United States, won countless converts to the Crockett approach to growing things. William Louis Stern is Professor of Botany at the University of Maryland, College Park. Carl A. Totemeier Jr. is Director of Old Westbury Gardens, Old Westbury, New York.

THE COVER: A Boston ivy vine displays its autumn colors—scarlet leaves and blue-black berries—while clinging tenaciously with tiny aerial roots to the side of a brick house. Boston ivy is an excellent deciduous vine for city gardens; within a few years it can cover a five-story building with its exuberant foliage.

For information about any Time-Life book, please write: Reader Information, Time-Life Books, 541 North Fairbanks Court, Chicago, Illinois 60611.

Library of Congress Cataloguing in Publication Data
Cravens, Richard H.
  Vines.
  (The Time-Life encyclopedia of gardening; 26)
  Bibliography: p.
  Includes index.
  1. Ornamental climbing plants. I. Time-Life Books. II. Title
SB427.C73        635.9'74        78-31771
ISBN 0-8094-2597-1
ISBN 0-8094-2596-3 lib. bdg.
ISBN 0-8094-2595-5 retail ed.

TIME-LIFE is a trademark of Time Incorporated U.S.A.

CONTENTS

# The vigorous, versatile climbers 1

A woman in Houston, Texas, who lives in a small apartment that opens onto a little balcony six stories above the street, has devised a high-rise, low-maintenance garden perfectly suited to her needs. On either side of the balcony she has planted clematis vines, which grow upward from tubs onto wide-mesh netting stretched from her balcony railing to the lower railing of a friend's balcony above. In the morning, when she steps outside for a cup of coffee, the big white, blue, pink and purple clematis blooms welcome her with a dazzling display; when she comes home after work, the handsome foliage screens her not only from the view of neighbors but also from the heat and glare of the late afternoon sun.

To complete her aerial bower, she has mounted a window box of English ivy on the front railing, and has trained a sweet-smelling jasmine vine to frame the glass doors leading to the living room. Just inside, she has more ivy curling around the door, flanked with hanging baskets of gracefully drooping black-eyed-Susan vines.

The Houston woman's ingenious use of four kinds of vine illustrates but a few of the many virtues of these plants—virtues often overlooked in crowded urban areas and in suburban and rural ones as well. Vines are among the most versatile and useful plants in a gardener's repertoire. Given almost any available support, from thin wires to solid masonry walls, vines provide a maximum vertical display while taking up hardly any ground space. Around outdoor living areas, vines can screen unwanted views as effectively as a solid wood fence; but they are more attractive and allow the passage of air and light. Trained to climb on overhead structures like arbors and pergolas, they can cool terraces and windows with dappled shade in the heat of summer and—if deciduous types are used—will lose their leaves to admit welcome winter sun.

Vines can enhance a decorative architectural feature, such as a fine chimney or an iron balustrade, or cover and soften an unsightly

*A 100-year-old creeping fig vine wanders across walls and rafters at the Dumbarton Oaks estate in Washington, D.C. The vine is pruned several times a year and is watered and misted almost daily in summer.*

one, such as a bare concrete wall, a chain-link fence, a downspout, an old tree stump or a storage shed. Used as ground covers, vines not only hide bare ground in short order but hold the soil on slopes and provide patterns of greenery under densely foliaged trees where grass will not easily grow.

A FEAST FOR THE EYE

Vines will also lend a wealth of color and interest to a garden. Some, like winter creeper and creeping fig, are valued for the lovely tracery of their foliage alone, while a few, like Boston ivy and Virginia creeper, are noted as well for their brilliantly changing leaf color in fall. Many have beautiful flowers, some as spectacular as the hanging purple clusters of wisteria or the orange-to-red cones of trumpet vine, while vines like jasmine and sweet autumn clematis offer the added dividend of perfumed scents. Still others have decorative fruits: the bright orange berries of bittersweet, the novel seed pods of balloon vine, the odd and varied shapes of gourds. The beauty of these features can be enjoyed inside the house as well. Sweet peas and climbing roses make fine cut flowers, while asparagus fern and English ivy make handsome foliage sprays. In addition, many vines can be grown as house plants, including many gorgeous tropical species that cannot survive outdoors in northern winters.

As a group, vines are not only versatile but have the added advantages of being vigorous, fast-growing, relatively pest free and, with some vigilance, easy to maintain. If chosen and located with care, a vine can perform one or more valuable functions with a minimum of problems and a maximum of rewards. Wrongly employed, on the other hand, it can itself turn into a persistent pest. Precisely because they are so vigorous and fast-growing, many vines can get out of hand, spreading into adjoining areas, competing with and smothering other plants, even tearing boards off a fence or shingles from the side of a house. So before using them you should know something of their nature: how they grow and what they can—and cannot—do.

STRENGTH IN WEAKNESS

First of all, it is important to realize that vines are a mode of plant behavior rather than a botanical family. Essentially, vines are any plants whose long stems are structurally so weak that they must either trail, creep along the ground, or rely on some other object (a tree, a fence post) for climbing support. Vines come in all shapes and sizes, from miniature ivy, with dainty runners a foot or two long that can curl prettily over the edge of a flowerpot, to giant jungle lianas, with stems as big around as a man's leg that can grow more than 500 feet long, clutching tall trees of the tropical rain forest in a deadly embrace. Strawberries can be grown as vines; they are relatives of climbing roses, which are also treated as vines in gardens. English ivy, one of the most popular vines used in home landscapes and interiors, is a member of the vast ginseng family of plants that includes American ginseng, used as a medicinal herb, and rice-paper plant, from which Oriental rice paper is made. Ivy's unpopular namesake, poison ivy, is also a vine but is completely unrelated botanically; somewhat surprisingly, poison ivy is a close cousin of the trees that produce delectable cashew and pistachio nuts.

Vining as a habit of growth is no accident of nature, but a trait that helped many plants survive as the rigorously competitive vegetable world evolved. More than a hundred years ago, the curious behavior of vines caught the interest of Charles Darwin, who devoted an entire book to the subject in 1875. In *The Movements and Habits of Climbing Plants*, Darwin reasoned that plants become climbers in order to reach the light. "This is effected by climbers with wonderfully little expenditure of organized matter," he noted, "in comparison with trees, which have to support a load of heavy branches by a massive trunk. Hence, no doubt, it arises that there are so many climbing plants in all quarters of the world, belonging to so many different orders."

In studying vines, Darwin and other researchers made some astounding discoveries. Perhaps the most startling was that plants, which had long been thought to be distinguished from animals by

## CLIMBING TO SURVIVE

"Watch out, Fred! Here it comes again!"

Drawing by Geo. Price; © 1939, 1967 The New Yorker Magazine, Inc.

*The reputation of vines for unceasing aggressiveness was the subject of this famous George Price cartoon, first published in 1939.*

## Circling for support

In order to raise its leaves toward the sun, a vine must find some way to attach its weak stem to a supporting object. Vines have developed a number of devices for this purpose, including coiling, threadlike tendrils, which may be modified stems, leaves or flower stalks. But a vine must locate a support before it can hold onto it. The plant does this by sweeping its growing tip or tendril in a continuous elliptical motion called circumnutation.

Charles Darwin was one of the first to recognize the circumnutation of vines, he did so while studying a milkweed vine. "The weather being hot, it was allowed to stand on my study table," he wrote in 1865, "and it was an interesting spectacle to watch the long shoot sweeping, night and day, this grand circle in search of some object round which to twine." Darwin hypothesized that all plant movements are modifications of circumnutation. The tip of every branch and every root circumnutates, although the movement is seldom as sweepingly dramatic as it is with a vine.

The circumnutation of a garden pea plant is demonstrated below in left-to-right time-lapse photographs. The plant, photographed in a laboratory under controlled conditions, made its complete elliptical sweep in 90 minutes.

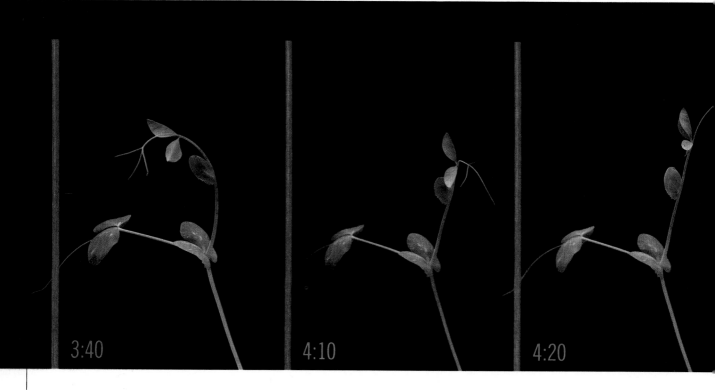

3:40    4:10    4:20

*At 3:40 p.m., a red stick is placed next to a two-week-old pea plant. The plant's three top tendrils, modified leaves, are already circumnutating. These tendrils are located at the plant's fifth node (nodes are points on the stem that bear leaves). The higher a pea plant grows, the more critical is its need to find support, so it produces successively more tendrils at each additional leaf node. The fourth node has only a single tendril, which is also circumnutating, but erratically. Although*

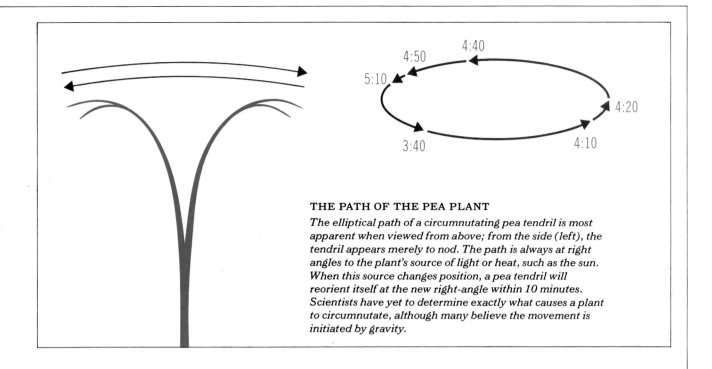

## THE PATH OF THE PEA PLANT

*The elliptical path of a circumnutating pea tendril is most apparent when viewed from above; from the side (left), the tendril appears merely to nod. The path is always at right angles to the plant's source of light or heat, such as the sun. When this source changes position, a pea tendril will reorient itself at the new right-angle within 10 minutes. Scientists have yet to determine exactly what causes a plant to circumnutate, although many believe the movement is initiated by gravity.*

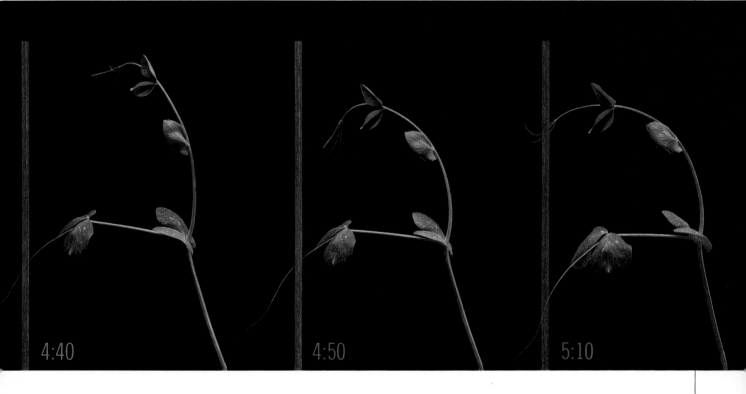

4:40
4:50
5:10

*this tendril is in contact with the stick, it is no longer "irritable"—sensitive to touch—hence is unable to coil around the stick. By 4:10, the top tendrils have swung counterclockwise toward the camera. They near the end of their ellipse by 4:20 and then swing away from the camera (4:40) and back toward the stick (4:50). By 5:10, their path brings them in contact with the stick and circumnutation stops as the tendrils begin to coil themselves around the stick.*

their lack of the power of movement, could actually move—and move so ingeniously they almost seemed to think—in situations where it was to their advantage to do so. In the evolutionary scheme, vines seemed to be a highly aggressive and resourceful intermediate form between earth-hugging shrubs and sky-reaching trees. The phenomenon was most strikingly observed in tropical rain forests where the growth was so dense and luxuriant and the competition for sunlight so keen that a species had little chance of survival unless it either adapted to living in the shade or somehow broke through the canopy above.

**ONLY WAY TO GO: UP**

Faced by this challenge, many species became scandent—from the Latin *scandere,* to climb—developing a variety of methods of scrambling, twining, hooking or otherwise grasping at anything in their path, including one another, in order to go one way: up. Not unlike some humans, these vines seemed programed to succeed at all costs, even if they smothered, strangled or pulled down their fellows. Moreover, they gained their places in the sun with remarkable economy and speed. By using any rigid support within their reach, they dispensed with the long, energy-consuming task of building up strong structural fibers like those of trees. A cross section of a vine's stem was found to resemble a thin-skinned pipe, or a collection of pipes, masterfully designed for quick growth, flexibility and the efficient conduction of water and nourishment to leaves and growing shoots that might be several hundred feet away, high in the jungle canopy.

What continued to intrigue and confound many botanists, however, was the utter changeability of these plants, apparently depending on the circumstances in which they grew. A South African species named *Podranea brycei* was reported by one expert observer to be a shrub 1½ to 2 feet high; another observer in a different location said it was a climbing shrub with long, flexible stems growing 6 to 8 feet in a season; a third referred to it as a strong-growing, showy vine that sent out long, waving branches that turned woody and thickened with age; and a fourth crowned the argument by calling it a full-fledged tree. Another African species was found to grow as a shrub in full sunlight, but if crowded by taller plants it became scandent and climbed 30 feet or more to their tops in a vining example of one-upmanship.

**A FATAL SUPPORT**

That many vines are in reality frustrated trees is probably most dramatically illustrated by a number of so-called "stranglers" or "murderers," including members of the fig or *Ficus* genus native to Brazil. Some fig species grow into sizable trees in normal fashion, but many begin as vines and use trees as their supports while they are getting started, eventually throttling their hosts in order to take their places as trees.

The seed of a strangler fig, carried aloft by a fruit-eating bird or bat, often lodges in a small pocket of organic debris high in the branches of a tree. As the seed sprouts, it begins to send roots down along the trunk toward the earth and leafy stems twining up toward the sun. When the roots find nourishment in the soil of the jungle floor, the strangler's growth quickens; its leaves mingle with and gradually overshadow those of the tree; new roots and stems form, thicken and harden around the trunk, slowly enveloping the tree in an ever-tightening strangle hold that cuts off water and food. By the time the host tree finally succumbs, the roots of the strangler have fused together into a stout, almost continuous buttress-like structure around the tree's trunk so that the fig, which started as a vine, can now stand independently as a tree, with a self-supporting trunk and a rigid, branching canopy of leaves. In its final stage the strangler may show no visible signs of its murderous history, looking just like any other jungle tree. Cut through the massed roots of its trunk, however, and you would find a good-sized cavity—a tomb for its victim's decomposed remains.

Few gardeners in temperate zones will ever witness a life-and-death struggle on such a scale, for the twisting, twining world of vines, exemplified in the fierce competition of the tropics, dwindles in intensity with distance from the equator. The farther north one goes the fewer and less vigorous the climbers become; even a southerly state like Texas has less than a score of native vines, compared with the 870 species of Burma, a region of about the same size. Still, there are plenty of vines that will grow in the cooler regions, and some, such as wisteria, are vigorous and competitive enough to recall, on a smaller scale, the habits of jungle vines. Examples of arborescence—the phenomenon of a vine becoming treelike in appearance or behavior—can be seen in such vines as creeping fig and English ivy. In their youth these plants will cover a wall with neat, small-leaved, well-behaved foliage, then in maturity pull a Jekyll-and-Hyde act by reaching out beyond side walls and roof line in a forest of stiff, coarse-leaved branches that look like a fright wig unless pruned every year.

Probably the most familiar characteristic of vines, however, particularly in the warmer, moister sections of the South, is their tendency to grow—and grow and grow—wherever they are planted and in a lot of places they are not. One observer reported a single wisteria vine, with a trunk as thick as a python's body, that had been trained to encircle its owner's entire yard. Another over-

## THE GRAPEVINE TELEGRAPH

*The popular phrase for passing on gossip and rumor, "heard it through the grapevine," originated in 1859 and described the sad fate of a telegraph line laid over the Sierra Nevada mountains, linking Placerville, California, and Virginia City, Nevada. Wind and snow soon stretched and snapped the line, which was strung from tree to tree, tossing the wires to the ground in useless, tangled loops. Local journalists disparagingly dubbed the failed project the "grapevine telegraph." The phrase caught on during the Civil War, when unreliable word-of-mouth accounts of often fictitious battles were said to have arrived via the "grapevine telegraph."*

## TOO MUCH TOO SOON

zealous plant is the famous—or infamous—kudzu vine, a common sight along Southern roadsides where its stems grow as much as 60 feet a year. Originally imported from Asia and put to work as a ground cover to save eroding lands, this handsome member of the pea family has taken over thousands upon thousands of acres, not only the cut banks and ravines where it was first planted but whole fields, forests and buildings as well. Growth-regulating chemicals sprayed around its edges have held it more or less at bay in critical areas, but it has more than earned its reputation as "the vine that ate the South."

FIVE CLIMBING METHODS

All vines grow by elongating their stems, some faster than others, though fortunately not even kudzu is able, like Jack's beanstalk, to reach the sky overnight. More interesting, and a good thing to keep in mind when considering their garden use, is how the lengthening stems of vines manage to climb. A leading student of vines, Dr. Edwin A. Menninger, counts 30 distinct methods of climbing, all essentially variants of five basic processes. Plants like allamandas and cape honeysuckles are "leaners" or "trailers" that flop around more or less helplessly, reclining against other plants or objects unless tied to posts or trellises to keep them upright as they grow. Others like bougainvillea and rambler roses are equipped with thorns that help keep their stems from backsliding by catching onto anything they touch. (The biggest of the thorn climbers are the giant rattans or climbing palms of the tropical forests, which thrash around with spiked whips until they catch onto a support; though hardly suitable for gardens, such monsters are sources of split rattan useful in home furnishings.) "Weavers" are a bit more efficient in their

(continued on page 19)

# Queen of the climbers

*Among the rare plants that Elizabethan sailors brought home to England in 1569 was a captivating Spanish clematis vine, C. viticella. It had dainty saucer-shaped flowers and was initially dubbed virgin's bower as a tribute to Queen Elizabeth I. England eagerly imported other small-flowered clematis species, but American gardeners showed little interest in the vine until 1866 when Francis Parkman, historian and ardent horticulturist, exhibited Jackman clematis, the first large-flowered hybrid, in Boston. Now one of America's most popular flowering vines, clematis offers gardeners hundreds of species and hybrids in a wide range of shapes, sizes and colors. Many are winter hardy in the northern United States.*

*Clematis' ropelike branches have leaf stalks that act like tendrils, winding around supports. Its flowers, which consist of enlarged sepals rather than petals, are often fragrant and are followed by decorative feathery seed heads. Trained over a trellis, wall or slope, clematis will bloom profusely as befits its modern appellation, queen of the climbers.*

*Two clematis hybrids, The President (right) and Nelly Moser (center) brighten a stone wall with their flowers.*

# A kaleidoscope of bloom

BIG PETAL CLEMATIS: *A native of China and Siberia, its nodding lavender flowers have a feathery texture.*

WILLIAM KENNETT: *It grows up to 20 feet, producing large summer flowers eight inches in diameter.*

HENRYI: *Large bright-eyed flowers appear on this vigorous hybrid, here growing over a holly shrub.*

VILLE DE LYON: *Given a southern exposure, it will be awash with red flowers from July to September.*

RAMONA: *Introduced in 1874, this hybrid's lavender flowers resemble a child's whirligig.*

SWEET AUTUMN CLEMATIS: *Displaying a sea of starlike flowers, this dense vigorous and very fragrant vine climbs the side of a brick house.*

DUCHESS OF EDINBURGH: *Its scented flowers appear on branches 10 feet tall.*

SCARLET CLEMATIS: *A hardy native of Texas, it blooms profusely in late summer.*

JACKMAN CLEMATIS: *A fast climber, it was the first large-flowered hybrid.*

ERNEST MARKHAM: *This fall bloomer was named after a famous English hybridizer.*

**GOLDEN CLEMATIS:** *Its bell-shaped flowers, an unusual golden color, start blooming in late summer and are followed by stunning silky seed pods.*

method; Confederate jasmine, for example, holds itself up by growing in and out of a wire mesh or trellis.

"Rooters" make up the fourth broad category of vines. These produce clusters of small roots at each junction of stem and leaves or branches as they grow. Rooters include many familiar vines like English ivy and periwinkle, which make good ground covers because they anchor the soil with their roots and cover it with foliage as they spread. Species like English ivy will creep along the ground, then ascend wherever they encounter a vertical surface, anchoring their roots in every crack or rough spot they can find. Thus, they can be planted to climb brick or stone walls unaided by trellises, but because they wedge strong stems between boards they can also cause damage if they are allowed to come in direct contact with clapboard or shingle siding.

Most vines, however, come under the general heading of "graspers," of which there are in turn several basic kinds. The biggest group consists of the "twiners," which include such old favorites as morning glories, climbing jasmines, wisterias and sweet peas. Twiners simply go around and around the nearest vertical support, guided by their sensitive growing tips. Some, like the hop vine, habitually circle in a clockwise direction (viewed from above); others, like the morning glory, move counterclockwise; but most do not seem to care and will go either way. The growing tip of a twiner shoots up through the soil and immediately begins to perform a trick called circumnutation, a slow rotary movement that might more simply be called "feeling around." If the tip comes into contact with a horizontal object like a fence rail, it will usually back off and keep on circling, but if it strikes a vertical object like a fence post or the trunk of a tree, it will concentrate its rotary movement on this support, twining around it as it grows.

Another large group numbered among the grasping vines are the "clingers," which produce delicate, threadlike organs called tendrils. Depending on the species, tendrils may grow from the petioles, or leaf stalks, from the leaves themselves, from the flowers or from the plant's main stems. In their early stages of growth, tendrils reach outward exploring for a contact, often circumnutating to increase their chances of a hit. Once a contact is made, friction produces a stimulus that automatically causes the tendril to stop circumnutating and to coil around the object, faster and faster as the friction on the inside surface intensifies. Some tendrils have an extraordinary sensitivity and reaction time, starting to coil in as little as five seconds after contact is made; those of the bur cucumber will respond when a length of thread weighing only seven billionths of an

**CIRCLING WITH A GOAL**

**HOW TENDRILS WORK**

ounce is drawn across them, a contact that produces no sensation whatever on human skin. As a tendril makes itself fast to an object, it becomes strong enough to support the vine's growing weight, at the same time forming an elastic spiral, much like a shock absorber, that protects the vine from being torn loose in a wind.

Other vines are "stickers," gluing rather than coiling themselves to a support. At the ends of tendrils, branchlets or aerial roots, these vines develop small adhesive discs that attach to flat surfaces like walls where other types of vines cannot get a grip. A familiar

## The vine's art of escalation

Except for leaners like allamanda, most vines are equipped with some built-in means of clambering up any available support.

Thorn-climbers such as rambler roses have prickles that prevent the plants from backsliding, while

## Adapting for the climb

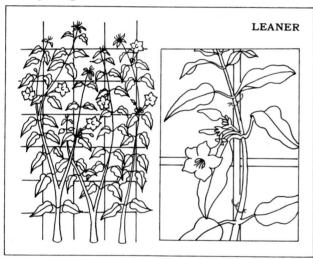

LEANER

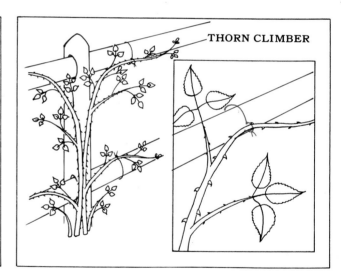

THORN CLIMBER

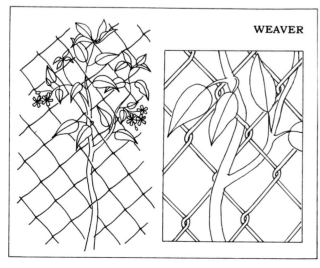

WEAVER

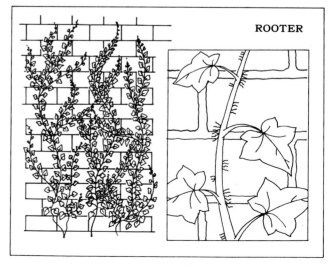

ROOTER

example is the ivy that covers the walls of the Ivy League colleges in the northeastern United States; it is called Boston ivy, though it might more accurately be called by its alternate name of Japanese creeper, being a native of the Orient. Like many clinging vines, Boston ivy needs the stimulus of a rough surface like brick to develop its sticky fingers; when it contacts a smooth surface like glass, no discs form. It is also an example of the adaptability of many vines that respond to the situation at hand. If planted next to a wire-mesh fence, Boston ivy will not develop discs but instead will climb

weavers like star jasmine will wend their way in and out of chain-link fences and trellises. English ivy has tiny aerial rootlets that attach it to almost any surface, while the twining stems of a morning glory will climb a taut string or wire.

Delicate-looking tendrils of surprising strength secure grapevines to their supports; and Boston ivy's tendrils sprout adhesive discs at their tips. Finally, some heavy jungle vines, needing substantial support, grow sharp, effective hooks.

## Four kinds of graspers

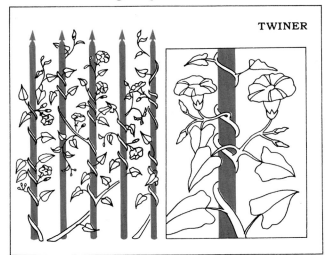

TWINER

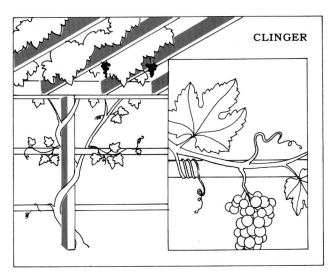

CLINGER

STICKER

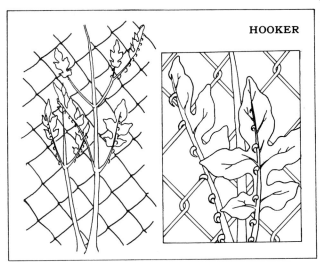

HOOKER

## MYTHS OF IVY AND GRAPE

by the simpler method of weaving in and out. Similarly, grapevines commonly hang onto thin supports like wires by means of coiling tendrils, but if planted next to walls they may develop adhesive discs on the ends of the tendrils or force their tips into crevices where they swell into balls of sticky tissue that cement the vines to the walls.

A fourth kind of grasper develops hooks on its branches, shoots or leaves to grip any object and support the vine's weight. These vines are natives of tropical jungles; one bears the odd name *Quisqualis*—Latin for "who? what?" reflecting the emotions of the Dutch botanist, George Edward Rumpf when he discovered it.

Because vines grow, climb and cling so actively and in so many ways, they are a source of satisfaction for the plant-watching instinct in every gardener. People have also found vines satisfying for other than strictly botanical reasons. Through history, undoubtedly the most widely domesticated vines have been members of the genus *Vitis,* the grape; in many languages the word for vine has been either a synonym for, or closely allied to, the word for wine. In ancient civilizations much industry went into the planting of grapes, and the harvest was celebrated with a special abandon that occurred with no other crop and at no other time of year. In Greek mythology, the god of the vine, Dionysius, and his Roman counterpart, Bacchus, presided over rites in which all cast restraint to the winds. Women were said to throw themselves into the festivities with exceptional vigor, dancing, singing, banging on musical instruments and—according to the myths—tearing limb from limb sacrificial wild animals.

Somewhere along the way another well-known vine, ivy, got tangled up in the tradition of the grape. In Greece it was called Cissos after a nymph who danced with such joyful frenzy at a feast of the gods that she fell dead at the feet of Dionysius. He was so moved by her death that he turned her into ivy, so that she could continue with her joyous and graceful embrace of everything near. Bacchus and his guests are usually pictured wearing ivy wreaths, as often as not a little askew. The Roman emperor Nero, too, whether drunk or sober, reputedly wore a crown of ivy as he fiddled away while Rome burned. Whether or not ivy was worn in hopes of avoiding total intoxication or painful hangovers is a matter of dispute, but its association with Bacchus persisted into Chaucerian times. Probably the first signs made to advertise commercial saloons were alestakes, poles garlanded with ivy and placed near the entrances of wayside huts and tents, and before long many pubs in England sported names like "The Ivy Inn" or "The Ivy Green."

In the late 19th Century the British passion for ivy—not only in bars but in ivy-covered castles and universities as well as in

Wedgewood china, which was decorated in ivy motifs—took root in America, where "English" ivy, *Hedera helix,* became all the rage, climbing on buildings, sprouting indoors in pots and appearing in designs on wallpaper, objets d'art and Tiffany dinner plates. (In point of fact, there are now more than 100 different varieties of *Hedera helix*, varying widely in leaf shape, size and color; what most people confidently call English ivy when they encounter it in gardens and on walls is more likely to be Irish ivy, *Hedera helix hibernica,* a large-leaved variety that is the fastest-growing of the winter-hardy ivies used outdoors.) Most of the ivies are still favorites, not only for their handsome foliage and their connotations of tradition and Old-World charm, but for their ability to survive in shade and for their undemanding way of growing steadily and remaining green year round in all but the coldest climates.

Other vines have their devotees too. For many gardeners who remember fondly the vine-covered porches and gardens of their childhood, no summer would be complete without the colorful flowers of clematis or morning glories, the sweet fragrance of honeysuckle, the flaming early autumn leaves of woodbine or the bright orange berries of bittersweet.

**CHILDHOOD MEMORIES**

Vines, indeed, seem to have a special charm for children of all ages. They summon up images of Jack the giant-killer climbing his beanstalk or Tarzan with his liana vine swinging through the trees, or they recall the products of fruiting vines like squashes, gourds and pumpkins and in turn the old-fashioned pleasures of harvest season and the magic of Halloween.

Perhaps the ultimate fascination of vines, though, is simply their vitality as growing things—their remarkable ability to spring swiftly from the ground, search out their places in the scheme of nature and cling tenaciously to life under the most unlikely circumstances. Because of such traits, vines were put to the highly practical, if unaccustomed, use of military camouflage during World War II. In parts of Southeast Asia, British units used morning glories to conceal gun emplacements and ammunition dumps. Within three months of planting, the sites had been so nicely overrun they were undetectable even in the sharpest aerial photographs. A particular species with pinkish flowers that grew naturally on sandy beaches was pressed into service to hide a battery of long-range coastal guns from enemy view. Each time the big guns were fired, the blast blew every bit of greenery clean off the concrete aprons in front of them. But the battery commander was undismayed. "In a fortnight," he explained, "we persuade new runners from the old roots to grow across from both sides."

**WARTIME CAMOUFLAGE**

# Choosing and using outdoor vines 2

"A physician may bury his mistakes," architect Frank Lloyd Wright once said, "but an architect can only plant a vine." The camouflaging value of vines is indisputable. In just a few short months, a Virginia creeper, a silver lace vine or a sweet autumn clematis can spread a soft green blanket over a raw expanse of concrete wall, the side of a humble tool shed or a fence that is strictly utilitarian. But this is barely half the story. Other equally valuable functions that vines can perform include enhancing desirable architecture, providing shade, covering and holding an eroding slope, or adding texture and color— sometimes in unexpected ways.

Along a Long Island country road, for example, a homeowner has adorned a row of towering locust trees with climbing hydrangeas that mount the bare, high-branching trunks. In late spring, large white flower clusters bedeck the stately trees, making them look like elegant ladies dressed for a ball. In nearby Brooklyn, a single venerable wisteria dominates a small garden behind a brownstone house. The fragrant purple flower pendants hang from an arbor attached to a brick wall built before the Revolutionary War by Robert Livingston, a member of the Continental Congress. Nor are vines notable only for flamboyant bloom. The foliage of many species is also decorative, ranging from the finely fringed ¾-inch leaves of a wire vine to the 10-inch pads of the crimson-glory-vine grape; from the coarse texture of Dutchman's-pipe to the waxy sheen of Algerian ivy. Leaf growth may be dense and impenetrable, or it may be loose and open, yielding glimpses of wall texture beneath.

Given such a wealth of characteristics, the main challenge lies in selecting the right plant for the purpose. Several things must be weighed: personal taste, the design of house and garden, your general climate zone and conditions that prevail in the microclimate of the garden itself. Equally important is the vine's behavior: how fast it grows, how large it can get, how it attaches itself to a surface or

*Rising from the ground through planting pockets in a concrete step, Boston ivy creates pillars of lush foliage outside an enclosed porch. The large deciduous leaves turn a brilliant crimson color in autumn.*

what kind of support it needs, whether it is a perennial or an annual that will have to be replaced each year, whether it is deciduous or will remain evergreen the year around. All of these traits are described for individual vines in the encyclopedia chapter *(page 89)* and are summarized in the chart that begins on page 148. In choosing any vine, however, there are certain broad guidelines that you should follow.

First, of course, is climate, which restricts choices in most of the country, especially in northern regions where many vines cannot survive the winter cold. Whenever you consider a specific vine for your garden, consult the map on page 146 to determine the zone you live in, then check the vine's listing in the encyclopedia chapter to see if it will thrive where you live.

WINTER HARDINESS    Even in Zone 2, the lower Canadian interior, a few vines can be grown, among them the American bittersweet, a remarkable plant that is actually a native as far south as South Carolina and Tennessee. Zone 3 adds such vines as trumpet honeysuckle and Virginia creeper, but a broad selection really begins with Zone 4, a band that extends from southern Maine to the north-central Plains states, where winter temperatures drop as low as $-30°$. Many vines valued for their foliage, flowers or fruit can be grown in this region, among them clematis, silver-lace vine, porcelain ampelopsis, climbing hydrangea and Japanese wisteria. Only a few, however, will remain evergreen in this region, even through mild winters; these include periwinkle, Hall's honeysuckle, five-leaf akebia and the hardier varieties of English ivy, such as Baltic ivy.

As a general rule, the vines that will survive in Zone 4 will do even better farther south, growing more vigorously and becoming more evergreen as the climate becomes balmier. There are exceptions; some deciduous vines of the north require a period of cold because they must go through a dormant phase each year. But in the subtropical climate of Zones 9 and 10, including Florida, southern Texas and parts of California, the list of choices expands greatly, embracing the whole spectrum of flamboyant tropical climbers—bougainvillea, jasmine, wax plant, passionflower, blood-red trumpet vine and flame vine among them.

THE SHADE HANDICAP    Wherever you live, check your selections with a local nurseryman, an agricultural extension agent or a knowledgeable gardening neighbor. Special conditions in your garden may influence your choices. Dense shade, for example, may suggest English ivy or common periwinkle. In partial shade, flowering clematis, climbing hydrangea and silver-lace vine will grow, but the darker the shade the less likely they are to bloom. Another common problem is soil

# Dangerous dead or alive

*"Leaflets three, leave it be."* That simple rhyme has taught countless school children to avoid poison ivy, the most virulent of all North American vines. Since Colonial days, poison ivy has been notorious for the serious rash it inflicts when touched.

The rash is caused by an oil in the plant. Some people are more allergic than others—although sensitivity may vary with age or the changing chemistry of the skin.

Like many allergies, poison ivy sometimes is treated by desensitizing the sufferers with shots or capsules, but the best protection against it may be simply to recognize it and avoid it.

As the children's rhyme suggests, poison ivy has distinctive compound leaves. Each leaf has three oval leaflets, glossy on top and hairy beneath. In autumn, the leaves turn a brilliant red-orange, which sometimes causes the plant to be confused with Virginia creeper. The leaves of the latter,

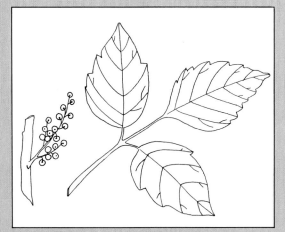

however, have five leaflets (in addition, its autumn berries are blue; those of poison ivy are white).

Needless to say, poison ivy should be eradicated as soon as it appears. To do so successfully, you must kill all its roots *(below)*. Remember that, even when dead, poison ivy is dangerous to touch. Never burn it, for the toxic smoke can cause an infection more serious than one caused by contact with the plant itself.

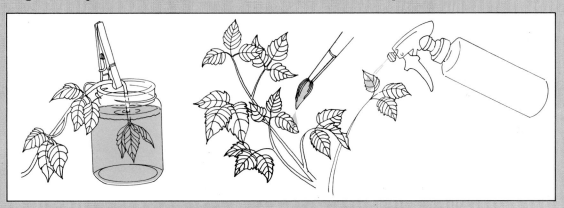

To eradicate poison ivy without endangering nearby plants, fill a wide-mouthed jar with the herbicide sold for this purpose at garden centers and hardware stores. Dip the top of the vine into the jar *(left)*, using a wooden clothespin to hold it in place. The poison will travel down to the roots, killing them. The herbicide can also be applied to a few leaves with a small paintbrush *(center)*. For larger infestations, use a sprayer that emits the fluid in a narrow, concentrated jet *(right)*. Always wear protective gloves and clothing. After handling the vine, wash with strong laundry soap.

that is constantly moist; vines such as yellow star jasmine, virgin's-bower clematis or trumpet vine will tolerate wetness around their roots. In the opposite situation—a dry, windy hillside with sandy, fast-draining soil—plants like trumpet honeysuckle, Boston ivy and creeping fig will survive without a constant need for watering. A wider range of vines can be grown in either situation if the drainage is altered—in wet places by the addition of a layer of gravel under the soil or the use of a raised bed, in dry areas by mixing a generous amount of moisture-retaining humus or peat moss into the soil and then covering the surface with a protective mulch *(page 57).*

VINE WALLS AND FLOORS

As you narrow your choices to plants that will thrive in your garden, consider the functions you want them to perform. Most vines grow rapidly and take little ground area, so they are useful in defining outdoor living spaces. In landscape design, these outdoor spaces are often regarded as extensions of indoor living spaces, with their own "floors," "walls" and "ceilings." All of these functions may be filled by vines; since vines climb, they suit the vertical dimension naturally, but many can be equally utilitarian, and decorative, when grown along the ground.

Grass is the most common outdoor flooring material, but there are many places where it does not grow well or is hard to care for. In such troublesome areas, vines provide an inexpensive, handsome ground cover, blanketing rocks and concealing other uneven areas as they creep along and send down roots to anchor the soil.

THE GROUND COVERS

Near other plantings or the house, the best horizontal vine choices are those that will not quickly get out of control. Among the best is common periwinkle *(Vinca minor),* also known as creeping myrtle. It thrives in sun or shade, bearing small, glossy leaves that form a low mat and are evergreen even in northern zones. Though it spreads rather slowly, it requires almost no attention. In milder climates its relative, greater periwinkle *(Vinca major),* has longer runners and larger leaves but otherwise possesses the same engaging traits. Its variegated form has white-striped leaves. Northern gardeners know this plant as vinca vine and let it trail over the edges of the plant containers that they move indoors in winter.

Other reasonably well-mannered vines—they need only an occasional trimming to keep them neat—are winter creeper, especially the variety with leaves that turn reddish purple in winter, and that jack-of-all-trades, English ivy, whose winter-hardy varieties stay green the year around even in northern states. English ivy, like periwinkle, can be grown in the shade around trees, where grass is hard to maintain. It provides a background for spring-flowering bulbs, concealing their yellowing foliage after the flowers are gone.

There are other vines that are valued as ground covers for large areas, where a bolder scale is desirable and where there is ample room to spread. Hall's honeysuckle, notable for its fragrant white flowers in late spring and early summer, is widely used to control erosion on open, sunny slopes. If there is a chance that it might intrude where it is not welcome, a better choice might be Henry honeysuckle, which resembles Hall's but spreads less vigorously and remains green in winter farther north. Akebia, whose five-leaflet leaves have a fine, distinctive texture, thrives in almost any soil and remains green late in the year, but it can spread as much as 15 feet in a single season and it will twine up anything within reach. Bittersweet is also an enthusiastic twiner, even entwining its own stems to form lumpy mounds when grown as a ground cover. Virginia creeper provides a quick ground cover, especially if runners are occasionally lifted and moved over bare patches of ground. Pruning Virginia creeper from time to time will induce dense, compact growth; used near a tree or stone wall, it will ascend to create a picturesque effect.

This ability of some vines to climb so willingly makes available an even broader selection of plants that can be used to define or embellish the vertical walls of outdoor rooms. Familiar to everyone is the traditional ivy-covered wall, which has a cooling effect in summer as it softens awkward angles and stark architectural lines. Though English ivy and Boston ivy are most commonly used, they are not the only choices, nor necessarily the best. Although a stucco surface might need to be totally concealed by a dense-foliaged ivy, a handsome brick or stone wall can be partly revealed through the delicate tracery of a lighter, more graceful vine like common winter creeper, with its inch-long leaves, or Low's creeper, with dainty foliage that turns brilliant red in fall, or climbing hydrangea, with lacy white flowers in early summer. If only a single feature needs softening—a porch pillar, for example, or a bare drainpipe—consider a light but vigorous twining species like silk vine, fleece vine or five-leaf akebia. Even more dramatic in the South is Chinese gooseberry, a climber with young red leaves that turn dark green with silvery undersides.

Being spread over an expanse of wall exposes a maximum amount of any vine to light and warmth, including that reflected from the wall. This in turn encourages maximum formation of flower buds, resulting in rich displays of flowers and berries. Most vines will produce their largest leaves and most abundant flowers in full sun, assuming they have ample moisture and nourishing soil. However, the evergreen leaves of vines like winter creeper and English ivy

A FOLIAGE WINDOW FRAME

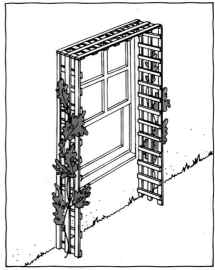

*To make a small trellis to guide vines around a window, build a frame the width of the window and the height from the ground to the window's top. Use lengths of 2-by-2 redwood or other rot-resistant lumber. Staple or nail lath strips onto the frame to form a lattice. Set the trellis in place and nail it to the window casing or the wall of the house. For a higher window, a shorter trellis can be fastened to a window box or an outdoor shelf that will hold potted vines.*

A WALL DISPLAY

sometimes die back in winter where they are exposed to the sun. This is often attributed to cold, but it is more likely due to the drying effects of the winter sun and wind; leaves lose moisture that the frozen roots are unable to replace and thus become desiccated. For this reason, it is wise to favor a northern or eastern exposure for such evergreen vines in cold-winter regions.

**TO CAMOUFLAGE A FENCE**

Vines can be used to beautify freestanding walls and fences as well as houses. The barrier that most often requires disguising is the common chain-link fence, chosen for reasons of privacy or security rather than beauty, or perhaps because it is required by a zoning code to surround a swimming pool. A dense, large-leaved, fast-growing grape or Dutchman's-pipe vine will, in short order, all but obscure such a fence. A flowering variety such as silver fleece, bougainvillea, trumpet vine, yellow-flowered Carolina jessamine or twining akebia will make it beautiful as well, causing it to resemble a flowering hedge more than a wire fence. A quick camouflage for any fence can be achieved with a vigorous annual vine like a morning glory, sweet pea or scarlet runner bean. One of these can be used to cover an unattractive surface while a slower but permanent perennial vine is becoming established.

Climbing vines can be used to solve many problems of screening in the garden—perhaps to intercept a neighbor's view of your terrace (and vice versa), or perhaps to separate a formal outdoor living area from a cluttered play space, a vegetable or cutting garden, a compost pile or even a service yard with garbage cans. If a nearly solid screen is wanted, you may need a sturdy framework built of posts or pipes *(page 33)* and covered with a broad-leaved vine like a porcelain ampelopsis, which has close-growing 5-inch leaves and decorative berry clusters that change from lilac to yellow, then to blue as they mature. But if your object is merely to suggest a division, without cutting off light and breeze, a more open-textured vine such as a large-flowered clematis or a trumpet honeysuckle can be grown on wires, strings or netting.

**BLOCKING THE SUN**

Finally, vines can also be used overhead as the final element of an outdoor room, the ceiling, providing pleasant, sun-dappled shade for sitting areas and house windows, with dividends of flowers, fragrance and fruit at close range. A popular choice for an overhead trellis or pergola is Chinese wisteria; several growing seasons may pass while it is getting established, but eventually it will develop strong stems that will produce handsome foliage and hanging clusters of scented lavender flowers for a generation or more. But if you live in the Deep South, you may prefer the traditional porch decoration, one of the brilliantly colored varieties of bougainvillea.

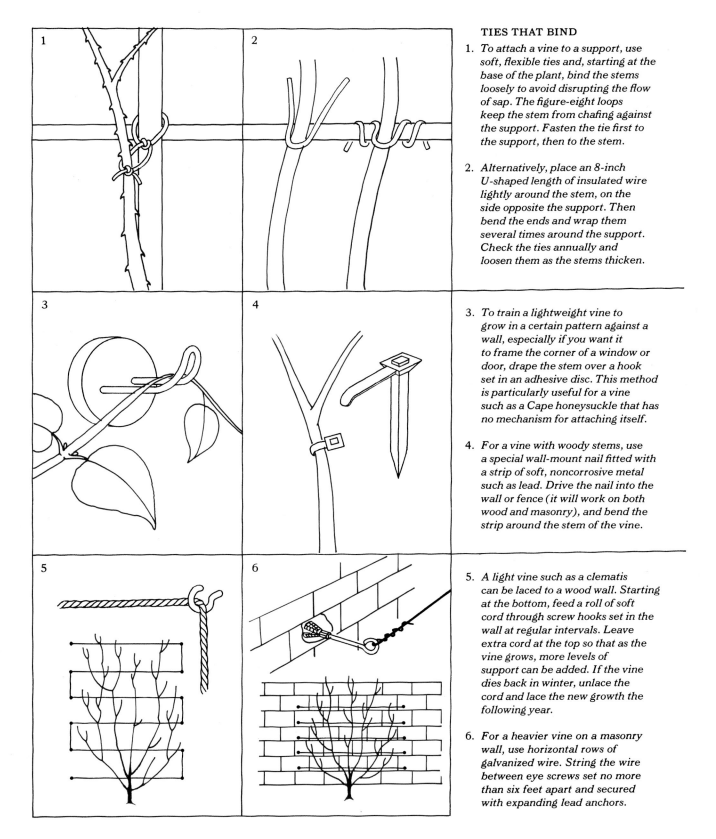

## TIES THAT BIND

1. *To attach a vine to a support, use soft, flexible ties and, starting at the base of the plant, bind the stems loosely to avoid disrupting the flow of sap. The figure-eight loops keep the stem from chafing against the support. Fasten the tie first to the support, then to the stem.*

2. *Alternatively, place an 8-inch U-shaped length of insulated wire lightly around the stem, on the side opposite the support. Then bend the ends and wrap them several times around the support. Check the ties annually and loosen them as the stems thicken.*

3. *To train a lightweight vine to grow in a certain pattern against a wall, especially if you want it to frame the corner of a window or door, drape the stem over a hook set in an adhesive disc. This method is particularly useful for a vine such as a Cape honeysuckle that has no mechanism for attaching itself.*

4. *For a vine with woody stems, use a special wall-mount nail fitted with a strip of soft, noncorrosive metal such as lead. Drive the nail into the wall or fence (it will work on both wood and masonry), and bend the strip around the stem of the vine.*

5. *A light vine such as a clematis can be laced to a wood wall. Starting at the bottom, feed a roll of soft cord through screw hooks set in the wall at regular intervals. Leave extra cord at the top so that as the vine grows, more levels of support can be added. If the vine dies back in winter, unlace the cord and lace the new growth the following year.*

6. *For a heavier vine on a masonry wall, use horizontal rows of galvanized wire. String the wire between eye screws set no more than six feet apart and secured with expanding lead anchors.*

Whether you use a vine on a wall, a fence or an overhead structure, you can often play off its basic character and texture against the character and texture of the supporting surface underneath. If, for example, you would like to focus attention on a particularly graceful brick chimney, a handsomely pillared entrance or a well-crafted stone wall, try an elegant, small-leaved, open-growing vine such as a scarlet katsura or a creeping fig. Small or finely textured leaves will also emphasize, by contrast, the character of a surface that is naturally bold and rough; a glossy winter creeper, for example, will accentuate the rustic effect of a mortarless field-stone wall or an old, weathered split-rail fence. Conversely, a fine-textured or smooth surface such as a wall of concrete blocks or stucco can often be made more appealing if a bold, rough-leaved vine like a Boston ivy or a climbing hydrangea is used. If the surface is something you would just as soon not call attention to—a tumble-down brick wall or a fence that has long since seen better days—a coarsely textured, densely foliaged fast-growing vine will mercifully bury it under a mantle of greenery.

BOLSTERING THE SUPPORT

As you choose a vine for any given situation, bear in mind its method of climbing and holding, how heavy it may get, what kind of support it may need. Vines that cling or stick by means of aerial rootlets or adhesive discs, such as Boston and English ivy, creeping fig or Virginia creeper, rarely need any help in climbing up a rough surface like stone or brick *(page 21)*. On a smoother masonry surface, such as poured concrete or painted concrete blocks, they may need horizontal wires every four to six feet to help support their weight *(page 31)*. The best wire to use is copper, which does not rust and weathers to an inconspicuous dark color, or wire covered with a weatherproof dark plastic such as that sold for electrical work. Stretch the wires tautly between pairs of rustproof masonry nails hammered into masonry joints, or use a masonry drill bit to make holes into which you can set expansion anchors and rustproof eye screws or hooks. Supporting wires are desirable on any masonry surface, rough or smooth, for such heavier sticking vines as climbing hydrangeas or bigleaf winter creeper. These project out from the wall as they grow; unsupported, they may be torn away by wind.

VINES ON TREES

Sticking clingers can be allowed to grow up a tree trunk without adverse effects, so long as they are not allowed to grow into the foliage of the upper crown. But robust twining vines like wisteria and bittersweet should be kept away from trees; they frequently wrap themselves so tightly around the trunks that eventually they may choke the trees by interrupting the flow of water and nutrients between the roots and the leaves.

It is not prudent to use a sticking or clinging vine on any fabricated wood surface such as clapboard or shingles. These vines need moisture to make their holdfasts stick; to get it, they pry into crevices, induce rot and may even dislodge the woodwork. When any repair or repainting is needed, the vines must be ripped down, a job that is easy on neither the houseowner nor the house, not to mention the vines.

However, if provision is made for a trellis or other support, many clingers and a large number of twining, weaving and leaning vines can be grown next to a wall or fence, even one of wood. A light twining vine like a morning glory or a cup-and-saucer vine may need

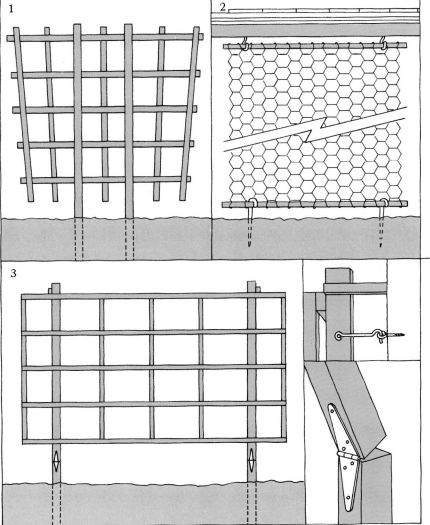

### A TRIO OF TRELLISES

1. *A freestanding fan-shaped trellis can be made with lath crosspieces nailed to 2-by-2 posts. Keep the supporting posts vertical for maximum strength. Angle the side supports outward to allow good air circulation and to spread flower distribution.*

2. *To grow small annual vines such as morning glories against a wall, make a trellis of chicken wire that is easy to remove at the end of the summer. Thread a dowel through the wire and suspend it from hooks in the eaves. Anchor the bottom with hooked stakes driven into the ground.*

3. *A hinged trellis is designed to swing away from the wall for easy maintenance of either the wall or the vine. Set 2-by-4 base posts about five feet apart and three feet deep. Attach the upper sections of the posts with galvanized strap hinges (inset). Make a lattice design with 1-by-2 slats. Nail a block of wood at the top of each post to keep the trellis at least six inches from the wall for good air circulation. A galvanized hook and eye (inset) holds the trellis to the wall. During painting or pruning, a rope tied to the trellis and the eye screw will hold the trellis any distance from the wall without damaging the vine.*

nothing more than a wire or nylon cord stretched between an overhanging eave and a stake driven into the ground. A larger decorative trellis for light vines can be made with a frame of light wood with wires or cords lashed across it. For plants like the Costa Rican nightshade that climbs by weaving, or like the ampelopsis that holds on with tendrils, you can use wide-mesh plastic-coated wire fencing or nylon garden netting for support. Even ordinary chicken wire will soon be masked by foliage.

A LADDER OF LACING

A vine of modest dimensions like a small-flowered clematis or an everblooming honeysuckle can be laced directly to a wall or fence as it grows. Install two rows of rustproof screw hooks, each a foot or two above the next, in vertical rows four to six feet apart. Tie nylon cord or wire to the lowest hook on one side, then string it over to the hook opposite, then up to the hook above and back, parallel to the ground, to the next hook on the first side, in a continuous ladderlike pattern *(page 31)*. Leave excess cord in a small roll so you can use it whenever the growing vine needs a little more lacing up. If the surface needs painting, a leaning or weaving vine can be unlaced and laid temporarily on the ground, then tied back in place when the work is done. In the case of an annual or perennial that dies back to the ground in fall, the dead vine can be easily removed and the cord saved for the following year.

BUILDING A TRELLIS

For more permanent support, several kinds of prefabricated wood, aluminum or plastic trellises are sold at garden centers. Or you can build your own. Such a trellis should be strong enough to provide support for large evergreen vines, or to look attractive even when a deciduous woody-stemmed vine is bare of leaves. The frame can be built of galvanized pipe, aluminum sections or wrought iron, but most home handymen find wood easiest to work with. Make the framework of 1-by-1s, 2-by-2s, 2-by-4s or a combination depending on the size of the trellis and the weight of the vine you intend to grow. You can paint the trellis the color of the house or a neutral white, or use a rot-resistant wood like redwood, cedar or cypress that will weather to a driftwood gray without being painted. Use rot-resistant wood for any posts in contact with the soil, or soak the post ends with a nontoxic wood preservative such as one containing copper naphthenate. Do not use creosote; it is harmful to plant roots. For stability, trellis posts should be sunk at least two feet into the ground, and farther in regions of deep frost.

When you place such a trellis next to a wall or fence, do not let them touch. Allow at least three or four inches of space—six inches or more for a large vine—to give the foliage good ventilation and to prevent moisture condensation that can cause rot and encourage fungus disease. A vine that stands apart from a wall is also spared damage from reflected heat from the sun, and it will be easier to prune. Galvanized angle irons, brackets or blocks of wood can be used to space the trellis out from the wall, or it can be allowed to stand on its own posts embedded in the ground with a wall connection only at the top.

If you install hinges at the bottom of the framework and hook-and-eye connectors at the top, you can swing the trellis away from the wall whenever necessary *(page 33)*. If you are growing a perennial vine that dies to the ground each winter, for example, you can unhook the trellis and lay it flat on the ground while you remove the dead vine. You can also lower the trellis whenever it is necessary to repaint the wall behind it. If the trellis is covered with a woody vine that might break, swing the trellis just far enough away from the house to allow painting.

Many vines and some plants such as climbing roses that are treated like vines can be trained against vertical surfaces to yield distinctive patterns, ranging from informal ones that accentuate natural growth lines to formal, geometric designs like the ones used in true espaliers. Such patterns relieve bare expanses of wall and make striking focal points for a terrace, a garage wall or a garden fence. Easily disciplined vines like Low's creeper, English ivy and winter creeper can be guided to form quick swags and garlands, tree shapes, zigzags, crisscrossed diagonals or open rectangular grids. The more complicated the pattern, of course, the more time it will take, for you will have to tie up shoots that are headed in the right

## GEOMETRIC PATTERNS

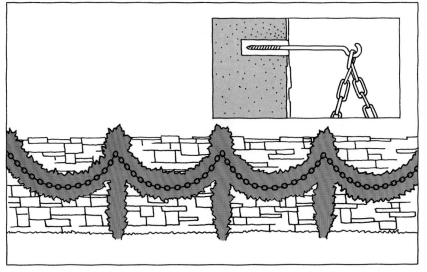

### GRACEFUL SWAGS OF IVY

*To make ivy swags against a wall, screw 4-inch hooks into lead anchors (inset) placed in the wall at 3-foot intervals. Loop a lightweight plastic or aluminum chain through the hooks and curve it into scalloped shapes. Plant ivy at both ends of the swags. After the ivy has grown up the wall to form pillars, train it onto the chain by tying it at 4-inch intervals with soft cotton cord. The chain will keep the ivy free of the wall, where it would be more difficult to control. Clip ends of ivy shoots regularly to encourage bushier growth. If you prefer, freestanding swags can be made with ivy trained on a chain connecting wooden posts set at 4-foot intervals.*

direction and clip off others that are not. To tie a vine to supporting wires or nails, you can use soft garden twine, raffia or the paper-covered plant ties sold in garden stores. Never tie tightly; ties must always be loose enough to allow growth without cutting into the stems. Heavy, large-stemmed vines need sturdy ties of nylon cord or strips of cotton cloth to hold up their weight.

A trellis or grid can be used not only against a wall but as a free-standing, self-supporting screen almost anywhere in the garden. The posts of the framework can be sunk in the ground and, for additional sturdiness, anchored with concrete collars. Or the structure can be attached to a long wooden planter box—a good solution if the soil is poor, if you may want to move the screen around, or if it is to be used on a paved terrace or rooftop where there is no soil at all.

**AN ARCH OVERHEAD** Variations on the freestanding trellis can be used for more elaborate structures. One is the arch, which can stand astride a garden path, serve as an ornamental bower for a garden bench, or frame a garden gate.

To build a simple square-topped arch, start with the sides. For each side, use a pair of 2-by-4 or 4-by-4 wooden posts and nail crosspieces between them like ladder rungs. Sink the lower posts of each ladder into the ground, then nail a similar unit across the top. For an airier design reminiscent of an old-fashioned lattice arbor, make the crosspieces of lighter, more closely spaced battens, grape stakes or laths. By extending this single flat-topped arch into a series, you can create an arbor or pergola, a shade structure for a terrace or a vine-covered breezeway.

**SHADING A TERRACE** Sturdy uprights are required if you plan to use a vine like wisteria, which becomes thick-trunked and foliage-heavy with age. Lighter supports can be used with thinner-stemmed akebia or ampelopsis. Overhead, you can choose a vine to produce just the degree of shade you want. Those with small or finely divided leaves like the honeysuckles will cast light, filtered patterns of sun and shadow. An actinidia, grape or Dutchman's-pipe will give denser, more cooling shade in areas that are subjected to blazing summer heat. In a southern garden, an evergreen vine like a madeira or a bougainvillea will yield shade year round, while in the north a deciduous vine like a wisteria, Boston ivy, grape or ampelopsis will provide shade in the summer when it is needed, then drop its leaves to allow the warming rays of the winter sun to enter.

In addition to shade, vines on a terrace arbor can provide flowers and fruit. Grapevines like Concords, Delawares and Niagaras are old favorites for their edible dividends; some gardeners relish actinidias for their sweet, figlike fruits. But before you plant a flowering or fruiting vine near a sitting area, bear in mind that other creatures in you garden may like them even better than you do. You may enjoy having birds eat the berries of a bittersweet or a Virginia creeper, but you may not enjoy cleaning up squishy fallen grapes, which attract insects. If you are allergic to the sting of a bee or a wasp, a sweetly scented honeysuckle or jasmine might better be planted some distance from your lounge chairs.

Vines can also be used to disguise other utilitarian features besides chain-link fences. A mailbox near the road or an old-fashioned lamppost, planted with an English ivy or a winter creeper, can become a welcoming note, and a leafy trumpet vine or climbing hydrangea will soften the thrust of an unattractive utility pole.

Or you can set up a simple structure just to display a vine. A 4-by-4 redwood or cedar post, eight feet long and sunk two feet into the ground, will show off a clematis, a hoya or a pillar rose. To make sure the vine clings, insert short dowels into drilled holes at one-foot intervals or, in the case of the rose, tie the canes loosely to the post with twine. For a fuller, more robust plant like a hop vine, make a tripod of three lengths of 2-by-2 lumber, grape stakes or bamboo. Lean the stakes on each other tepee fashion and lash the tops together. Plant vines inside the tripod and guide the stems up the stakes. Vining vegetables can also be grown in this fashion. Cucumbers, for example, have lovely yellow flowers and large, padlike leaves in addition to the cucumbers themselves. Handsome flowers, foliage and fruit are also borne by peas, pole beans, tomatoes and melons, not to mention ornamental gourds.

More than one imaginative gardener has found ways to make such vines do double duty. Among the most ingenious is a gardener in St. Louis who likes cantaloupes but had not room to accommodate their sprawling growth in his tiny backyard. Then it occurred to him to build a raised wooden planting bed and train the melon vines on a wooden trellis attached to the wall of the house.

Now the St. Louis gardener grows abundant crops of such midget melons as Honeygold, a golden-skinned honeydew, and Minnesota Midget cantaloupe. He starts them indoors in early spring in pots placed near a window; by late May, soil in the raised outdoor bed is warm enough for him to transplant the seedlings, a week or more ahead of ground-level beds. All he has to do is tie the growing stems to the trellis as they ascend, watch the flowers unfold and the bees go to work. As the fruits swell he supports their weight in little fishnet slings that he attaches to the trellis. By August, for the price of a packet of seeds, he is starting every breakfast with a mouth-watering melon fresh from his vertical garden.

## A PORTABLE LEAFY SCREEN

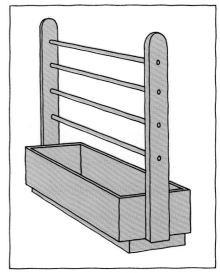

*To shade a sunny patio or create a privacy screen, convert a standard redwood planter into a trellis for vines. Round one end of two 2-by-4 uprights, clamp them together, and drill ¾-inch holes through them at desired intervals; horizontal supports at 8- to 10-inch intervals are usually adequate. Fasten the uprights to the planter's ends with rustproof screws, then slide ¾-inch dowels through the holes and glue in place. For a portable trellis, use a lightweight soil mix.*

## MELONS ON THE WALL

# Pretty and practical problem solvers

Vines were among the first plants to be cultivated. The ancient Egyptians considered the grapevine sacred and eagerly harvested its fruit to make wine. At first, the plants were grown on simple wooden structures. But as their decorative value became more appreciated, vines were given elaborate supports. By the reign of young King Tutankhamen (1358 B.C.), an exquisitely painted circular pergola draped with vines was often the central and most conspicuous feature of an Egyptian garden.

Thousands of years later, vines are still playing a dual role in garden design: they are both decorative and functional. A winter creeper vine, with its glossy foliage, can provide a lush evergreen screen to mask an unsightly wall or fence. A creeping fig (*opposite*) can turn a blank concrete wall into an exotic gallery of delicate leaf patterns. A trumpet vine can climb a drainpipe, clothing it with dense foliage and vivid trumpet-shaped flowers. A prickly rambler rose or common matrimony vine can add a splash of color to a steep bank while holding the soil in place. And, as the Egyptians learned so many centuries ago, a grapevine grown over an arbor will provide a shaded sitting area—and delicious fruit as well.

Vines are ideal for a small city garden; many kinds grow quickly without taking up much space. Study the way a particular species of vine grows before you plant it. Vines that cling to flat surfaces with rootlike appendages, like a climbing hydrangea, can be planted against a brick wall or board fence to which they will cling. Vines that climb with twining stems, like a wisteria, or with grasping tendrils, like a grapevine, need a different kind of support, perhaps a wire trellis or a lath arbor. Some trailing vines will need even more help to grow upward; they should be fastened to their supports with soft cotton cord or other mechanical means.

Young vines that tend to shoot upward quickly should be trained horizontally at first to make sure the lower area of a wall or fence will be covered as well as the top. They may form only a high mass of foliage if left to their own devices.

*The golden trumpet-shaped flowers of an allamanda vine accent a slatted gate in a Southern garden. Clinging gracefully to the wall is a young creeping fig.*

# The winter-hardy wisteria

*Draping a 19th Century balcony, a hardy Japanese wisteria offers a breathtaking display of its long fragrant flower clusters.*

*Viewed at close range, the flower clusters of a Japanese wisteria reveal their habit of opening progressively from branch to tip.*

A coral vine climbs a wrought-iron fence by using its clinging tendrils. It has long strands of tiny heart-shaped flowers. The tuberous roots are valued in Mexico for their nutlike flavor.

Trained on a wire trellis, a bleeding-heart vine scales the side of a house. The dainty flowers of this twining evergreen vine consist of tiny red petals and white sepals.

## Color for the sunny South

Flowering vines seem to revel in gardens of the Deep South where the moist, frost-free climate enables them to bloom almost year round. Such tropical renegades as cypress vine and scarlet star glory run wild in the South, sprinkling abandoned cotton fields with their tiny star-shaped flowers. In the garden, Southern vines can be equally rebellious, yet with regular pruning their luxuriant growth is easily kept under control. Some of the South's spectacular fast-growing perennial vines, such as lantana and morning glory *(pages 44-45)*, are treated as annuals in the North.

*A Cape plumbago blankets a brick wall with its powder-blue phloxlike flowers, which bloom continuously throughout the year.*

Imperial morning glories, planted in
large clay pots, offer a year-round
display of heart-shaped leaves and
ruffled flowers in New Orleans. Rapid
climbers, these morning glories are
grown as annuals in the north.

A sweeping border of trailing
lantana lines the top of a concrete wall
in Southern California, where it
blooms all year. In colder climates,
lantana is grown in hanging pots that
can be moved indoors.

# Fast growers for quick covers

With the help of its tiny aerial roots, a winter-hardy trumpet vine climbs the side of a brick house and camouflages a drainpipe.

*A twining silver-fleece vine, trained on transparent fishing line, conceals an electrical meter at the side of a pillared portico.*

# Climbers with shady habits

*A climbing hydrangea crowns a wooden garden gate with its creamy flower clusters. Whether grown in partial shade, as here, or in full sun, this woody vine will cover a wall or building to a height of 20 feet.*

*A two-year-old porcelain ampelopsis drapes a brick townhouse. Climbing by tendrils, this shade-tolerant vine is grown for its decorative berries, which turn as they ripen from pale lilac to yellow to porcelain blue.*

*Laden with several varieties of European grapevines, a strong wooden archway decoratively frames the entrance to a flower garden. Although grown here for their ornamental value, grapevines have the bonus advantage of producing tasty fruit that can be harvested for jellies.*

51

# Plants to tend and plants to tame 3

To some it is a mythic image: the unstoppable surge of life itself. Poems have been written to it, rock music groups and beauty contests have been named after it—and thousands of tons of deadly poisons have been dumped on it in a vain attempt to throttle its growth. Originally from Japan, the kudzu vine was planted during the 1930s to save the South's soil from erosion. But in many places this large-leaved, ropy-stemmed, very persistent import has outstayed its welcome. In a few weeks, anything in the vine's path, from automobiles to barns to tall forests, can be engulfed in a suffocating blanket. As one longtime foe put it, "Three things that make life miserable are mosquitoes, city living and kudzu."

Despite its detractors, the plant does have its uses, holding erosion-prone banks or rapidly filling in bare spots around a new house—as long as the gardener remains ready with the pruning shears. For kudzu is perhaps the ultimate example of the trait that makes vines such practical additions to the landscape: their nearly unmatched vitality. To get started, however, most vines need a bit more help than kudzu does. Like other garden plants, they benefit from properly prepared soil, water and nourishment, and protection from weather extremes and occasional pests. Finally, timely training and pruning are needed to keep vines attractive and well-behaved.

The best initial insurance of success with vines is to start with a healthy plant that will present few maintenance problems later. Some nurseries stock only the smallest, most popular and least riotous vines like periwinkle and ivy, so if you want something like a wonga-wonga or a beaumontia you may have to buy from a specialist grower or a mail-order house. If you do find the plant you seek at a nursery, check its general appearance. Look for specimens that have been tied to stakes or spread evenly over small trellises; avoid those that have been allowed to trail or that show signs of insect infestation. Beware also of plants that are tangled and matted or that have

*A small wrought-iron arbor, laced with glory bower vines, arches over a small statue in a southern garden. Planted in rich, well-drained soil, these evergreen vines produce sprays of tiny flowers in summer.*

obviously outgrown their containers; you may lose a good portion of the plant in pruning the foliage or untangling the roots.

Mail-order houses usually ship perennial vines such as English ivy and winter creeper as one- or two-year-old plants, potted and wrapped to withstand the ordeals of transit, and accompanied by some sort of guarantee. You may also order packets of seeds for growing morning glories, moonflowers and other annual flowering vines as well as fruit-bearing vines such as cucumbers, melons and ornamental gourds.

Seeds can be planted directly in the garden as soon as all danger of frost is past, but with late bloomers like balloon vines, many gardeners get ahead of the game by starting seeds indoors four to six weeks before the last frost is due, or as much as eight weeks for slow starters like morning glories. The seeds of morning glories and moonflowers have tough seed coats; to hasten germination, nick this outer casing with a file, or soak the seeds in warm water overnight to soften their coats. Seedlings may be started in commercial potting soil and planted in the garden when all danger of frost is past. Those grown in flats must be pried up gently to preserve their roots, while those in peat containers can go directly into the ground—container and all; but crush the peat slightly so the roots can grow out.

A convenient alternative is the peat pellet, which requires no potting soil. Place the pellets, one for each vine, in a shallow tray of water, where they will absorb moisture and expand to several times their original height. Poke three holes in the top of each pellet with a pencil, insert a seed in each hole to the depth prescribed on the seed packet, then pinch the moist peat to cover the seeds. Set the tray in a bright warm spot out of direct sunlight, and keep the pellets moist but not soggy by occasional watering or by covering them loosely with plastic. When the seeds sprout, remove the covering and place the seedlings in a sunny window, and when they begin to crowd one another, snip off all but the largest and healthiest one in each pellet. Rotate the seedlings periodically to keep them growing evenly, and set them outside for a few hours a day in good weather until it is warm enough to transplant them into the ground.

Annual vines are started in the spring, of course, as are perennials such as passionflower that need the whole summer to get established in the north before facing the rigors of winter. Bare-rooted nursery plants are best planted as soon as the ground can be worked in spring, while they are still dormant. Vines grown in their own soil-filled containers can be planted later in spring or summer, but they also need time to achieve solid growth before winter arrives. A few tough-stemmed woody vines such as woodbine and

## A NICK IN TIME

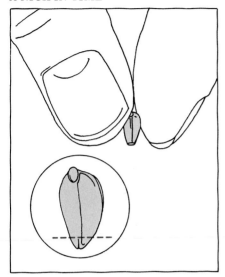

*A hard-coated seed, such as that of a morning glory (above), sweet pea or cypress vine, will germinate more quickly if the shell is nicked, or scarified. Hold the seed between your thumb and forefinger. With a file or fingernail clipper, cut off the tip of the seed opposite its eye, to avoid damaging the embryo. Soak the seed for four hours in warm water before planting. Some seeds are sold already scarified.*

## THE PLANTING SEASONS

54

trumpet vine can be planted quite late in fall, as long as their roots have a month or two to grow before the ground freezes.

Whether you are starting seeds, seedlings or nursery-grown stock, careful preparation of the planting bed is essential. Most vines will grow well in the mildly acid soil found in many parts of the country (6.5 to 7.0 on the pH scale). Some, such as clematis, prefer slightly alkaline soil, while Boston ivy grows best with more acid conditions. Test the soil of your planting bed with an inexpensive kit from a garden center, or submit a sample to your local agricultural extension service. You can raise the pH of soil about one point, making it slightly more alkaline, by mixing in five pounds of finely ground limestone for every 100 square feet of planting area. Or you can lower the pH ½ to 1 point, making the soil slightly more acid, by mixing in ½ pound of finely ground sulfur per 100 square feet. In either case, do the mixing a month or two before planting so the chemicals will have time to work. A faster-acting alternative for lowering the pH is to mix in 3 pounds of iron sulfate per 100 square

## Does ivy harm brick walls?

In England, ivy is sometimes credited with protecting centuries-old stone castles and brick manor houses from moisture damage. The vine's supporters contend that its overlapping leaves shield the buildings from driving rain, while its roots absorb moisture from foundation walls.

But ivy-covered walls are not always a boon. Occasionally the plant forces its way between a brick and a window frame, leaving an opening for moisture to enter the building. Dampness from ivy can also stain and discolor light-colored bricks. Worst of all, ivy's aerial roots have been known to invade weak mortar joints in both old and new brick buildings, damaging their structure.

The strength of a mortar joint can be detected by scraping it with a key: if it crumbles, the wall is too weak to support ivy. In an old wall, weak mortar is usually the result of years of weathering; in a new wall, it occurs more often when too much sand has been used in proportion to cement. A good strong mortar mixture consists of 1 part portland cement, 1 part hydrated lime and 6 parts builder's sand. A retaining wall that is holding back soil requires an even stronger formula: 1 part portland cement, ¼ part hydrated lime or fire clay and 3 parts sand.

If a building's mortar is crumbling because of age or poor workmanship, you can train ivy to grow on a trellis that will hold it a few inches away from the wall. And if you are building a new brick wall on which you intend to grow ivy, you might want to use a special convex jointing tool that indents the mortar, allowing the vine to get a foothold on the brick surfaces between the joints without doing the mortar any damage. The indented joint also helps the mortar shed water.

feet of planting area. However, iron sulfate leaches away more rapidly than sulfur and must be replenished every two years or so.

Nearly all vines grow well in soil that is moderately moisture-retentive yet drains well. A liberal amount of organic matter such as leaf mold, compost or peat moss will not only open up heavy clay soil to air and better drainage but will also hold moisture around plant roots in sandy ground. In extreme cases, it may be more practical simply to grow your vines in tubs, raised beds or wooden planters equipped with drainage holes and filled with a commercial soil mix.

PLANTING TECHNIQUES    When preparing for planting, excavate to a depth of at least 2 feet (3 feet for deep-rooted woody vines such as wisteria and grape), and give your plants growing room by making the hole 2 to 3 feet wide. Place the rich, dark topsoil and the lighter-colored subsoil in separate piles. Mix into each pile 1 part organic matter to each 2 parts of soil. Given this rich planting medium, most vines will not need additional fertilizer at this time.

Now start to fill the hole with the topsoil mix. Position the plant at the same depth it was previously growing at. There are a few exceptions: some vines such as clematis will get a better start if they are set 2 to 4 inches below their previous depth. Fill in around the plant with more topsoil mix and firm the soil to eliminate air pockets. If the root ball is wrapped in burlap, simply loosen the ties and spread the cloth; it will eventually disintegrate. For a bare-rooted plant, keep the roots wrapped and moist while you shape the soil into a mound, then unwrap the roots and spread them gently over the mound. Continue filling in around the plant. For a large plant in a large hole, fill the hole with water when it is about ⅔ full of soil, let it drain, then complete the filling. Make a 1- or 2-inch saucer of soil around the hole and fill this gently with water. Wait while the water soaks in, then fill the saucer a second time.

ADJACENT TO THE HOUSE    If you are planting vines that will cover the wall of your house, there are several things to keep in mind. First, the soil next to the foundation may be quite alkaline because of lime that leaches out of the concrete. Or it may contain masonry rubble used as backfill around the foundation. In either case you may need to replace the soil in the planting bed. Second, make certain the plants will receive moisture by planting them away from the wall, at the edge of the eave drip line. Finally, to help prevent disease, provide good air circulation behind the vines by training them to grow on trellises or wires that are propped out from the wall (page 31).

One annual vine, the sweet pea, requires a special planting technique. The secret is to provide a deep, rich, moist planting bed (see Lathyrus, Chapter 5). Feeding established sweet pea plants two or three times during the summer with a balanced fertilizer will encourage flowering.

Watering and mulching are beneficial to all vines. These plants are generally deep rooted and need a thorough soaking every week or 10 days during the growing season unless there has been at least an inch of rain. Light sprinkling will not do any good and may actually harm the plants by encouraging the growth of surface roots that suffer during periods of drought. Vines also benefit from periodic hosing of foliage to remove accumulated grime and insects. This is best done in the morning so leaves and stem joints do not remain wet overnight, which would encourage mildew and fungus diseases.

Mulching can reduce watering needs and keep the roots of vines cool and moist. A mulch can be almost any organic material: bark or

### CREATING A WALL COVERING

1. *To create an ivy-covered wall that is attractive, healthy and easy to maintain, plant a rooted cutting of English ivy 6 to 10 inches long in rich, moist soil at the base of the wall in the spring. Encourage the ivy to grow upright against the wall; do not prune. The following spring, cut all the ivy shoots back to the ground (blue).*

2. *In late spring, after the ivy has sent up strong new shoots, select four of the most vigorous and train them upright against the wall in the shape of a fan, guiding them if necessary with twine or wire. Prune away all other growth.*

3. *The following spring, cut back the trained shoots by one third of their length to stimulate lateral branching. Remove any new vertical shoots that sprout between the four main shoots.*

4. *Later in the year, lateral branches will begin to fill in bare areas between the trained shoots. Each spring, cut back the new top growth by one third. Remove new vertical shoots at ground level and cut off branches that project out from the wall. With this training, a single ivy cutting can cover 20 square feet of wall with a single layer of neat, healthy foliage.*

wood chips, salt-marsh hay, leaves, pine needles, decayed sawdust, buckwheat hulls or cocoa-bean hulls. The mulch should not touch the stems and should allow water and air to reach the roots, so it should not be put on thickly or be allowed to become matted. Use about 2 inches of a firm material like bark or wood chips, or 3 or 4 inches of compressible matter like hay or leaves. If you use peat moss, buy the coarse, chunky kind often labeled "poultry grade"; the finely shredded peat moss usually mixed into soil tends to form an impervious blanket that sheds water. In addition to keeping the soil moist, a mulch will keep most weed seeds from germinating and make the few weeds that do poke through easier to pull. As a mulch of leaves or hay disintegrates, it adds some nourishment to the soil. You may need to put down a fresh layer every year or two.

THE RIGHT FERTILIZER    Many vines will grow satisfactorily for years in soil enriched at planting time and protected with a mulch. However, creeping fig, English ivy and other robust growers tend to deplete soil nutrients and need fertilizer annually, when new growth starts in spring. A few vines, notably sweet autumn clematis and silver fleece vine, benefit from a second application in midsummer. Unless you seek a mass of leaves to cover a large area quickly, or unless a foliage vine like ivy seems anemic, it is best to use fertilizer that is relatively low in leaf-stimulating nitrogen. A good all-purpose fertilizer to use is one marked 5-10-5 (5 parts nitrogen, 10 parts phosphorus, 5 parts potassium). For strong roots and better flowers without excessive foliage, many gardeners use slow-acting bone meal, high in phosphorus and low in nitrogen, or a no-nitrogen chemical formula such as 0-10-10. With any fertilizer, use a little less than is recommended on

*(continued on page 63)*

# Ivy: in a league of its own

*Long before ivy became associated with the debauchery of Bacchus, it represented fidelity and immortality. Poets, from Homer to Keats, revered it, as did several emperors. Nero is said to have worn an ivy wreath around his head while Rome burned. Eighteen centuries later, Napoleon took with him on his exile to the island of St. Helena chinaware that was stamped with a beautiful, bold ivy pattern.*

*Although Thomas Jefferson grew ivy at Monticello, it is not native to North America. Jefferson imported his ivy from Europe. Yet not until after the Civil War, when tourists began bringing back pictures of ivy-covered English castles, did this evergreen vine really catch the fancy of American gardeners. Indoor screens, luxuriantly covered with ivy, became faddish, as did ivy-framed paintings, mirrors and windows.*

*Today, ivy is primarily grown outdoors, where it thrives in moist, shaded soil. There are five cultivated species of evergreen ivy, but English ivy (Hedera helix), with more than 100 varieties, is the most popular.*

*Trained on hidden nails, English ivy snakes its way across the side and up the stately portico of a brick house.*

*Baltic ivy, a hardy outdoor variety of Hedera helix, forms an all-year wreath against an old brick wall. The wreath's frame is a band from a barrel.*

*English ivy, grown vertically and clipped to a wooden fence, creates a sculpturesque backdrop for a patio. At the sundial's base is glacier ivy.*

*Trained on strands of aluminum wire bolted to a brick wall, English ivy produced this lush diamond pattern about a year after planting.*

An owl 6 feet tall, made of small-leaved Patricia ivy, perches before a concrete wall. Its eyes, nose and feet were fashioned from clay.

Trained up brick pillars and tied to a swagging chain, English ivy creates a formal leafy backdrop for a clipped hedge of white azaleas.

the label. Scatter the fertilizer at the base of the plant and scratch it lightly into the soil, then water it in to start dissolving the nutrients.

Probably the single most important aspect of caring for vines is training and pruning. Prune regularly, beginning while the young plant is still easy to control. Postponing the chore means the vine will grow so large that severe cutting will either produce an unsightly butchered look or stimulate even more rampant growth.

Pruning starts at the planting stage, when any dead or broken roots or stems should be removed. If the plant came bare rooted, trim about ⅓ of the top growth after planting (unless the nursery has already done so) to compensate for roots sliced off when the plant was dug. As soon as possible, start training the vine to its support. Pinch off stem tips just above growth buds to encourage branching and dense growth; otherwise, a vine such as a goldflame honeysuckle or most clematis may become almost bare at the base. Remove suckers and diseased stems as soon as you notice them.

AN INITIAL TRIMMING

Foliage that becomes dense and matted provides a breeding ground for insects and fungus diseases as well as a nesting place for birds. A solid wall of ivy looks attractive but a colony of chittering sparrows that awakens you at dawn may be unwelcome. Selective thinning from time to time can avoid such problems; remove individual branches rather than shearing the vine as if it were a hedge.

Most perennial woody vines need a general pruning once a year. A foliage vine can be pruned whenever necessary, but in northern areas it is better to do major work in late winter or early spring, so that new growth will have ample time to mature before the next winter. Greater care should be taken with flowering vines. Wisteria, for example, blooms in spring from buds formed the previous summer; it should be pruned soon after it finishes flowering. But Henry honeysuckle and silver fleece vine bloom in late summer or autumn from buds formed earlier the same year; they should be pruned early in the spring before new growth starts.

IF IN DOUBT, WAIT

The tender stems of a non-woody perennial such as the passion flower, when grown in the north, die down to the ground each year, sprouting fresh growth in the spring. The dead vines can be cut off a few inches above the ground after cold weather has set in. Do not be too hasty about this, though; the woody stems of Boston ivy and many hybrid clematis may seem dead in winter, only to come back to life in spring. Whether a vine's top growth will live through a winter is not always easy to predict. If in doubt, leave the old stems in place and remove them only if they fail to grow in the spring.

There are several treatments for a vine that has become overgrown. To slow its growth while you stimulate more abundant

*Three living sculptures of English ivy grace a lath arch. The ivy is trained on aluminum wire attached to posts inserted into the soil.*

flowering, you can prune its feeding roots with a sharp spade, cutting around the plant one foot from the stem for each inch of the stem's diameter. To fill in around bare lower stems of a vine that is producing most of its foliage at the top, try bending a long shoot downward and tying it in place. A climbing rose, which grows less productive with age as the canes turn dark and rough, may be rejuvenated by cutting back one or two old stems to within six inches of the ground each spring. The new green shoots will supply far more luxuriant growth than their aged progenitors. A vine that is clearly out of hand or a clinger heavily matted against a wall may be cut to the ground in early spring, thus stimulating new growth. (Such surgery is not recommended for wisteria and other flowering vines that take several years to produce flower buds.) Finally, you may simply dispense with the old vine entirely and replace it.

COPING WITH PESTS

Vines are generally resistant to insects and disease. Indeed, trumpet creeper and five-leaf akebia seem almost immune to garden pests. Others, such as Virginia creeper, may attract Japanese beetles, and trumpet honeysuckle is susceptible to aphids. Many insects can be kept under control by simply spraying stem joints and the undersides of leaves occasionally with a brisk jet of water from the hose, but a heavy infestation requires insecticide treatment.

In northern and central states especially, one insect that can cause problems is euonymus scale. Named after the genus of the winter creeper, its favorite target, the insect sometimes attacks bittersweet and English ivy as well. The tiny white males and larger brown females hatch in spring when the weather warms. To keep eggs from hatching, apply a dormant oil spray as soon as the temperature is above 40°. After eggs have hatched, apply malathion two or three times at five-day intervals. If a severe infestation turns the leaves almost white, cut the vine to the ground, destroy the foliage and spray the stumps and the area around them with dormant oil or malathion. The roots will produce new pest-free vines.

WINTER INSULATION

Some vines, particularly woody ones grown near the limits of their hardiness zones, may be injured by winter cold. Where winters are severe, protect marginally hardy vines by mounding soil 6 to 12 inches high around the bases of the plants. Bring the soil in; do not scrape it from above the roots. Or pile a mulch of hay, straw or evergreen boughs around the stems. For even greater protection— for climbing roses, for example—either pull the canes together inside a snug wrapping of burlap, or arch them gently over until they touch the ground and bury them under an insulating mound of earth.

While vines are generally inexpensive, some species are not readily available, and you may want to duplicate a specimen.

Cuttings are the easiest answer. One horticulturist has a novel method of adding to his collection. Whenever he encounters a plant he especially admires, he goes right up to it, ostensibly to sniff the fragrance of its flowers or examine the luster of its leaves. Innocently lifting the stem close to his face, the gentleman bites off the tip and quickly slips his treasure into a plastic bag—leaving the donor plant a little shorter, but otherwise none the worse for the experience.

Most perennial vines are easily propagated from such softwood cuttings, taken less surreptitiously in late spring or early summer, when the stems are young and green but have well-developed leaves. Snip off tips 5 or 6 inches long, about ¼ inch below leaf nodes; sprinkle the cuttings with water and keep them moist in a plastic bag until you can put them in a rooting bed. Remove flowers and flower buds. Dip the bottom ½ to 1 inch of each cutting into a hormone rooting powder, available at most garden stores, and tap off the excess. For a rooting medium, use a 3- to 4-inch layer of coarse sand or peat moss, or a mix of equal parts of the two. Just as good are vermiculite, perlite or finely ground sphagnum moss.

With a pencil, make holes about two inches deep to receive the cuttings, firm the medium around the stems, then water lightly until the medium is evenly moist. Cover the cuttings with clear plastic to maintain humidity, propping the plastic up with sticks, and set the miniature greenhouse in a warm place out of direct sunlight. Keep the medium moist until the cuttings show signs of rooting by putting out new leaves—two or three weeks for quick-rooting vines such as euonymus and ivy geranium, as long as three months for slower ones like clematis and trumpet vine. Then replant each cutting in an individual pot, using packaged potting soil. In warm climates, vines such as plumbago and bougainvillea can be set out in the garden as soon as they are rooted; in cooler regions, they should spend the winter in a greenhouse or a cold frame, or in a sunny window indoors, moving outside when all danger of frost has passed.

Their ease of propagation seems quite in keeping with the adaptability of vines generally: circumnutating cautiously, sprouting adhesive discs or hooks when necessary, weaving or twining as the situation demands. But a vine's life is not without problems. The popular British performing-songwriting team of some years ago, Michael Flanders and Donald Swann, commemorated the star-crossed romance of a right-twining honeysuckle and a left-twining bindweed, who were discouraged by a passing bee. Consider the confusion of their potential offspring, the bee advised. How would it know which way to twine? "Right, left, what a disgrace—or it may go straight up and fall flat on its face!"

OFF TO A STRONG START

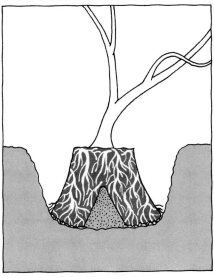

*Because many vines are naturally deep rooted, one purchased in a container of loose, light soil is likely to have long, tangled roots. To help the roots become quickly established in heavier soil, remove the container and split the bottom part of the root ball one half to two thirds of the way up from the bottom with a sharp spade or knife. Prepare a planting hole twice the diameter and depth of the root ball. At the bottom of the hole, shape a mound out of topsoil, then spread the roots and plant as usual.*

# The indoor trailers and clingers 4

Many a gardener fondly recalls his first experience with the spectacular growth potential of vines when, as a child, he pushed a few toothpicks into a sweet potato and suspended it in a glass of water on the kitchen window sill. Within a few days, tiny roots appeared below the tuber. Soon afterward, fragile shoots emerged and began to grow upward, sprouting delicate, heart-shaped leaves. With practically no effort, the young gardener soon was the proud owner of a fine vine several feet long, which could be trained around the window or transplanted to the garden to produce more tubers.

You and your children can evoke the same magic if you can find a garden-fresh sweet potato (many sold in supermarkets have been treated with a chemical to prevent sprouting). Failing that, there are scores of other vines that can be grown in the house with equal ease, requiring little more than a vase of water or a pot of soil. Most vines are as easy to grow indoors as out, and like those in the garden they can provide all sorts of decorative dividends in limited space.

The simplest to grow, and most popular, are the common foliage vines sold for indoor use. One of these, the heart-leaved philodendron, virtually launched the modern house-plant industry in the 1930s, when a Florida nurseryman began to market it through dime stores as well as florists' shops. Though the philodendron is still the best-selling house plant, it has been joined by a host of other vines that offer a great choice of foliage size, color and shape and will tolerate the low light and dry, heated air found indoors.

A particular favorite is the split-leaf philodendron; its rounded leaves resemble those of an ordinary philodendron when they are young but in time become deeply notched and perforated and up to a foot long. At this point a more vivid description is provided by its botanical name, *Monstera*. Given a tall, bark-covered slab of wood to climb, this Central American native will become a ceiling-scraping giant. At the other end of the scale are such dainty vines as creeping

*A variegated Canary Island ivy, flanked by two gloxinias in bloom, adds a cheerful note to an enclosed sun porch. Grown from an 18-inch pot, the vine clings to a trellis and the wall with rootlike appendages.*

*Many indoor vines, such as grape ivy, philodendron and wandering Jew, can be grown in water. Select a tinted or opaque container and line the bottom with charcoal granules to soak up impurities. Cover the charcoal with washed aquarium gravel to ⅓ the depth of the container. Fill with tepid water and place the vine in it, using the gravel as an anchor. To aerate the water without changing it, squirt air into it weekly with a kitchen baster or an automobile battery syringe.*

pilea, with minuscule leaves that will trail neatly over the edge of a hanging basket, and string-of-beads, with curious spherical leaves about the size of peas that hang like tiny beaded curtains.

Among the most decorative indoor foliage vines are those that have "ivy" in their names, though not all are true ivies *(Hedera).* Swedish ivy, initially popular as a house plant in Sweden, is a *Plectranthus,* native to Australia and Africa. Its waxy, scallop-edged leaves make a lustrous display cascading from a pot or bowl. Grape ivy *(Cissus),* named for grapelike tendrils but possessing three-part leaves more like those of poison ivy—is another vine easy to grow in a hanging container, as is its larger-leaved cousin, kangaroo ivy. Equally amenable are German or parlor ivy, with bright green spike-lobed leaves; devil's ivy or pothos, with heart-shaped foliage flecked or marbled with gold or white; and Kenilworth ivy, a delicate charmer with small, scalloped leaves.

And of course there are the true ivies, as widely grown indoors as out. Five species make up this *Hedera* genus: Canary Island, Persian, Japanese, Nepal and—the most popular—English. More than a hundred varieties of English ivy are available, from the large-leaved Hibernica or Irish ivy to the dainty Minima, with leaves no more than ½ inch across, and their foliage ranges from dark green to buttercup yellow, from curly to starlike.

Foliage vines are treasured in many homes because they grow with modest amounts of light, filtered through curtains or reflected from ceilings and walls. Many will live even in dim corners, though their growth will slow and they may become sickly unless moved occasionally to brighter light. Plants with variegated foliage will generally lose their distinctive markings without sunlight.

As a group, flowering vines are more demanding than foliage vines, needing more light to produce good blooms. A few, like rosary vine, firecracker vine and star jasmine, will flower in reflected or curtain-filtered sunlight. But most require at least four hours of direct sunlight a day. Among popular flowering vines grown indoors are the hoyas, also called wax plants, with long-lasting clusters of waxy, fragrant, star-shaped flowers in several colors; Mexican flame vines, with daisy-like blooms of a brilliant orange red; black-eyed-Susan vines, with yellow, orange or white flowers that have dark centers; the spectacular bougainvilleas, which come in a wide variety of colors; as well as ivy geraniums, passionflowers, jasmines, nasturtiums, glory lilies and many more.

The best location for any of these, in all but the hottest climates, is the sunniest window in the house. One facing south or east is best. A western exposure may be as good, but delicate species like the flame violet may need a sheer curtain in summer to prevent burning by the afternoon sun. Many gardeners give each pot a quarter turn when they water, so all sides of the plant receive equal light.

Vines can be grown in many kinds of containers, from dainty teapots to massive ceramic urns; the choice depends on the size of vine you choose, where you want to put it and what effect you want to achieve. Clay flowerpots are perfectly adequate for many vines grown on the floor or on a window sill. Their warm, earthy color goes with most color schemes, they are heavy enough to resist tipping and, because they are porous, the danger of overwatering and thus drowning a plant is lessened.

Plastic pots, on the other hand, are generally less expensive than clay pots, less susceptible to breakage, available in many colors, and easier to clean. Because they are not porous, they retain moisture, requiring less frequent watering but more care to avoid overwatering. Lightweight plastic containers are particularly well suited for hanging plants, especially large ones; the kind designed for this purpose comes with a drip saucer attached to the base and with hanging wires or chains attached to the sides.

Many trailing vines lend themselves admirably to a hanging display, their long runners draped gracefully over the edges of a pot—which may be hidden inside a handsome basket if you like. By suspending plants from the ceiling, a wall bracket or the top of a window frame, you can enjoy them at eye level and also display more plants without crowding a room. Hang them where they look best and get enough light but will not block traffic—at the center or sides of a window, in a bare corner, high over a stair well, under a skylight, or over a piece of furniture that is not apt to be moved, such as a dining-room table, room divider, bookcase or planter box.

Even a plant in a plastic pot may be quite heavy after it has been watered, so make sure it is securely anchored to the ceiling or wall. A hook or bracket for a large plant should be screwed into a ceiling joist or wall stud. If you do not find a joist or stud in just the right spot, anchor the hook with an expansion or toggle bolt.

Many garden and hardware stores carry special plant-hanging fixtures, including a few ingenious ones. Among the most useful are pivoting brackets that let you swing a plant to follow sunlight (or avoid it) and swivel hooks that allow you to rotate a plant without taking it down, either to provide equal light or to show its best side. Another handy gadget is a self-locking pulley that lets you lower a plant to a convenient level for watering and pruning.

While most vines will cascade from containers suspended in the air or placed at the edge of a window sill, many can also be trained to

## FRAMED FOR A WINDOW VIEW

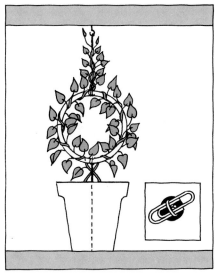

*To make a decorative curtain of vines for your window, thread a length of nylon fishing line through the hole in the bottom of a flower pot and tie it to a paper clip flattened against the pot's exterior (inset). Tie the other end of the nylon line to one edge of an embroidery hoop—or any circular frame. Then tie another length of line to the opposite edge, stretching it to the top of your window and tying it to a screw hook. Fill the pot with soil and plant the vines, which will assume the frame's shape.*

## HANGING DEVICES

climb vertical supports. A philodendron that grows slowly as a trailing plant, for example, will increase its growth rate and leaf size substantially if allowed to climb something resembling the trunks and branches of its native jungle. The support can be as simple as a wooden dowel pushed into the soil of the pot. More attractive, and easier for many vines to cling to, is a branch of weathered driftwood, a section of bark-covered log, or a length of tree fern. Or you can improvise a log by placing long-fibered sphagnum moss, well moistened, on a rectangle of wire mesh. Then roll the mesh to form a tube two or three inches in diameter. Chicken wire will do, though a 1-inch garden mesh coated with dark green plastic is less visible. Set the cylinder upright against the inside edge of a container, then plant the vine next to it, using the potting soil to anchor the cylinder. Fasten the vine to the mesh with pieces of bent wire to give it a start, and encourage aerial rooting by keeping the moss moist.

CLIMBING GUIDANCE

Vines can be trained on other kinds of supports. Climbers can be coaxed into framing a window by providing a simple latticework of string, crisscrossed back and forth between push pins imbedded at intervals around the window. A colorful vine for this purpose, and an easy one to grow, is the morning glory. Plant a few seeds *(page 54)* in a pot in late summer, thin to the strongest seedling when they are a few inches high, and set the pot on the sill, guiding the stems onto the string lattice so the tendrils can get a grip. You will be rewarded with bright flowers at your window into the winter.

Foliage vines, which need less light, can be trained in similar fashion to provide filigrees of leaves elsewhere in the house. Nylon cord or plastic-coated clothesline can be looped between eye screws, hooks or nails to form a freestanding screen.

A LIVING WREATH

With ingenuity, you can train vines to do other indoor tricks. You may enjoy practicing a form of quick topiary, using ivy, creeping fig or other foliage vines grown on wire frames to make ornamental forms. A swan or a poodle made of ivy may appeal to you, or you may prefer simple geometric shapes. Among the latter, one of the easiest to construct is a hoop or ring. Cut a length of galvanized or aluminum wire, bend it into a circular shape, bend the ends outward and anchor them in a potful of soil. Put a young plant or rooted cutting at each base of the wire and tie the stems loosely to it until they grow up to meet at the top of the hoop. With pinching and pruning to stimulate branching, you will have a living wreath that can be decorated with ribbons and used as a holiday ornament.

Almost as easy to make is an ivy tree. Insert several lengths of split bamboo or green plant stakes in a soil-filled urn and tie them together, tepee-fashion, at the top. Young vines trained up the stakes will soon form a convincing tree shape, which can be trimmed with a few baubles for the Christmas scene. Vines like Chilean jasmine or Mexican flame vine, grown at a sunny window, will bear their own ornaments in the form of flowers; move them temporarily to a place of honor for a special occasion. A pair of outdoor vine trees flanking a doorway provide a welcoming note in summer and can be moved indoors when the weather turns cold.

However vines are displayed, they will grow best if given a compatible growing medium and the right care. Some popular foliage vines—heart-leaved philodendron, devil's ivy, English ivy, wandering Jew—will grow in nothing more than a bowl of water. Use an opaque bowl to prevent formation of a scum of algae, and change the water every month or six weeks, adding a few drops of liquid fertilizer for nourishment and a few spoonfuls of charcoal to absorb odors. Most vines, however, grow more satisfactorily in soil. A commercial packaged potting soil for house plants is adequate, sterilized and supplemented to give it nutritive value and a texture that is moisture-retentive but not mushy. Some indoor gardeners think such potting soils are too dense, however, and open them up by adding peat moss or leaf mold and perlite, vermiculite or sand. A few vines require an even more specialized potting mixture; these are detailed in the encyclopedia. Plants like episcias and treebines

**TAILORING A PLANTING SOIL**

**A POLE OF MOSS TO CLIMB**

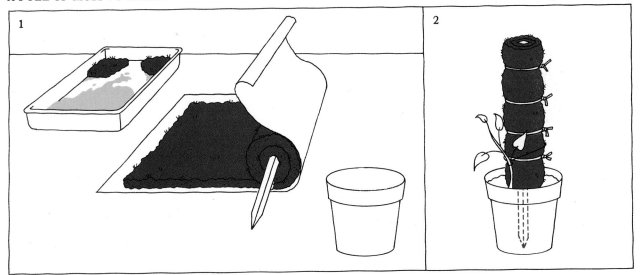

To make a mossy support for a vine with aerial roots, soak loose, long-fibered sphagnum moss in water for 10 minutes. Squeeze out excess moisture and spread the moss in a ½-inch layer over a sheet of brown wrapping paper. Lay a pointed stick at one end of the moss, allowing it to extend far enough beyond the moss to reach the bottom of the pot. Roll the moss tightly around the stick, using the edge of the paper to get started.

When the moss pole is the desired thickness, wrap garden ties or twine around it to hold the moss in place. Push the pointed end into a pot and plant the vine, tying it to the pole. Keep the moss damp by misting daily.

prefer somewhat alkaline conditions; add a tablespoon of ground limestone or crushed eggshells per gallon of potting mix.

When you move a new plant into its permanent pot, or repot an older one that needs more room, line the bottom of the new container with broken pieces of clay pot or a 1-inch layer of coarse gravel to help excess water drain out the bottom hole. Large urns without holes require even deeper drainage layers to keep water from standing around the roots. Place the plant in the container, filling in with soil mixture so the top of the root ball will be half an inch below the pot's rim, or an inch in the case of pots 6 inches or more in diameter. Hold the plant upright and fill around it with more soil, pressing down with your fingers to eliminate air pockets. When the soil is level with the base of the stem, firm it with your thumbs. Water the plant until water dribbles out through the drainage hole.

## A WATERING SCHEDULE

How often you water the plant thereafter will of course depend largely on the varying requirements of different species. A baby's tears or German ivy, for example, should be kept almost constantly moist, while a burro's tail will do better if it is allowed to dry almost completely between waterings. The cycle of growth also influences watering; a dormant plant needs far less water than one actively growing or producing flowers. Other considerations are the type of container and its location. As noted earlier, a plastic pot will retain moisture longer than a clay pot, a solid urn longer than one with drainage holes. A plant in a dark corner will stay moist many days longer than one exposed to sunlight and good air circulation.

As with any house plant, the greatest threat to vines grown indoors is too much water, which prevents air from reaching the roots. Before watering, first probe the soil in each pot with your finger. If it is dry and crumbly, apply enough water to do a thorough job. Many gardeners find it easier to take smaller plants and those in hanging containers to the kitchen sink or bathtub, soaking them in water up to their rims for half an hour before setting them aside to drain. It is a simple matter at the same time to spray the leaves or swirl the foliage around in the water to remove dust and wash off pests. However you water your plants, use tepid rather than cold water. If the water is heavily chlorinated, let a bucketful stand overnight before using it. Water plants in the morning so the leaves and stems will have a chance to dry before nightfall, thus forestalling diseases such as rot that are encouraged by excess moisture.

## UP WITH THE HUMIDITY

While house-plant vines often suffer from too much soil moisture, they also suffer from too little moisture in the air around them. Vines do especially well in kitchens and bathrooms, where the humidity tends to be high. In a dry, sunny living room, group plants so they can take mutual advantage of the moisture that they all transpire constantly, or raise the humidity still more by setting the plants on evaporating trays containing an inch or so of gravel or crushed rock. Keep the bottoms of the trays filled with water, but take care that it does not rise above the gravel. Most vines, especially tropical ones like philodendrons and wandering Jews, also benefit from frequent misting; use a bottle atomizer, and mist the plants in the morning or afternoon so the leaves can dry by dark. Most vines also grow and flower more satisfactorily if night temperatures are cool; ideal ranges are given in the encyclopedia entries *(Chapter 5)*. Actual temperatures may vary within a room, however, and a wall thermostat can only give you an approximation. For more accurate readings, place a thermometer near the plants; if possible, use a maximum-minimum type that records the high and low for the day.

Although vines need nourishment, they require surprisingly little indoors, where dim light slows the process of photosynthesis that enables them to use plant food. Next to overwatering, overfeeding probably kills more house plants than anything else. Too much fertilizer, applied to give a plant rich, shiny foliage, may have the opposite effect; the chemicals build up in the soil without being assimilated, burning the roots until leaves begin to wilt and fall off. Most vines bought at a nursery or garden center have been growing

**EASY ON THE FEEDING**

**TOPIARY IN THE ROUND**

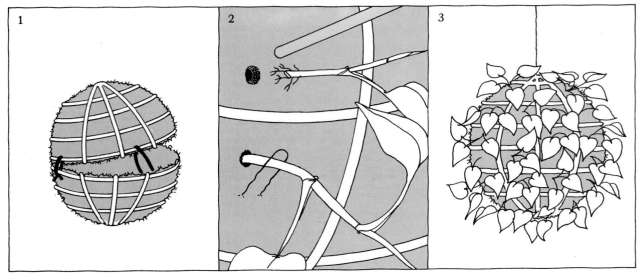

*You can make this leafy green ivy ball in a few simple steps: first, fill two round wire baskets with moist, long-fibered sphagnum moss. Using short lengths of rustproof wire, join the baskets together to form a sphere.*

*Use your fingers or a stick to push rooted ivy cuttings through the wire frame into the moss, anchoring the stems against the moss with bent wire or hairpins. Space the cuttings so that the ivy has room to spread.*

*Your topiary ball needs regular trimming to maintain its shape. It also needs to be kept moist by misting daily and by immersing it in water and letting it drain about as often as you would water any house plant.*

lustily in a well-lighted greenhouse, and have probably been given enough fertilizer to last them for months. While they adjust to their move to less-than-perfect conditions, they will not need additional nourishment for at least three months and more likely six. In addition, most indoor foliage vines require no feeding at all from November through February. Flowering vines should not be fed during winter dormancy; wait until new growth begins to appear.

When you do fertilize, follow the directions given in the encyclopedia for the species you have chosen. Most house-plant fertilizers have their principal minerals in a general ratio of 1:2:1—high in phosphorus for strong root growth, and relatively low in nitrogen and potassium. Never exceed the dosage indicated on the label; many experienced gardeners, in fact, use one half or one fourth the recommended strength. When applying fertilizer, even in dilute liquid form, moisten the soil first to avoid burning the roots. Do not feed a plant that is dormant, ailing or newly potted. A seedling should not be fertilized until it is 3 or 4 inches tall, a cutting until it has put out new growth; then apply the fertilizer at half strength or less. A white crust of minerals on the soil or on the sides of a porous pot indicates a build-up of harmful fertilizer salts; water the plant generously two or three times to leach out the salts, or immerse it, pot and all, for half an hour in a pail of tepid water.

**INDOOR INSECT CONTROL**    Pests and diseases are less of a problem with vines indoors than they are outside. When you buy a plant, check it carefully to make sure it is as trouble-free as possible. Keep any new plant isolated for a couple of weeks, examining it for any previously undetected ailment that might spread to other plants. If you note a colony of insects under leaves, along stems or on tender new growth, remove the plant promptly to the bathtub. Common pests like spider mites, whiteflies and aphids can be washed down the drain by a stiff spray from the shower. Smaller plants can be inverted and swished around in soapy water, and the leaves of larger ones wiped clean with a soapy sponge before being rinsed.

A few insects may defy the floodwaters. Scales—small, oval insects that cling tenaciously—can be soaked with soapy water and scrubbed off with an old toothbrush. Cottony blobs of mealy bugs will succumb to a cotton swab dipped in rubbing alcohol. Larger garden imports like slugs and snails can be picked off by hand or lured to drown in a saucer of grape juice, beer or other tasty liquid set next to the plant. If an insect infestation reaches alarming proportions or a disease starts to blotch foliage, you have two last resorts. You can treat the plant with a chemical targeted for the specific affliction, taking it outdoors to dissipate noxious fumes and scrupulously following the label directions. Or you can spare your other plants the same fate by consigning the infested one to the trash.

After a winter indoors, your vines will be as eager as you are to get out of dry, heated quarters into the fresh air and sunshine. They will benefit noticeably from a summer vacation outdoors. Wait until any danger of a late spring frost has passed, then make the transition gradually so that foliage accustomed to dim indoor light and still air will not be shocked by bright sunlight and damaging winds. Put the plants in a shady, sheltered spot for a couple of weeks, then move those that prefer more light into brighter sun. To keep plants from drying out quickly and to reduce watering chores, slip the pots into larger containers lined with a moisture-holding material like sphagnum moss, or bury them up to their rims in a trench filled with gravel or cinders topped by coarse peat moss, dead leaves or some other moisture-retentive mulch. The coarse lining material will make it less likely that earthworms or slugs will invade the pots.

Summer is also a good time to check a plant's need for repotting and to take cuttings to start new plants. By autumn your vines should be refreshed and flourishing. When outdoor temperatures drop to about the same level you maintain in your house in winter, you can move your vines back inside. Prune away dead stems and exuberant growth, spray the foliage to eliminate any insects picked up in the garden, and return the plants to their indoor places, perhaps trying a new arrangement for your growing collection. Trailing or climbing, lustrous green or splashed with color, your vines will be ready to give you pleasure for another winter.

**A SUMMER VACATION**

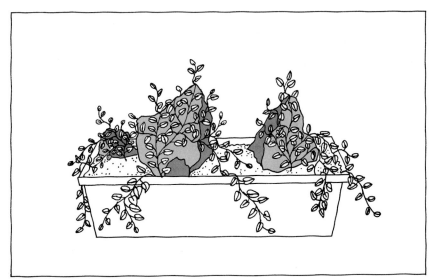

**INDOOR ROCK CLIMBERS**

*Vines whose small aerial roots cling naturally to rocks outdoors, like creeping fig or Canary Island ivy, can continue to do so as house plants, offering an intriguing display of their leaf and stem patterns. To compose such a naturalistic planting, use a plastic or lined redwood planter that will not drip. Put a 2-inch layer of drainage gravel in the bottom. Place one or more rocks on top of the gravel, positioned and partially buried in the soil so that they make a natural-looking miniature landscape. Add potting soil and plant a vine at the base of each rock, pressing down firmly on the soil around the roots to eliminate air pockets.*

# A variety act to fill the house

In a cameo scene in the movie *Desk Set,* Spencer Tracy incredulously surveys a single philodendron vine that winds and curls its way across the walls of Katharine Hepburn's office. "Green thumb," Hepburn crisply states. "Ah!" replies an enlightened Tracy.

Despite the actress' explanation for her plant's flourishing condition, a green thumb is not a prerequisite for successfully growing a philodendron—or any other vine—indoors. Many vines adapt readily to indoor living, thriving in room temperatures of 65° to 75° and sometimes in limited light.

As house plants, vines are vibrant and versatile. They come in an astonishing array of sizes, shapes and colors. Some are grown for the beauty of their foliage, others for their spectacular blooms. There are delicate dwarf vines such as the miniature creeping fig, and giant climbing vines such as the monstera, which indoors can reach a height of more than six feet. Some, like the wandering Jew, are rampant growers and are best started anew each year; others, like the devil's ivy, are so restrained in their growth that they will remain a convenient size for years.

Because their stems are flexible, vines can be trained to fit the line or curve of almost any space. A variegated English ivy can be made to frame a window or alcove, or it will climb lattice strips to form a stunning pattern against a bare wall or ceiling. A grape ivy will weave its way up strands of taut wire to create a floor-to-ceiling room divider. Trailing vines, such as a purple passion vine or a Swedish ivy, will fill an empty corner with shimmering foliage when hung from a wall bracket or planted in a hanging basket.

Most indoor vines need to be periodically thinned and shaped to admit sunlight and air and to keep them in bounds. A bougainvillea, if left unpruned, can overwhelm a picture window in a single season. Such flowering vines need pruning in early spring or after their flowers fade, but foliage vines can have their stems pinched back at any time to keep them shapely. With this easy care, most vines reward their gardeners with vigorous green-thumb growth.

*A glossy-leaved grape ivy hangs suspended over a banister. One of the most popular vines for the house, it thrives in cool nooks where it receives a moderate amount of light.*

# The drama of diverse foliage

From the plumy fronds of a Japanese climbing fern to the wide, perforated leaves of a monstera, indoor vines offer an endless variety of foliage patterns. And many foliage vines are as versatile in use as they are varied in form. A flat-leaved creeping fig can climb a wooden window frame—or the glass of the window itself. A fleecy Sprenger asparagus fern will trail three feet or more from a hanging basket or, if guided, will climb ten feet up a wire trellis.

*The ½-inch paper-thin leaves of a miniature creeping fig lie flat, creating a delicate mat. The vine climbs with rootlets that cling to smooth surfaces.*

*A durable house plant, the monstera is a jungle vine that climbs by sending out aerial roots from its stems. Its glossy leaves may become a foot long.*

*The purple passion vine has 3- to 4-inch lance-shaped leaves covered with purple velvety hairs on both sides. It does best in direct sunlight.*

*The needles of the plumosus asparagus fern (left) and the Sprenger asparagus fern (above) are really short flattened stems that act as leaves. Both climb by twining; without support, their stems arch downward.*

The broad heart-shaped leaves of an elephant's-foot yam dangle from a clay pot. The tuberous root visible in the pot is grown for food in tropical areas.

A Japanese climbing fern weaves its way through a dried cactus stem. The feathery fronds (top) are fertile; the larger ones (bottom) are sterile.

# The many faces of cissus

A large group of mostly tropical and subtropical evergreens, cissus vines (also called treebine or grape ivy) offer a remarkable range of shapes and sizes. Cissus leaves can be broad, thick and bold or as delicate as downy feathers. Climbing with twining tendrils, cissus vines are closely related to grapes, but their fruits are inedible. Most species prefer bright indirect or curtain-filtered sunlight and soil that is allowed to become dry to the touch between thorough waterings. Stem tips should be pinched back to encourage bushiness.

*The toothed foliage of marine ivy tumbles from a pot atop a cylindrical pedestal. Marine ivy tolerates widely fluctuating room temperatures.*

The thick heart-shaped leaves of
an Arabian wax cissus reach out from a
basket. The succulent leaves help
the plant tolerate dry indoor air.

A slender pink cissus displays
velvety leaves colored burgundy on the
undersides. Pink cissus grows
quickly in bright sun.

A jointed, sparsely leaved branch of
a succulent veld grape trails toward the
floor. In summer, it produces green
flowers and pea-sized red fruit.

A miniature grape ivy shows off its
daintily divided leaves. A jungle native,
it needs a warm, humid atmosphere
to grow this luxuriantly.

# Vines that show their colors

Many of the tropical flowering vines grown in northern gardens as annuals, such as black-eyed-Susan vine and ivy geranium, can be coaxed into year-round bloom indoors. Other flowering vines that bloom outdoors only in the Deep South, such as bougainvillea and passionflower vine, also make splendid house plants. They can be used to make a spectacular frame for a south-facing window. Most such vines require constant moisture and frequent fertilizing.

*Swedish ivy produces spikes of tiny orchid-like flowers. If it is grown as a hanging plant, its stems will trail as much as two feet.*

*Rose dipladenia bears salmon flowers that bloom continuously through the year.*

*Bougainvillea has brilliantly colored bracts—scalelike leaves that surround its inconspicuous flowers.*

*The furled flowers of ivy geranium appear in clusters on slender stems that can grow up to four feet long.*

*Two black-eyed-Susan vine flowers peer out like unblinking eyes from a backdrop of raveled foliage. This vine needs cool nights and moist soil.*

*A passionflower vine reveals a large, intriguing flower. A spectacular framing vine for a sunny window, it grows best with cool nights.*

# An encyclopedia of outdoor and indoor vines 5

Vines are like the little girl with the curl in the middle of her forehead: when they are good they are very, very good, and when they are bad they are horrid. The problem is that their habit of growth, taking them perpetually in search of the light, may cause them to exceed the limits of best-laid garden plans. To help you pick a plant that suits your needs, the following encyclopedia describes the ways and means each vine travels and its rate of growth.

You should know before planting, for example, that wisteria is as pushy as a rush-hour bus rider. Place it near a tree and it will thank you by twining to the top and choking the tree to death. Other vines are so polite that their vining habits may hardly be noticed. The asparagus fern, for example, has soft stems equipped with small thorns that enable it to twine on a support. Outdoors or in a greenhouse it can reach lengths of 20 feet. Most people, however, do not recognize it as a vine, since they plant it indoors in hanging containers where the stems cascade under their own weight.

Knowing a vine's habit of growth allows you to choose a flat creeper to cover a rocky slope, a vine that arches in graceful mounds to disguise a stump, a flowering vine to weave through a latticework arbor or an evergreen vine to cling to a brick wall. But habit of growth is not the only important consideration; you also need to know the optimum conditions for a vine's survival. Those that grow outdoors are keyed in the encyclopedia to the climate zone map on page 146, showing where they will survive winter cold. And to help you pick the best time for planting, pruning, mulching and taking care of other garden chores, the maps on page 147 give the dates of the first and last frosts in each of these climate zones.

Plants are listed alphabetically by their Latin botanical names, followed by their common names, and common names are cross-referenced to botanical ones. The chart on pages 148-152 provides a quick reference to the traits of all the vines in the encyclopedia.

*Beautiful baggage carried by traveling vines includes cobaea's cups (top left), sprays of lonicera (top right), thunbergia's black-eyed blooms (bottom right) and the striped foliage of zebrina (bottom left).*

CHINESE GOOSEBERRY
*Actinidia chinensis*

KOLOMIKTA ACTINIDIA
*Actinidia kolomikta*

# A

ACTINIDIA

*A. arguta* (bower actinidia, tara vine); *A. chinensis* (Chinese gooseberry, kiwi berry); *A. kolomikta* (Kolomikta actinidia); *A. polygama* (silver vine)

Actinidia vines twine rapidly around vertical supports as they grow to heights of 15 to 50 feet. These perennials quickly cover arbors, wire fences, and other garden structures with their shiny, heart-shaped deciduous leaves. All bear edible fruit, but male and female flowers are borne on separate plants, so vines of both sexes must be grown to ensure pollination.

The bower actinidia is used as a screen or shade vine for its dense cover of 3- to 5-inch glossy dark green leaves on long red stalks; inconspicuous, mildly fragrant white flowers appear in midsummer and are followed by 1-inch greenish-yellow fruits. Young stems and leaves of Chinese gooseberry are covered with velvety red hairs; its cream-colored 1½-inch flowers appear in midsummer. They turn orange-yellow as they age and are followed by 1½- to 2-inch fuzzy green fruits that taste like gooseberries. The 5- to 7-inch leaves are dark green. Kolomikta actinidia's 4- to 6-inch leaves are blotched at the tips with white or pink; male plants have more leaf color than female ones; leaf colors are brighter if the soil is rich in calcium. The silver-to-white sheen of the male plant's young leaves gives the silver vine its common name; the shiny, bright green mature leaves, 3 to 5 inches long, occasionally are splotched with yellow. This species so excites cats that they claw it to shreds. Bower actinidia, Kolomikta and silver vine grow in Zones 5-10, while the less hardy Chinese gooseberry grows in Zones 7-10.

HOW TO GROW. Actinidias thrive in full sun or partial shade. They grow well in any good garden soil and can become rampant in rich soils. Plant in locations that are moist but well drained; be sure the soil does not become dry in hot weather. Feed sparingly in spring with a general-purpose garden fertilizer. Prune the vines annually in late fall after fruiting or in early spring, cutting back to about one third of the previous year's growth to produce more numerous blooms. Flowers are borne on growth of the previous year. The vines are relatively pest-free. Propagate additional actinidia plants from seeds planted in spring or from stem cuttings taken in midsummer, rooted in moist sand and set out the following spring.

AESCHYNANTHUS

*A. marmoratus; A. radicans*, also called *A. lobbianus; A. speciosus* (all called lipstick plant, basketvine)

Displayed in hanging pots, lipstick plants trail cascades of glossy evergreen leaves and brightly colored tubular flowers on stems 2 to 3 feet long. One species, *A. radicans*, may also be grown on a trellis, but its thin stems need to be tied at intervals. *A. marmoratus* bears 1½-inch yellow-green flowers with brown blotches through the summer. It has light green leaves marbled with dark green, with reddish undersurfaces. The 1½-inch yellow-throated red blooms of *A. radicans* appear in late spring and early summer. *A. speciosus* has 3-inch orange flowers, scarlet at their tips, from midsummer to early autumn.

HOW TO GROW. Lipstick plants grow best with at least four hours of direct sunlight in winter and filtered sunlight in summer, or with 14 to 16 hours a day of medium artificial light. Maintain night temperatures of 65° to 70° and day temperatures of 70° to 75°, with humidity of 50 to 60 per cent. Plant in a packaged potting soil recommended for African violets. Keep the soil constantly moist throughout the growing season and fertilize every two weeks with a house-plant fertilizer diluted to half the recommended strength.

In winter, allow the plants to rest with nearly dry soil, no fertilizer and night temperatures as low as 55°. Do not let new plants flower the first year: instead, pinch back stems when new shoots are 3 or 4 inches long to encourage bushier plants and thus more abundant flowers the following year. When established plants finish blooming, cut stems back to about 6 inches to encourage branching. Repot every three years to ensure good drainage. Plants may become infested with spider mites. Propagate in spring by rooting stem cuttings in moist sand or vermiculite.

## AIR-POTATO YAM See *Dioscorea*

## AKEBIA
### *A. quinata* (five-leaf akebia)
An extremely fast-growing vine, five-leaf akebia twines on any vertical support to a height of up to 15 feet in its first year. It can also be used as a ground cover. The smooth, dark green leaves, composed of five oval leaflets each 1 to 3 inches long, create a delicate texture and a dappled shade for arbors, trellises and other garden structures. A perennial, five-leaf akebia grows to a height of 30 feet or more. From Zone 7 south, the foliage remains green on the vine all year, while in northern areas it remains on the plant well into winter. In the spring the vine bears inconspicuous clusters of fragrant flowers—the females 1 inch wide and purplish brown, the males smaller and light purple.

HOW TO GROW. Five-leaf akebias thrive in full sun and tolerate partial shade in Zones 4-10. A light, moderately rich soil is best but the vine will grow in almost any soil that drains well. Fertilize once a year in spring with a general-purpose garden fertilizer. Annual pruning just after spring flowering is necessary to keep the plant in bounds and to remove weak shoots. The whole plant can be cut back to the ground; it will grow back quickly. Plant in spring, setting the plants about 2 feet apart. Provide a strong support. Five-leaf akebia resists pests and diseases. Propagate from seeds, root division or stem cuttings taken in early summer.

## ALGERIAN IVY See *Hedera*

## ALLAMANDA
### *A. cathartica* (allamanda)
The evergreen tropical allamanda is not a strong climber; it must be tied at intervals to a sturdy permanent support, such as a trellis, fence or pergola, or to horizontal wires strung 3 feet apart. Outdoors in a warm climate, this fast-growing plant can reach a height of 30 to 50 feet, or it can be pruned to form a shrub 2 to 4 feet tall. The large, glossy, dark green leaves, 4 to 6 inches long, form a dense backdrop for the fragrant, brilliant yellow trumpet-shaped flowers, 3 to 5 inches across, that bloom much of the year, most abundantly from late spring to fall. Though it can be grown outdoors in Zone 10, throughout the rest of the country it is grown as a house plant in a sunny window.

HOW TO GROW. An allamanda grows best outdoors in full sun. An indoor plant should be given four hours of sunlight a day except in midsummer, when curtain-filtered light is desirable. Maintain night temperatures of 60° to 65° and day temperatures of 70° or more. Plant the vine in packaged potting soil. Keep the soil moist but not soggy during the growing season and fertilize it every other week with a liquid fertilizer at half the strength recommended on the label. To maintain abundant bloom for nine months of the year, let the

LIPSTICK PLANT
*Aeschynanthus radicans*

FIVE-LEAF AKEBIA
*Akebia quinata*

*For climate zones and frost dates, see maps, pages 146-147.*

ALLAMANDA
*Allamanda cathartica*

PORCELAIN AMPELOPSIS
*Ampelopsis brevipedunculata*

plant rest through the winter; water it so sparingly that the soil is kept nearly dry, and withhold fertilizer. Night temperatures can fall to 55° at this time without damaging the plant. To keep allamanda bushy, prune in late winter, cutting back new shoots to within two or three swollen nodes of the old wood. Train the new growth that will follow while the stems are young and supple.

Propagate allamanda in spring by rooting 3-inch stem cuttings in moist sand or vermiculite over bottom heat of 75° to 80°. When roots have formed, in about three weeks, move cuttings to 3- to 4-inch pots; transfer them to 6-inch pots later in the year. Repot to the next larger container early each spring, when new growth is less than 6 inches long.

**ALLAMANDA, PURPLE** See *Cryptostegia*
**AMERICAN BITTERSWEET** See *Celastrus*

**AMPELOPSIS**
*A. brevipedunculata* (porcelain ampelopsis)

A member of the grape family, the porcelain ampelopsis has deeply lobed green leaves that provide good shade and create a lacy pattern on walls, fences and arbors. It also provides good ground cover, growing in hard, rocky soil and tolerating other adverse conditions. The vine is grown for its clusters of ¼-inch berries that ripen in late summer and autumn, before the vine loses its leaves. The berries of the porcelain ampelopsis change from light green to turquoise, lavender, deep purple and porcelain blue, with all colors frequently appearing in the same cluster at the same time. With forked tendrils, these perennial vines rapidly climb any vertical support, growing up to 15 or 20 feet in their first year. The vine is hardy in Zones 5-10.

HOW TO GROW. The porcelain ampelopsis thrives in either full sun or partial shade. It grows best in light soil but tolerates dry, rocky soil. Feed once a year with a general-purpose garden fertilizer. Prune severely in early spring to thin and shape the vine and restrict its growth. Use pesticide as necessary to control leaf spot and caterpillars. Propagate additional plants from seeds, stem cuttings or by pegging stems to the ground in the spring, then cutting the rooted tips from the mother plant the following spring.

**ANCHORLEAF PHILODENDRON** See *Philodendron*
**ANGELWING JASMINE** See *Jasminum*

**ANTIGONON**
*A. leptopus* (coral vine, Mexican creeper)

With curling tendrils the coral vine will quickly climb 30 to 40 feet up a vertical support outdoors, but it may also be grown in a greenhouse and trained up strings or wires. This vine will cover a trellis, arbor or wire fence with arrow- or heart-shaped leaves up to 4 inches long. Trailing sprays of bright pink flowers bloom abundantly from late summer into fall. The coral vine is hardy outdoors in Zones 9 and 10, where it is evergreen in warm regions but may drop its leaves in cooler areas.

HOW TO GROW. In a greenhouse, the coral vine grows best in full sun where the temperatures range from 60° to 70° at night and from 75° to 85° by day, with humidity of 40 to 60 per cent. Plant in packaged potting soil and keep the medium moist but not soggy. Fertilize infrequently for slow growth and abundant flowers; use house-plant fertilizer diluted to half the strength recommended on the label. Cut the vine back severely after it flowers each year to keep its size under control. Allow the vine to rest over the winter, watering sparingly so the soil remains nearly dry.

Outdoors, plant the coral vine in full sun in light, well-drained soil. Fertilizing is unnecessary; the best flowering is produced on plants growing in infertile soil. Keep the ground moist but never soggy during the growing season. Prune hard, even to the ground, in late fall; the vines will return quickly in the following spring. The vine is relatively pest-free. Propagate from seeds or stem cuttings, or by dividing the tuberous roots at any time during the growing season.

**ARABIAN JASMINE** See *Jasminum*
**ARALIA IVY** See *Fatshedera*

## ARISTOLOCHIA

*A. durior* (Dutchman's-pipe, pipe vine); *A. elegans* (calico flower)

Dutchman's-pipe is a perennial vine grown for dense shade or as a screen in Zones 5-8. Its broad heart-shaped deciduous leaves, glossy dark green and up to 12 inches long, create an overlapping curtain that quickly reaches 20 to 30 feet in height. In the spring of its second season, inconspicuous 1½-inch flowers bloom, curved in the shape of tiny pipes, greenish-yellow at the stem and brownish-purple at the bowl. Their odor is objectionable.

Brazil's calico flower, an evergreen vine, is best grown in a greenhouse or outdoors in Zones 9 and 10, placed where it can climb to a height of 10 feet or more. In the summer, scentless 3-inch-wide flowers grow among the 3-inch heart-shaped leaves. The cups of the flowers are white with purple veins outside, purple-brown with white marks inside.

HOW TO GROW. Dutchman's-pipe thrives in full sun or partial shade and is tolerant of a city environment. It will grow in any good garden soil that is well drained. Before planting, prepare the soil by working in leaf compost or peat moss. Use a general-purpose garden fertilizer once a year. In northern areas, provide winter protection the first year with a heavy mulch. Pinch back stems once or twice during each growing season to encourage branching. Prune severely in late winter to reduce density. Propagate additional plants from stem cuttings in midsummer.

In a greenhouse, calico flower grows best if given full sun in winter and bright indirect light in summer. Night temperatures of 60° to 65°, day temperatures of 70° to 80° and humidity of 40 to 50 per cent are ideal. Pot the vines individually, using a packaged potting soil, or plant 12 to 18 inches apart in greenhouse benches. Provide wire supports for the vines to climb. While the vines are growing actively, keep the soil moist and fertilize once a month with a house-plant fertilizer diluted to half the strength recommended on the label. Let the plants rest in winter by dropping night temperature to 55°, keeping the soil drier and withholding fertilizer. Prune in the spring and repot the plants at the same time. Outdoors in Zones 9 and 10, provide calico flowers with rich, moist, well-drained soil and plant where they will be sheltered from strong wind. Propagate in the spring from seeds or by rooting stem cuttings in moist sand or vermiculite. A container-grown calico flower can be moved outdoors in summer. Both the Dutchman's-pipe and the calico flower may be infested with red spider mites or aphids.

**ARROWHEAD PLANT** See *Syngonium*

## ASARINA

*A. barclaiana,* also called *Maurandya barclaiana* (maurandia); *A. erubescens,* also called *Maurandya erubescens* (creeping gloxinia)

The perennial asarinas are frequently grown as annuals in

CORAL VINE
*Antigonon leptopus*

CALICO FLOWER
*Aristolochia elegans*

MAURANDIA
*Asarina barclaiana*

SPRENGER ASPARAGUS
*Asparagus densiflorus* 'Sprengeri'

northern areas because they quickly become 6 to 10 feet high and bloom in their first year, even when started from seed. The delicate stems will twine around thin vertical supports or cascade from hanging containers. Numerous 3-inch flower trumpets, pink to deep purple on maurandia and rose-red on creeping gloxinia, bloom from spring to autumn against a backdrop of 1- to 3-inch leaves shaped like arrow-heads. Evergreen perennials in Zones 9 and 10, asarinas can be grown in Zones 5-9 as annuals.

HOW TO GROW. Outdoors, grow asarinas in full sun. They will thrive in any moist, well-drained garden soil that has been enriched with leaf mold or peat moss. To grow these plants as annuals, start seeds indoors six to eight weeks before the last expected frost and move the seedlings, in their pots, to the garden when all danger of frost is past. Asarinas bloom most abundantly if their roots are crowded in their pots. Provide strings, wire or a trellis for support.

## ASPARAGUS

*A. asparagoides* (smilax asparagus, florists' smilax); *A. densiflorus* 'Sprengeri,' also called *A. sprengeri* (Sprenger asparagus); *A. plumosus,* also called *A. setaceus* (asparagus fern)

Perennial asparagus vines have lacy fernlike foliage that combines attractively with cut flowers. Smilax asparagus and asparagus fern are both climbers that will twine around a heavy string or wire. Smilax asparagus grows rather quickly to 10 feet; the asparagus fern may ultimately twine to a height of 10 to 20 feet. The delicate evergreen foliage of either species makes an attractive border when grown in beds, boxes or pots along the walls of a greenhouse or a sunny room. Both plants have inconspicuous greenish-white or white flowers in spring. The 2- to 6-foot branches of the Sprenger asparagus arch up and over to form a cascade of needle-like foliage when planted in a pot or hanging container. It may produce fragrant white or pale pink flowers in spring and early summer.

HOW TO GROW. Asparagus vines grow best with bright indirect light, or with 12 to 14 hours a day of medium artificial light. Temperatures of 50° to 55° at night and 68° to 72° in the daytime, with humidity of 40 to 50 per cent, are ideal. Plant the vines individually in pots or 12 inches apart in beds or boxes. Use commercial potting soil and keep the growing medium moist but not soggy. Wait four to six months before feeding newly purchased or potted plants, then fertilize every other week with house-plant fertilizer diluted to half the strength recommended on the label. Allow plants to rest in winter by watering sparingly and withholding fertilizer. Remove yellowing branches as they appear so new ones can take their place. Repot whenever roots appear crowded in the container. The vines may be infested with red spider mites, aphids or thrips. Propagate by dividing the thick, fleshy roots, or start new plants from seeds.

AUSTRALIAN FLAME PEA See *Chorizema*
AUTUMN CLEMATIS, SWEET See *Clematis*

# B

BABY'S TEARS See *Soleirolia*
BABY WINTER CREEPER See *Euonymus*
BALLOON VINE See *Cardiospermum*
BANKS' ROSE See *Rosa*
BANKSIA ROSE See *Rosa*
BASKETVINE See *Aeschynanthus*
BEACH PEA See *Lathyrus*
BEAN, HYACINTH See *Dolichos*
BEAN, SCARLET RUNNER See *Phaseolus*

## BEAUMONTIA

*B. grandiflora* (herald's-trumpet, Easter-herald's-trumpet); *B. jerdoniana* (beaumontia)

In subtropical climates, the beaumontias can rapidly twine their stout, woody stems to a height of 15 to 30 feet. The herald's-trumpet has glossy evergreen leaves up to 8 inches long. In spring and summer, hundreds of trumpet-shaped white flowers 4 inches long and equally as wide appear on the previous season's growth. The large blooms resemble those of Easter lilies and have a fragrance similar to that of the gardenia. The beaumontia vine has smaller leaves and smaller, fragrant trumpet-shaped flowers. Outdoors in Zone 10 either of these perennial vines can be tied to a sturdy trellis or fence, or their arching, semitwining stems can be allowed to climb a tree. They can also be grown in greenhouse beds and kept short by pruning.

HOW TO GROW. Beaumontia vines grow best in full sun in Zone 10 where humidity is high. In a greenhouse, maintain night temperatures of 60° to 65°, day temperatures of 70° to 85° and humidity of 60 per cent. The plants thrive in rich, moist, well-drained soil. Greenhouse vines should be planted in benches rather than pots, since their roots will not tolerate confinement. Keep the soil moist but never soggy; reduce the amount of water in late winter to produce more flowers. Fertilize in the spring with a general-purpose garden fertilizer. Immediately after the vines bloom, prune them severely to reduce size and density and to stimulate lateral growth for the following year's bloom. Beaumontias are relatively free of pests. Propagate additional plants from seed or by rooting stem cuttings in moist sand, vermiculite or equal parts of peat moss and perlite.

HERALD'S-TRUMPET
*Beaumontia grandiflora*

## BEGONIA

*B. tuberhybrida* 'Pendula' (hanging tuberous begonia)

Suspended in a greenhouse or sunny window, hanging tuberous begonias quickly grow into spectacular specimen plants. The 2- to 4-foot stems that spill gracefully over the edges of their containers are covered with masses of flowers throughout the summer. Often frilled, ruffled or tinged a contrasting color along their edges, the flowers may be large or small, single or double, depending on the variety. In bright scarlet, rose, pink, orange, yellow or white, they are borne among shiny heart- or arrow-shaped leaves with serrated edges. Plants growing indoors can be moved to partly sunny locations outdoors during the summer.

HOW TO GROW. Hanging tuberous begonias grow best if they are started in direct sun in spring, but they need indirect or curtain-filtered sunlight during hot summer months while they are flowering. Night temperatures of 55° to 60°, day temperatures of 68° to 72° and humidity of 40 to 50 per cent are ideal for growth. In early spring, start the tubers in shallow pots of moist peat moss mixed with sand. When the leaves appear, pot three to four plants to a 6- to 8-inch pot. Use packaged potting soil, keep the soil moist but not soggy and feed the plants every two weeks during the growing season with a liquid house-plant fertilizer diluted to half the strength recommended on the label. For large flowers, pinch off all of the first set of flower buds, then remove all but the central bud on each stem when the second set appears. In fall, stop fertilizing, gradually withhold water, and allow the foliage to die back. Store the tubers over the winter in a cool, dry place at a temperature between 40° and 50°.

The tubers will increase in size over several growing seasons. Large tubers can be divided in late winter just as they break their dormancy and buds begin to appear. Hanging tuberous begonias can also be propagated by stem cuttings

HANGING TUBEROUS BEGONIA
*Begonia tuberhybrida* 'Pendula'

*For climate zones and frost dates, see maps, pages 146-147.*

taken in early summer and rooted in moist vermiculite; these will form tiny new tubers during their first season and can be stored over the winter and gradually grown to full size.

BEGONIA TREEBINE See *Cissus*
BELLFLOWER, CHILEAN See *Lapageria*
BELLFLOWER, ITALIAN See *Campanula*
BELLS, CATHEDRAL See *Cobaea*
BENGAL CLOCK VINE See *Thunbergia*
BIG-LEAF WINTER CREEPER See *Euonymus*

## BIGNONIA

*B. capreolata* (crossvine)

Climbing by means of twining, branched tendrils that have sticky discs at their tips, the crossvine grows quickly up to 50 or 60 feet, covering walls, fences or trellises with 2- to 6-inch oblong leaflets. In Zones 7-10, this climber makes an effective screen of evergreen foliage that is slightly red in fall and winter. In Zone 6 it grows as a rambling ground cover that is killed to the ground by extreme cold but readily sprouts with the onset of warm weather. Clusters of yellow to brownish-orange trumpet-shaped flowers up to 2 inches long bloom in late spring and early summer and are followed by flat 5- to 7-inch seed pods in fall.

HOW TO GROW. The crossvine grows in full sun or partial shade in any well-drained garden soil. Fertilize the plants with a general all-purpose fertilizer only to get young vines established or when growth is poor, since crossvine tends to be a rampant grower. In early spring, prune 3 to 10 feet from each branch to stimulate new growth and to encourage profuse flowering. At the same time remove any weak branches and prune to improve the vine's shape. Mealy bugs sometimes infest crossvine. Propagate additional plants from seed or by rooting stem cuttings in a mixture of half moist peat moss and half sand.

BIGNONIA See also *Pyrostegia*
BITTERSWEET, AMERICAN See *Celastrus*
BITTERSWEET, EVERGREEN See *Euonymus*
BITTERSWEET, LOESENER See *Celastrus*
BITTERSWEET, ORIENTAL See *Celastrus*
BITTER NIGHTSHADE See *Solanum*
BLACK-EYED-SUSAN VINE See *Thunbergia*
BLACK PEPPER See *Piper*
BLEEDING HEART VINE See *Clerodendrum*
BLUE PASSIONFLOWER See *Passiflora*
BOSTON IVY See *Parthenocissus*

## BOUGAINVILLEA

*B. glabra* (lesser bougainvillea, paper flower); *B. spectabilis* (Brazilian bougainvillea) (both called bougainvillea)

Bougainvilleas are notable for their colorful blooms, which are actually modified leaves called bracts that surround inconspicuous true flowers. Bougainvillea may bear a mantle of these blooms year round, though flowering is most profuse in summer. The two species and their hybrids offer a spectacular range of colors from white through cream to yellow, pale mauve through purple to crimson and orange. The lesser bougainvillea's flowers last longer than those of the Brazilian bougainvillea, but they are smaller and the vine is less vigorous. Brazilian bougainvillea has showier bracts, but its rampant growth requires more pruning. Both bougainvilleas have weakly twining stems and hooked thorns which enable them to climb, but they need to be tied to vertical supports so they do not fall of their own weight. These vines are grown as screens or coverings for arbors and porches

CROSSVINE
*Bignonia capreolata*

outdoors in Zone 10 and in protected locations in Zone 9; elsewhere they are grown in greenhouses.

HOW TO GROW. Outdoors, grow bougainvillea in full sun in any well-drained garden soil. Bougainvillea grows best when the soil is kept moist but not wet, though it will withstand periods of dryness. Fertilize the vine annually in spring with a general-purpose garden fertilizer, and again in summer if needed. Mulch in autumn with leaf mold or compost. Prune after flowering to shape the vine, restrict its growth and remove deadwood. Cut off suckers whenever they appear at the base of the plant.

In a greenhouse, grow bougainvillea in any commercial general-purpose potting soil. Allow the soil to become moderately dry between waterings and feed the plant monthly during the spring and summer growing season with a liquid house-plant fertilizer diluted to half the strength recommended on the label. Before new growth appears in spring or after the vine flowers, cut it back to control its size. During the winter, withhold fertilizer and reduce water. Winter temperatures of 45° to 50° at night and 55° to 60° during the day suit bougainvillea. Summer temperatures of 60° to 65° at night and 70° to 85° by day are ideal. Repot an overcrowded vine in late winter or early spring, being very careful not to damage its roots. Bougainvillea may be attacked by scales, aphids and mealy bugs. Propagate in late spring or early summer by rooting stem cuttings in moist sand.

BOWER ACTINIDIA See *Actinidia*
BOWER, GLORY See *Clerodendrum*
BOWER PLANT See *Pandorea*

## BOWIEA

*B. volubilis* (climbing onion)

An unusual, leafless vine, the climbing onion is a succulent with twining, fleshy green stems that grow from a large green bulb. These stems become 3 to 6 feet long with many forking branches. You can let the stems trail or train them up a light trellis or stake. Hardy in Zone 10, the plant produces inconspicuous green or greenish-white flowers in winter. In spring and summer it is dormant, with the branches dying back.

HOW TO GROW. Climbing onion grows best with four hours or more of direct sun or 12 hours of very bright artificial light daily. During active growth in fall and winter, temperatures of 50° to 55° at night and 68° to 72° in the daytime are ideal. When the plant becomes dormant, in spring and summer, keep it as cool as possible. Plant in a mixture of equal parts of packaged potting soil and sharp sand, adding 1 tablespoon each of ground limestone and bone meal to each gallon. Set the bulb so about three quarters of it projects above the soil. While climbing onion is growing actively, allow the soil to become moderately dry between thorough waterings. As it begins to yellow in spring, reduce watering, then withhold water altogether while the bulb is dormant. Resume watering when growth begins in fall; at the same time fertilize with one teaspoon of bone meal. Repot in fall when necessary.

Outdoors, climbing onion thrives in full sun. Plant it in well-drained sandy loam to which ground limestone and bone meal have been added. When the stems begin to yellow in the spring, let the bulb dry gradually; then dig it up and store it in a cool, dry place through its dormancy and replant it in the fall. Propagate in winter by planting seeds or separating and potting the bulblets that develop around the parent bulb in a moist mixture of soil and sand.

BRAZILIAN BOUGAINVILLEA See *Bougainvillea*
BRAZILIAN FIRECRACKER See *Manettia*

*For climate zones and frost dates, see maps, pages 146-147.*

LESSER BOUGAINVILLEA
*Bougainvillea glabra*

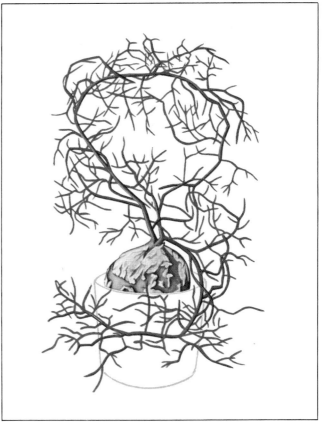

CLIMBING ONION
*Bowiea volubilis*

**WHITE ITALIAN BELLFLOWER**
*Campanula isophylla* 'Alba'

**TRUMPET CREEPER VINE**
*Campsis radicans*

BREADFRUIT, MEXICAN See *Monstera*
BRIDAL VEIL, TAHITIAN See *Tripogandra*
BURMESE HONEYSUCKLE, GIANT See *Lonicera*
BURRO'S TAIL See *Sedum*
BUTTERFLY VINE See *Stigmaphyllon*

# C

CALICO FLOWER See *Aristolochia*
CALONYCTION See *Ipomoea*

## CAMPANULA

*C. isophylla* (Italian bellflower); *C. isophylla* 'Alba' (white Italian bellflower)

Growing only 6 inches high but spreading into clumps 12 to 18 inches wide, Italian bellflowers are perennials suitable for gardens in the South, where their 1-inch heart-shaped or oval leaves form a dense yet delicate cover. Indoors they grow well in a pot placed in a sunny window or trailing from a hanging container. In late summer and fall, 1-inch blue flowers cover the Italian bellflower; the Alba variety has white flowers. The plant is hardy in Zones 8 and 9.

HOW TO GROW. Indoors, Italian bellflowers need moderately cool temperatures, 50° to 55° at night and 68° to 72° during the day. Provide four hours of direct sunlight daily except in midsummer, when curtain-filtered light is sufficient; alternatively, provide 14 to 16 hours of artificial light daily. Plant in a packaged potting soil recommended for African violets. Keep moist during the growing season and fertilize once a month with liquid fertilizer diluted to half the strength recommended on the label. Rest the plant in winter, watering less frequently and withholding fertilizer. In late winter when growth resumes, pinch back stem tips to encourage branching and more flowers.

Outdoors, plant Italian bellflowers in full sun or partial shade, but provide protection from summer noonday sun. Set plants 12 to 18 inches apart in any well-drained garden soil with compost added. Propagate in spring from stem cuttings or plant divisions in moist sand or vermiculite.

## CAMPSIS

*C. grandiflora* (Chinese trumpet creeper); *C. radicans* (trumpet creeper vine); *C. tagliabuana* 'Madame Galen' (Madame Galen trumpet creeper)

In midsummer, the perennial trumpet creepers are covered with spectacular clusters of brightly colored trumpet-shaped flowers, funnels of scarlet or orange 2 to 3 inches long. The deciduous vines provide an effective cover for stone walls, fences, tree stumps or pergolas, bearing compound leaves with 5 to 11 leaflets with saw-toothed edges. Climbing by means of aerial rootlets, the vines may grow 20 to 30 feet high on a rough surface. Seed capsules 5 inches long hang on the vines in winter.

Chinese trumpet creeper, hardy in Zones 8-10, is the least vigorous climber of the three and is therefore best suited for low structures, though its scarlet flowers are the largest. Both the trumpet creeper vine and the Madame Galen hybrid are hardier, surviving in Zones 5-10. Their flowers are bright orange to scarlet.

HOW TO GROW. Trumpet creepers grow best in full sun. Plant them in rich, moist, well-drained garden soil mixed with compost or leaf mold. A mulch of leaves or pine needles will help keep the soil moist. Fertilize young vines by applying a new layer of compost in the spring or by dusting bone meal around the plants in the fall; established vines rarely need fertilizer. Tie new vines to their supports until aerial rootlets appear; heavy mature vines may also need tying.

To control growth, prune established plants in late winter or early spring before new growth starts. Later, pinch back growing tips to promote branching near the base of the plant. As trumpet creepers send out shoots or suckers from underground runners, new plants can be obtained by root division in early spring. These suckers can be a nuisance as well, for new vines may sprout several yards from the main plant. Contain their growth by cutting the roots with a spade. Plants can also be propagated by planting seeds or rooting stem cuttings in moist sand or vermiculite in early spring.

CANARY-BIRD FLOWER See *Tropaeolum*
CANARY NASTURTIUM See *Tropaeolum*
CAPE HONEYSUCKLE See *Tecomaria*
CAPE PLUMBAGO See *Plumbago*
CARDINAL CLIMBER See *Ipomoea*

## CARDIOSPERMUM

*C. halicacabum* (balloon vine, heartseed, love-in-a-puff)

The balloon vine often reaches a height of 10 feet or more in a single season. It has twining tendrils and 2-inch leaves with finely cut leaflets. The inconspicuous white flowers that bloom in the summer are followed by ornamental fruit that appears in the fall. The seed pods are papery, green and balloon shaped; an inch in diameter, they contain black seeds, each with a heart-shaped spot on it. Grown as an annual in Zones 4-8, the balloon vine is an evergreen perennial in Zones 9 and 10. It makes a lightweight, fast-growing cover for trellises, arches, posts or wire fences.

HOW TO GROW. Balloon vines grow best in full sun and in any well-drained garden soil. Although they tolerate some wind, their roots need protection if the temperature falls to freezing. Sow seeds after all danger of frost has passed in the location where the plants are expected to grow so the roots will not have to be disturbed. Before planting, soak seeds overnight to speed germination. Seedlings that have been started in peat pots should be set 12 to 18 inches apart and given supports for climbing.

CAROLINA JASMINE See *Gelsemium*
CATHEDRAL BELLS See *Cobaea*

## CELASTRUS

*C. orbiculatus* (Oriental bittersweet); *C. rosthornianus,* also called *C. loeseneri* (Loesener bittersweet); *C. scandens* (American bittersweet)

The fast-growing bittersweet vine makes an ornamental cover for an arbor, trellis, fence or rocks—or for a wall if the plant is given vertical supports to twine about. But never use a young tree for a support; the twisting stems are so strong they can kill a sapling. Green leaves up to 5 inches long provide heavy cover until autumn when they turn yellow before dropping. On female plants, yellow-orange fruit capsules burst open to reveal spectacular scarlet fruits. These stay on the vines through the winter or until the birds eat them. Berried branches gathered before frost and dried will remain colorful for months indoors. Inconspicuous greenish-white flowers bloom in late spring or early summer.

Oriental and Loesener bittersweets are hardy in Zones 5-9. The vines grow 30 to 40 feet long and bear rounded leaves; fruits appear in small clusters along the branches. American bittersweet, hardy in Zones 3-9, grows only 20 feet long but spreads rapidly; its leaves are oval and berries cluster at the ends of the branches.

HOW TO GROW. Bittersweet vines thrive in full sun or partial shade, growing in any garden soil that is not constant-

**BALLOON VINE**
*Cardiospermum halicacabum*

**ORIENTAL BITTERSWEET**
*Celastrus orbiculatus*

*For climate zones and frost dates, see maps, pages 146-147.*

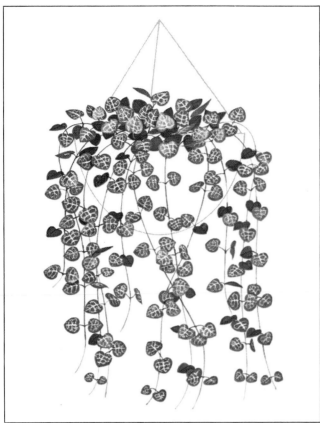

ROSARY VINE
*Ceropegia woodii*

AUSTRALIAN FLAME PEA
*Chorizema cordatum*

ly wet. Prune severely in early spring to increase fruiting and to keep the plants within bounds. Bittersweet may be infested with euonymus scale.

Often invasive, bittersweet vines have underground shoots that may produce new vines where they are not wanted. Cut these from the main plants with a spade. Propagate from such suckers or from stem cuttings taken in spring and rooted in moist sand. Grow male and female plants together to ensure that fruit will appear.

CELEBES PEPPER See *Piper*
CERIMAN See *Monstera*

CEROPEGIA
*C. woodii* (rosary vine, heart vine)

The wirelike purplish stems of the rosary vine are lined with pairs of ¼- to ½-inch, heart-shaped succulent leaves that are green marbled with white on top and purple underneath. In the fall, small clusters of tiny, waxy pink-to-purple flowers sometimes bloom in the leaf joints. Plants may flower for as long as six weeks. This fast-growing house plant can be tied to a small trellis, or its 3- to 4-foot stems can be allowed to trail gracefully from a hanging container.

HOW TO GROW. The rosary vine grows best in bright indirect or curtain-filtered sunlight, or in 12 to 14 hours a day of medium artificial light. Night temperatures of 50° to 55° and day temperatures of 68° to 72° are best. Plant in a packaged potting soil. Let the soil become moderately dry between thorough waterings from spring through fall; in winter, water only enough to keep the leaves from shriveling. Feed every two weeks from spring to midsummer with a standard houseplant fertilizer at half the strength recommended on the label. Do not feed at other times of the year. Pinching back tips causes bushier growth. Repot crowded plants in the spring; do not feed newly potted plants for a year. Propagate from cuttings. The small beadlike tubers that occasionally develop at the leaf joints can be cut off and rooted in moist sand or vermiculite to obtain more plants.

CHAIN PLANT See *Tradescantia*
CHALICE VINE, GOLDCUP See *Solandra*
CHILEAN BELLFLOWER See *Lapageria*
CHILEAN JASMINE See *Mandevilla*
CHILE-BELLS See *Lapageria*
CHINA FLEECE VINE See *Polygonum*
CHINESE GOOSEBERRY See *Actinidia*
CHINESE TRUMPET CREEPER See *Campsis*
CHINESE WISTERIA See *Wisteria*
CHINESE YAM See *Dioscorea*

CHORIZEMA
*C. cordatum* (Australian flame pea, flowering oak)

A sprawling evergreen, Australian flame pea has weak, wiry 3- to 4-foot stems that can be trained to climb a trellis or trail over low walls. From spring to early summer, the plant bears loose, multicolored flower clusters up to 6 inches long. The ¾-inch yellow, purple, orange and red flowers that make up each cluster resemble pea blossoms. The oval 1- to 2½-inch leaves may have jagged edges when mature. Its evergreen foliage makes the Australian flame pea useful for disguising unsightly garden structures in Zones 9 and 10.

HOW TO GROW. Outdoors, the Australian flame pea grows best in full sun in any well-drained slightly acid soil. Plant the shrub at any time of the year and keep it well watered. Cut flower stems back after they bloom. Pinch back young plants two or three times to promote branching. To train the shrub up a trellis, prune away all but three or four stems. In the greenhouse, the flame pea does best in full sun. Night temperatures of 50° to 55° and day temperatures of 60° to 70° are best. Plant in a packaged potting soil. Keep the soil evenly moist and feed every two months with a house-plant fertilizer diluted to half the strength recommended on the label. Do not feed newly potted or purchased plants for four to six months. Propagate the Australian flame pea by rooting cuttings of new growth in moist vermiculite.

CINNAMON VINE See *Dioscorea*

## CISSUS
*C. antarctica,* also called *C. glandulosa* and *Vitis antarctica* (kangaroo treebine); *C. discolor,* also called *C. velutina* (begonia treebine); *C. incisa* (ivy treebine, possum grape, marine ivy); *C. rhombifolia,* also called *Vitis rhombifolia* (grape ivy, Venezuela treebine)

Vines that cling to supports with grapelike tendrils, the treebines rapidly climb trellises, strings or posts. Outdoors, they can be trained to grow over a small arbor or pergola; one of them, the ivy treebine, is more commonly grown as a ground cover. Indoors, the plants' soft stems usually dangle over the edges of hanging containers. Kangaroo treebine's shiny, dark green oval leaves are 4 to 6 inches long with toothed edges. Its hairy branches remain under 8 feet indoors but grow from 10 to 15 feet long in the garden. It is hardy in Zones 9 and 10. Begonia treebine has velvety heart-shaped leaves 3 to 4 inches long that are marbled with purple and silver on top and have dark maroon undersides. During the winter, plants drop most of their leaves and the remaining foliage fades. On house plants, the trailing red stems grow up to 8 feet long but outdoors they may reach 20 feet. They are hardy in Zone 10.

Ivy treebine bears fleshy three-lobed leaves 1 to 2 inches long on woody stems that may reach 30 feet in length. This native American plant is usually grown only outdoors. Thick and shrubby, it is hardy in Zones 8-10. Grape ivy has three-lobed leaves, 4 inches long and almost equally wide. Bronze at first and coated with fine reddish hairs, they turn green as they mature. The hairy brown stems grow up to 8 feet long indoors; outdoors they may become 20 feet long. Grape ivy is hardy only in Zone 10.

HOW TO GROW. Indoors, the kangaroo and begonia treebines and grape ivy grow best in bright indirect or curtain-filtered sunlight or in 10 to 12 hours a day of medium artificial light. Kangaroo treebine and grape ivy need night temperatures of 50° to 55° and day temperatures of 68° to 72°. They tolerate humidity as low as 30 to 40 per cent. Begonia treebine grows best with temperatures of 65° to 70° at night and 75° to 85° by day, with humidity of about 50 per cent. Pot these three species in commercial potting soil, adding 1 tablespoon of ground limestone per gallon of soil. Allow the soil to dry slightly between thorough waterings. Feed plants weekly with a house-plant fertilizer diluted to one fourth the strength recommended on the label. To encourage bushy growth rather than trailing stems, pinch off stem tips in the spring.

Outdoors all treebines thrive in partial shade and in any well-drained soil, but in the northernmost parts of the growing zones, they all need protection from strong wind and winter cold. Water plants frequently in summer, then reduce watering for the rest of the year. Prune in early spring. Treebines are subject to infestations of aphids and mealy bugs. Propagate additional plants by rooting stem cuttings of new growth in moist vermiculite or sand.

*For climate zones and frost dates, see maps, pages 146-147.*

KANGAROO TREEBINE
*Cissus antarctica*

BEGONIA TREEBINE
*Cissus discolor*

JACKMAN CLEMATIS
*Clematis jackmanii*

ORIENTAL CLEMATIS
*Clematis orientalis*

## CLEMATIS

*C. jackmanii* (Jackman clematis); *C. montana rubens* (pink-anemone clematis); *C. orientalis,* also called *C. graveolens* (Oriental clematis); *C. paniculata* (sweet autumn clematis); *C. tangutica* (golden clematis); *C. texensis* (scarlet clematis); *C. viticella; C.* hybrids (all called clematis)

Vigorous, fast-growing clematis vines twist their tendril-like leaf stalks around any thin support as they climb and produce abundant, exquisite flowers as far north as Zone 5. The vines are perennials that have a dense mat of leaves to shade porches or conceal walls and fences. Depending on the species grown and the climate, the vines may be evergreen or deciduous, or they may die to the ground in winter. The flowers, 1 to 10 inches wide, have no true petals but 4 to 8 brightly colored petal-like sepals. Fluffy seed pods remain on some species long after the flowers fade. As cut flowers, clematises are long lasting; the seed pods are used in dried arrangements. Clematis flowers form either on the current season's growth or on that of the previous year. In the latter case, flowering is less certain in colder areas.

Jackman clematis grows up to 12 feet tall and bears clusters of deep violet flowers, 4 to 6 inches wide, from summer to fall on growth of the current season. Spring-blooming pink-anemone clematis often reaches 25 feet in height and bears rosy clusters of anemone-like flowers, 2 to 2½ inches wide, on the growth of the previous year. Its bronze-green leaves are red when they unfold. Oriental clematis grows from 10 to 20 feet tall; its autumn flowers are yellow, 1½ to 2 inches wide, with thick, curving sepals; they appear on the current year's growth.

Sweet autumn clematis grows up to 30 feet tall; its fragrant white flowers, 1½ to 4 inches wide, bloom on the current year's growth in late summer and fall and are followed by decorative silvery seed heads. It is attractive as a ground cover as well as a climber. Golden clematis usually remains under 10 feet tall, bearing yellow flowers 3 to 4 inches wide from summer to autumn on the current year's growth. Scarlet clematis, which grows 6 to 12 feet tall, usually dies to the ground in winter but reappears the following spring; its urn-shaped red flowers, 1 to 1¼ inches long, bloom in the summer. *C. viticella* grows 8 to 12 feet tall and bears single or clustered purple-to-rose bell-shaped flowers, 1 to 2½ inches wide, which appear on the current year's growth from midsummer to fall.

Many hybrid clematis vines have been produced with spectacular flowers that are up to 10 inches wide. Spring-flowering hybrids are Duchess of Edinburgh, with double white flowers, and Nelly Moser, with flowers that are lavender with purplish-red stripes.

Hybrids that flower late in the season on the current year's growth include Ernest Markham, with vivid red flowers; Hagley Hybrid, with pink flowers and purple anthers; Gipsy Queen, with deep violet flowers; Lord Neville, with plum-colored flowers; Mme. Baron-Veillard, with lavender to rose blooms; and Prins Hendrik, with light-blue flowers.

HOW TO GROW. Clematis grows best in partial shade, but in the northern zones the plants tolerate full sun. They thrive in moist, well-drained, slightly alkaline to neutral soil. Buy two-year-old plants. Set them out in the fall when they are dormant or, where winters are severe, plant in the spring. Place the crown of each plant 2 inches below the soil level. During the growing season keep the soil cool and moist by covering it with a 2- to 3-inch mulch of compost or peat moss supplemented with a cupful of ground limestone. Do not plant within six feet of the vines because the shallow roots are easily damaged. Provide a light trellis or other support.

The vines can remain undisturbed indefinitely and need only occasional pruning. Prune late-flowering species in the early spring; remove dead or weak stems and cut off seed heads from the previous year. Vines that bloom in the spring on growth of the previous year should not be pruned; if flowers are removed after they fade, new ones may follow in the fall. To encourage bushy growth on vines, cut shoots about 9 inches from the ground early in the second season. Clematis wilt sometimes causes vines to die to the ground, but if diseased vines are removed and the roots kept moist and shaded, new shoots often reappear either in the same season or by the following spring. Clematises can be propagated from stem cuttings taken in spring or early summer and rooted in moist sand or vermiculite.

## CLERODENDRUM
*C. thomsoniae* (bleeding heart vine, glory bower)

Dangling two-toned flowers that bloom in spring and summer make the bleeding heart vine a decorative indoor plant. Its twining evergreen stems are easily trained to a trellis and will cascade from a hanging container. Flower clusters up to 6 inches long and 3 inches wide begin blooming at the end of each stem when stems are but a foot long. The deep red petals hang from a white puffy base. The vine's deeply veined 3- to 6-inch leaves are covered with downy hairs.

HOW TO GROW. Bleeding heart vine grows best in bright indirect or curtain-filtered sunlight. It can also be grown under 12 to 14 hours of medium artificial light daily. Night temperatures of 60° to 65° and day temperatures of 70° or higher are ideal. Plant in a commercial potting soil and keep the soil evenly moist but never soggy. Feed the plants every two weeks during the growing season with a house-plant fertilizer diluted to half the strength recommended on the label. After the flowers fade, cut the branch tips back to encourage new growth and new flowers. Propagate by rooting stem cuttings of new growth in moist sand or vermiculite.

## CLIANTHUS
*C. formosus,* also called *C. dampieri* (desert pea); *C. puniceus* (parrot's bill, red kowhai) (both also called glory pea)

These two glory peas are sprawling shrubs, but their hanging 3-inch flowers, which are followed by 2- to 3-inch pods, are displayed best when the plants are trained against a wall or trellis. Desert pea grows up to 4 feet tall; its satiny red flowers are blotched with purple-black at their centers; they bloom in spring or summer amid 1-inch silver-gray leaves. Parrot's bill is a 6-foot bush in New Zealand, but it is usually trained for vinelike growth in the Northern Hemisphere. Its flowers are red, pink or white. Both glory peas are perennials in Zones 9 and 10.

HOW TO GROW. Glory peas thrive where they receive full sun in winter and partial shade in summer and in any well-drained soil. When night temperatures remain above 50°, sow seeds where the plants are to remain, since glory peas are difficult to transplant. Space plants about 1 foot apart and provide a trellis, string or wire support for them to climb. The desert pea is not easy to raise from seed; its seedlings are sometimes grafted onto the roots of *Colutea arborescens.* Parrot's bill can be propagated from stem cuttings rooted in moist sand or vermiculite.

CLIMBER, CARDINAL See *Ipomoea*
CLIMBING FERN, JAPANESE See *Lygodium*
CLIMBING FIG See *Ficus*
CLIMBING HYDRANGEA See *Hydrangea*
CLIMBING ONION See *Bowiea*

*For climate zones and frost dates, see maps, pages 146-147.*

BLEEDING HEART VINE
*Clerodendrum thomsoniae*

PARROT'S BILL
*Clianthus puniceus*

103

CUP-AND-SAUCER VINE
*Cobaea scandens*

COLUMNEA
*Columnea gloriosa*

CLIMBING PEPPER See *Piper*
CLOCK VINE See *Thunbergia*

## COBAEA

*C. scandens* (cup-and-saucer vine, cathedral bells)

A dense vine that can grow 15 to 25 feet in one summer, the cup-and-saucer vine clambers rapidly over a fence, trellis or wall. Its stems cling by branched tendrils that grow on the end of each leaf stalk. From early summer to midfall, the vine bears unique flowers about 2 inches long and 1½ inches wide; these resemble tiny greenish-purple, lavender or violet cups sitting on green saucer-like bases. The opening buds have an unpleasant smell at first but soon become honey-scented. In frost-free areas of Zones 9 and 10, this vine is a woody perennial; in Zones 3-8 it is grown as an annual.

HOW TO GROW. The cup-and-saucer vine thrives in full sun and in a moist, well-drained soil. A soil that is rich encourages leaf growth with fewer flowers. The plants are relatively pest free. In Zones 3-8, sow seeds indoors six to eight weeks before the last frost is expected. Once the danger of frost is past, move seedlings outdoors, spacing them 18 to 24 inches apart. Give the plants a support to climb, such as strings, wire netting, stakes or a trellis. In Zones 9 and 10, sow seeds directly in the garden in early spring. During the growing season, pinch back tips to stimulate branching and to encourage more flowering. Plants grown as perennials should be thinned in late fall to direct growth and reduce density.

## COLUMNEA

*C. allenii; C. gloriosa; C. hirta; C. tulae* 'Flava' (all called columnea)

Grown indoors in hanging containers, columneas, which are native to the tropics, bear spectacular tubular flowers 2 to 4 inches long that are shaped like goldfish. Occasionally, white berry-like fruit develops after the flowers fade. The stems, which grow up to 4 feet long if not pinched back, are lined with pairs of 1- to 2-inch leaves and are sometimes covered with fine hairs. From fall through spring *C. allenii* has red-orange flowers with yellow throats; *C. gloriosa*, red flowers with yellow throats in May and June; *C. hirta,* vermilion flowers from fall through spring; *C. tulae* Flava, yellow flowers from fall through spring.

HOW TO GROW. Columneas grow best when they are given bright indirect or curtain-filtered sunlight or 14 to 16 hours daily of low artificial light. Night temperatures of 60° to 65° and day temperatures of 70° to 75° are suitable most of the year, but *C. gloriosa* blooms best if it is given a winter rest period with night temperatures reduced to between 50° and 60°. At the same time withhold fertilizer and water sparingly. Maintain humidity as close to 60 per cent as possible. Plant columneas in a commercial potting soil recommended for African violets. Keep the soil evenly moist. If flowers wither prematurely, the plants have too much water; if the leaves yellow, the plants are not receiving enough water. Fertilize monthly during active growth with a house-plant fertilizer diluted to half the strength recommended on the label. To stimulate new growth, prune branches after the flowers fade. Propagate in spring or summer from stem cuttings rooted in moist sand or vermiculite.

COMPACT WAX PLANT See *Hoya*
COMPTON CORAL-PEA See *Hardenbergia*
CONFEDERATE JASMINE See *Jasminum*
CONFEDERATE STAR JASMINE See *Trachelospermum*
CORAL-PEA, COMPTON See *Hardenbergia*
CORAL HONEYSUCKLE See *Lonicera*

CORAL VINE See *Antigonon*
COSTA RICAN NIGHTSHADE See *Solanum*
CREEPER, ENGELMANN See *Parthenocissus*
CREEPER, JAPANESE See *Parthenocissus*
CREEPER, LOW'S See *Parthenocissus*
CREEPER, MEXICAN See *Antigonon*
CREEPER, ST. PAUL'S See *Parthenocissus*
CREEPER, SILVER-VEIN See *Parthenocissus*
CREEPER, TRUMPET See *Campsis*
CREEPER, VEITCH'S See *Parthenocissus*
CREEPER, VIRGINIA See *Parthenocissus*
CREEPER VINE, TRUMPET See *Campsis*
CREEPING FIG See *Ficus*
CREEPING GLOXINIA See *Asarina*
CREEPING JENNIE See *Lysimachia*
CREEPING MYRTLE See *Vinca*
CREEPING PILEA See *Pilea*
CRIMSON VINE See *Vitis*
CROSSVINE See *Bignonia*

## CRYPTOSTEGIA
*C. grandiflora* (palay rubber vine, purple allamanda)

The palay rubber vine is a woody African twiner with stems that wrap around any convenient support to create a dense evergreen screen in warm climates. The leathery leaves, 3 to 4 inches long, are paired along stems up to 20 feet long. Funnel-shaped purple flowers, 2 to 3 inches wide, resemble allamanda blooms. They gradually fade from purple to pale lavender in the sun and are followed by 4-inch wing-shaped pods. Latex taken from the plant can be used to make rubber. The palay rubber vine grows outdoors in Zone 10 or it can be grown in a warm greenhouse.

HOW TO GROW. Palay rubber vine does well in partial shade and in any well-drained garden soil. Water freely during hot summer months, more sparingly the rest of the year. Give the plant a strong support to climb, such as a wall, fence or trellis. Prune lightly to control the shape. Propagate additional plants in spring or summer by rooting cuttings in moist sand or vermiculite.

CUP-AND-SAUCER VINE See *Cobaea*
CUP-OF-GOLD See *Solandra*
CYPRESS VINE See *Ipomoea*

# D

DESERT PEA See *Clinathus*
DEVIL'S IVY See *Scindapsus*

## DIOSCOREA
*D. batatas* (cinnamon vine, Chinese yam); *D. bulbifera* (air-potato yam)

Fast-growing vines with large heart-shaped leaves, these perennials, evergreen in frost-free areas, use their stem tips to twine around vertical supports, growing up to 10 feet in a single season. They die to the ground in northern winters but reappear the following spring.

Cinnamon vine, named for the scent of its flowers, rises from an underground tuber 2 to 3 feet long. Its stems sometimes produce small secondary tubers at leaf joints. The stems of air-potato vine bear tubers 8 to 12 inches long on the vine. Both bear clusters of tiny pale flowers in late summer and need strong supports to grow on. Cinnamon vine is hardy as an ornamental in Zones 5-10, but for edible tubers ready to be harvested in the fall it should not be planted north of Zone 7.

HOW TO GROW. Both cinnamon and air-potato vines thrive

*For climate zones and frost dates, see maps, pages 146-147.*

**PALAY RUBBER VINE**
*Cryptostegia grandiflora*

**CINNAMON VINE**
*Dioscorea batatas*

ROYAL TRUMPET VINE
*Distictis* 'Rivers'

HYACINTH BEAN
*Dolichos lablab*

in full sun or partial shade. They should be planted in moist, well-drained garden soil. Give plants room to spread both below and above the ground. Set cut pieces of tubers out in the spring; in frost-free zones they can be planted at any time. Place tubers 6 to 8 inches deep. Water the plants frequently, then decrease the amount of water gradually as the plants die down; do not water them in winter. Where the soil in winter is cold and moist, dig up the tubers and store them indoors in dry sand in a cool place. In mild climates, prune the vines severely in late fall to control growth.

**DIPLADENIA** See *Mandevilla*

## DISTICTIS
*D. laxiflora* (vanilla trumpet vine); *D.* 'Rivers' (royal trumpet vine)

Fast-growing trumpet vines have tendrils at the ends of their leaves with which they grasp the arbors and pergolas they decorate in southern gardens. Sometimes growing 20 feet in one season, they branch freely and bear trumpet-shaped flowers at intervals all through the year. Vanilla trumpet vine is named for the scent of its flowers, which are 3½ inches long and 2½ inches wide. Their dark purple buds open lavender, then fade to white with red-striped throats. All of these colors often appear simultaneously. Thin, winged seed pods up to 3½ inches long follow the flowers. The hybrid royal trumpet vine has flowers that are often twice as big as those of the species. Both vines are evergreen in Zones 9 and 10 and can survive the winter in Zone 8 if they are planted in a sheltered position.

HOW TO GROW. Trumpet vines require partial shade during the hottest part of the day. They grow well in any moist, well-drained garden soil if they are protected from drying winds in the winter. In frost-free zones, sow the seeds outdoors in the early spring; in other areas, sow seeds when the night temperatures will remain above 50°. Space trumpet vines to grow about a foot apart. If there is no nearby trellis, provide strong wire supports. Prune away excessive growth as soon as the flowers have faded. Propagate additional plants from stem cuttings taken in the spring and rooted in moist sand or vermiculite.

## DOLICHOS
*D. lablab* (hyacinth bean)

A vine that climbs by twining, hyacinth bean grows from 10 to 30 feet in a single summer and will quickly cover a fence or trellis. Hyacinth bean, which is neither a hyacinth nor a bean, has 6-inch leaves and bears purple or white flowers 2 to 4 inches wide on long spikes in midsummer. These are followed by flat seed-filled pods. In Zones 3-8 hyacinth bean must be treated as an annual; it can be grown as a perennial in Zones 9 and 10, but it has a tendency to become woody and less attractive after several years.

HOW TO GROW. Hyacinth bean grows well in full sun in any well-drained soil, but in Zones 3 and 4 it needs a sheltered location. Since it is hard to transplant successfully, plant it in its permanent location. When night temperatures will stay above 50°, sow the seeds, spacing them about 1 foot apart. If no trellis is available, provide string or wire supports for the tendrils to grasp. Hyacinth bean is relatively free of pests. For earlier flowering in Zones 3-5, start seeds indoors six to eight weeks before the last frost is due. Sow seeds in individual 3-inch peat pots. Once the danger of frost is past, set the seedlings, pots and all, directly into the ground. Additional vines can also be propagated from stem cuttings rooted in moist sand.

DUTCHMAN'S-PIPE See *Aristolochia*

# E

EASTER-HERALD'S-TRUMPET See *Beaumontia*
ENGELMANN CREEPER See *Parthenocissus*
ENGLISH IVY See *Hedera*
EPIPREMNUM See *Scindapsus*

## EPISCIA
*E. cupreata* (flame violet); *E. cupreata* 'Acajou'; *E. dianthiflora* (lace-flower vine); *E. lilacina; E. reptans* (flame violet) (all called episcia, flame violet)

The plush-leaved episcias spread by sending out many runners to form new plants. The wrinkled foliage may be shades of red, purple, bronze, copper and silver as well as green. Episcias are grown indoors in hanging containers so their long stems and runners can cascade gracefully over the edges. Delicate tubular flowers ½ to 2 inches long bloom from early spring to early fall.

*E. cupreata* has slender branching stems with shoots bearing bright orange-red flowers; its wrinkled, downy leaves 2 to 3 inches long have copper, bronze or silver markings. The variety Acajou has silvery green leaves edged with mahogany or greenish-brown. Lace-flower vine makes a 4-inch mound of velvety 1½-inch oval green leaves with purple midribs; its 1¼-inch white flowers have fringed edges and purple-spotted throats. *E. lilacina* has lavender flowers and bronze-green leaves 3 to 4 inches long. *E. reptans* has hairy dark green leaves up to 5 inches long with a light green or silver pattern along the midribs; the 1½-inch flowers are red.

HOW TO GROW. Episcias grow best in bright indirect or curtain-filtered sunlight or under medium artificial light for 14 to 16 hours a day; too much light will bleach and burn the leaves. Night temperatures of about 65°, day temperatures of 70° to 75° and a humidity of 60 per cent are ideal. Dry air causes the leaf edges to dry and curl. Plant episcias in a packaged mix prepared for African violets and add a teaspoon of ground limestone per quart. Keep the medium evenly moist but not soggy and feed plants every two weeks after watering, using a standard house-plant fertilizer diluted to half the strength recommended on the label. Avoid splashing cold water on the leaves lest they develop brown spots. To encourage new growth, a more compact shape and more profuse flowering, pinch off runners and cut back straggly stems after flowers fade. Repot when roots fill the container; episcias do poorly if pot bound. Propagate additional plants at any time from runners or from stem cuttings rooted in moist vermiculite, sand or perlite.

## EUONYMUS
*E. fortunei* 'Colorata' (purple winter creeper); *E. fortunei* 'Minima' (baby winter creeper); *E. fortunei radicans* (common winter creeper); *E. fortunei vegeta* (big-leaf winter creeper, evergreen bittersweet)

Evergreen winter creepers cling to rocks, trees and walls by means of tiny roots that sprout along their stems as they slowly develop into mats up to 20 feet long and 6 feet wide. Sometimes pruned as shrubs, winter creepers can serve as ground cover, especially in places where erosion control on steep banks is needed. They will ramble over fences or boulders and can be trained up the side of a house or other support. Winter creeper is hardy in Zones 5-10.

Common winter creeper has dark green 1-inch leaves. Purple winter creeper has 1- to 2-inch leaves that turn purple or red in fall and winter. Baby winter creeper is a trailing plant that is used in rock gardens; its stems, seldom more

EPISCIA
*Episcia cupreata* 'Acajou'

BABY WINTER CREEPER
*Euonymus fortunei* 'Minima'

*For climate zones and frost dates, see maps, pages 146-147.*

**FATSHEDERA**
*Fatshedera lizei*

**CREEPING FIG**
*Ficus pumila*

than 3 feet long, are lined with tiny ½-inch leaves. A variety called big-leaf winter creeper, which is more shrublike in habit, has rounded 1½-inch leaves and bears orange-to-red berries in the autumn.

HOW TO GROW. Winter creeper grows well in full sun or partial shade; in Zones 5 and 6 it needs some shade to protect its leaves from sunburn during winter. Plant winter creeper in any moist, well-drained garden soil. Set the plants out in spring or fall, spacing them 1 to 2 feet apart, discouraging weeds with a mulch of ground bark or wood chips. Provide a sturdy support if vertical growth is desired. Propagate in the spring by rooting stem cuttings in moist sand or vermiculite. Spray with malathion or dormant oil in early and late summer to control euonymus scale.

EUROPEAN GRAPE See *Vitis*
EVENING TRUMPET FLOWER See *Gelsemium*
EVERBLOOMING HONEYSUCKLE See *Lonicera*
EVERGREEN BITTERSWEET See *Euonymus*

# F

## FATSHEDERA
*F. lizei* (fatshedera, tree ivy, aralia ivy)

Fatshedera is a semierect vinelike shrub resulting from an unusual cross between plants of two different genera, Irish ivy *(Hedera helix hibernica)* and Moser's Japanese fatsia *(Fatsia japonica* Moseri). Although it lacks ivy's aerial roots, its ropelike, elongated, 4- to 8-foot stems are easily tied and trained to a support. Fatshedera is far less bushy than fatsia, but regular pruning encourages leafy growth 3 to 4 feet wide. The glossy evergreen leaves are deeply cut into lobes like the Irish ivy but are 5 to 10 inches wide. Outdoors in Zones 8-10 the floppy stems will trail across the ground or drape low walls and banks. Either indoors or out, fatshedera grows well in containers.

HOW TO GROW. Fatshedera grows best indoors with at least four hours of direct sunlight or 12 to 14 hours daily of medium artificial light. It will grow fairly well in bright indirect light. Temperatures of 40° to 55° at night and 65° to 72° by day are best. Plant in a packaged potting soil and keep it barely moist at all times. Wait four to six months before feeding newly potted plants. Feed established plants monthly except in winter with a liquid house-plant fertilizer diluted to half the strength recommended on the label. Repot crowded plants before new growth starts in early spring. To encourage branching, cut plants back in the spring to within 4 to 6 inches of the soil.

Outdoors, fatshedera thrives in full sun or partial shade in any well-drained soil. Set out plants in the fall or spring. For a trailing ground cover, pin the stems down onto the soil when they are about 1½ feet long. Tie climbing plants to a support. Propagate in summer by rooting stem cuttings in moist sand or vermiculite.

FERN, ASPARAGUS See *Asparagus*
FERN, JAPANESE CLIMBING See *Lygodium*
FERNLEAF INCH PLANT See *Tripogandra*

## FICUS
*F. pumila,* also called *F. repens* (creeping fig, climbing fig)

Creeping fig is a clinging vine with crisscrossing stems that in time form a solid matted wall of 1-inch heart-shaped leaves with pronounced veins. Because its ivy-like aerial roots cling to concrete blocks, bricks and even stucco, this evergreen vine is a good cover for masonry surfaces; its dense, flat growth pattern also makes it useful as a screening plant. Hardy outdoors in Zones 9 and 10, the plant rapidly grows 20 to 60 feet tall. Unpruned mature creeping figs develop projecting branches with large, thick 2- to 4-inch leaves and 2-inch heart-shaped brown-to-purple fruit that is inedible. A dwarf variety has tiny ⅝- to ¾-inch leaves; the oak-leaved creeping fig has dark green leathery leaves less than an inch long with pronounced lobes; a variegated form has green foliage marbled with white. Creeping figs are also frequently grown as house plants that trail from hanging containers to climb small supports.

HOW TO GROW. Outdoors, creeping figs grow well in full sun or partial shade in any moist, well-drained soil. Water the plants generously in summer and spray them daily with a hose in very hot weather. For bushy growth, pinch off the growing tips of young vines. Each year, in late fall or early spring, thin the plants to reduce density, encourage young growth, and eliminate mature branches that project horizontally from the stems.

Indoors, creeping fig vines grow best in bright indirect or curtain-filtered sunlight or medium artificial light for 12 to 14 hours daily. Maintain night temperatures of 65° to 70°, day temperatures of 75° to 85°. Keep the humidity as close to 50 per cent as possible. Plant in a packaged soilless mix prepared for African violets and keep it barely moist at all times. Never allow the mix to become soggy, since the roots of creeping fig rot easily. Feed every two weeks with a liquid house-plant fertilizer diluted to half the strength recommended on the label. Repot only when the roots become crowded. To encourage compact growth, pinch back the stems. Creeping fig is rarely bothered by pests. Propagate by rooting stem cuttings in moist sand or vermiculite.

**FIDDLE-LEAVED PHILODENDRON** See *Philodendron*
**FIG** See *Ficus*
**FIRECRACKER, BRAZILIAN** See *Manettia*

## FITTONIA
*F. verschaffeltii* (red-nerved fittonia); *F. verschaffeltii argyroneura* (silver-nerved fittonia, mosaic plant)

An ornamental creeping plant that has papery, intricately veined leaves, fittonia is grown indoors in hanging containers with its 8- to 10-inch stems tumbling over the sides. The 3- to 4-inch oval leaves of red-nerved fittonia are prominently marked with a network of red veins; silver-nerved fittonia has smaller leaves veined in white.

HOW TO GROW. Fittonias grow best in the shadowless light of a north window or under medium artificial light for 12 to 14 hours daily. Provide temperatures of 65° to 70° at night and 75° to 85° during the day; maintain humidity as close to 50 per cent as possible by setting plants on a humidity tray. Plant in a packaged potting soil and keep it constantly moist but not soggy. Feed fittonias every month except in winter with a liquid house-plant fertilizer diluted to half the strength recommended on the label. When fittonias begin to look straggly, replace them with plants propagated by rooting stem cuttings in moist sand or vermiculite.

**FIVE-LEAF AKEBIA** See *Akebia*
**FLAME PEA, AUSTRALIAN** See *Chorizema*
**FLAME VINE** See *Pyrostegia*
**FLAME VINE, MEXICAN** See *Senecio*
**FLAME VIOLET** See *Episcia*
**FLEECE VINE** See *Polygonum*
**FLORISTS' SMILAX** See *Asparagus*
**FLOWER, PARADISE** See *Solanum*
**FLOWERING INCH PLANT** See *Tradescantia*

*For climate zones and frost dates, see maps, pages 146-147.*

SILVER-NERVED FITTONIA
*Fittonia verschaffeltii argyroneura*

CAROLINA JASMINE
*Gelsemium sempervirens*

PURPLE PASSION VINE
*Gynura aurantiaca* 'Purple Passion'

FLOWERING OAK See *Chorizema*
FOX GRAPE See *Vitis*

# G

## GELSEMIUM

*G. sempervirens* (Carolina jasmine, evening trumpet flower)

An evergreen perennial often found growing wild in the southeastern United States, Carolina jasmine grows up to 20 feet tall. All parts of the plant are poisonous if swallowed but are safe to touch. From late winter through spring, clusters of 1- to 1½-inch yellow trumpet-shaped flowers fill the air with fragrance. Hardy in Zones 8-10, the plants start blooming when they are young, so they are effective in container gardens. An airy, delicate texture makes the vine useful for shading or screening as well as for use as a ground cover. It may also be grown indoors, either trained up a trellis or allowed to trail from a hanging container.

HOW TO GROW. Carolina jasmine grows best when its roots are shaded and cool, but the vine tolerates either full sun or partial shade. Plant it in rich, well-drained soil with organic matter worked into it. Although a moist soil is ideal, the vine is able to withstand short periods of drought. While the plant is actively growing, apply a balanced fertilizer. Prune immediately after flowering, removing dead or broken branches and shaping the plant. Propagate in spring from stem cuttings of established young growth or from seeds.

Indoors, Carolina jasmine needs full sun or bright indirect light. Provide temperatures of 50° to 55° at night and 68° to 72° by day. A humidity of 50 per cent is ideal. Keep the soil around actively growing plants moist but let it dry slightly during the period of winter dormancy. Fertilize once a month during active growth with a liquid house-plant fertilizer diluted to half the strength recommended on the label. Pests rarely attack Carolina jasmine. Prune the vine in spring after flowering to maintain the desired size.

GERANIUM, IVY See *Pelargonium*
GERMAN IVY See *Senecio*
GIANT BURMESE HONEYSUCKLE See *Lonicera*
GIANT GRANADILLA See *Passiflora*
GLORY BOWER See *Clerodendrum*
GLORY PEA See *Clianthus*
GLORY VINE See *Vitis*
GLOXINIA, CREEPING See *Asarina*
GOLD VINE, GUINEA See *Hibbertia*
GOLDCUP CHALICE VINE See *Solandra*
GOLDEN CLEMATIS See *Clematis*
GOLDEN POTHOS See *Scindapsus*
GOLDEN VINE See *Stigmaphyllon*
GOLDFISH PLANT See *Nematanthus*
GOLDFLAME HONEYSUCKLE See *Lonicera*
GOOSEBERRY, CHINESE See *Actinidia*
GRANADILLA See *Passiflora*
GRAPE See *Vitis*
GRAPE, POSSUM See *Cissus*
GRAPE IVY See *Cissus*
GREATER PERIWINKLE See *Vinca*
GUINEA GOLD VINE See *Hibbertia*

## GYNURA

*G. aurantiaca* (Java, purple or royal velvet plant); *G. aurantiaca* 'Purple Passion,' also called *G. procumbens* and *G. sarmentosa* (purple passion vine) (both also called gynura)

For exotic indoor color, few vines equal the iridescent purple foliage of gynuras. Their trailing stems and irregularly lobed leaves are blanketed with so many purple hairs that their true green color is hardly visible. This purple down is especially thick on young leaves; on older foliage it is usually confined to the veins and leaf edges. The Java velvet plant bears triangular leaves 4 to 6 inches long; its stems grow upright at first but trail down as they grow older. The purple passion vine has slender stems that hang down but can be trained to climb if they are tied to a support. Both the stems and the undersides of the 3- to 4-inch lance-shaped leaves are wine red.

Indoors, these perennial vines will grow up to 3 feet long, but in their native tropics they may reach more than 9 feet in length. Small yellow or orange flowers may appear in late winter or early spring but they have an unpleasant scent and most gardeners pinch them off. Given a support, gynuras can be trained to grow upward but usually the stems are left to cascade over the sides of hanging pots.

HOW TO GROW. Gynuras grow best in direct sunlight—which intensifies their purple coloring—but they grow fairly well in bright indirect light. They will also grow well if given bright artificial light for 14 to 16 hours daily. Give them a humid atmosphere (50 per cent if possible) and temperatures of 65° to 70° at night and 75° to 85° during the daytime. Plant in packaged potting soil, adding a teaspoon of ground limestone per quart of soil. Keep the mixture barely moist at all times and feed the plants weekly with a house-plant fertilizer diluted to one fourth the strength recommended on the label. Because they are most colorful when young, gynuras are often replaced every two years, but they may be repotted when they become crowded. To encourage bushy growth, pinch off the branch tips. Propagate additional plants by rooting tip cuttings in moist sand or vermiculite.

# H

HALL'S HONEYSUCKLE See *Lonicera*
HANGING TUBEROUS BEGONIA See *Begonia*

### HARDENBERGIA

*H. comptoniana* (Compton coral-pea); *H. violacea*, also called *H. monophylla* (vine lilac)

Delicately colored flowers in winter or early spring make the hardenbergias unusual twining vines for a warm climate or cool greenhouse. Growing slowly, the Compton coral-pea has limp, tangled stems 10 to 15 feet long. Evergreen leaves are made up of three to five oval leaflets; the ½-inch blue-violet flowers bloom in spikes 6 to 8 inches long. The Compton coral-pea can be trained on a trellis to serve as a screen, especially on the north side of a house. The vine lilac, a weak climber, is more shrublike. It has single evergreen leaves and small lilac flowers singly or in pairs. Varieties of the vine lilac have rose-violet, pink or white flowers. This plant is most effective as a ground cover. Although the vine lilac is hardier, both hardenbergias can be grown outdoors in those parts of Zones 9 and 10 that do not have prolonged periods of freezing temperatures.

HOW TO GROW. Hardenbergias grow best in partial shade, tolerating full sun only in cool temperatures. Plant the vines in a well-drained sandy soil; they are able to withstand short periods of drought, so the soil does not need to be kept constantly moist. Feed the plants every two months with a fertilizer such as 5-10-5. Regularly prune sprawling branches and remove faded flowers.

Indoors, the plants require a cool greenhouse with bright indirect light and temperatures of 45° to 50° at night and 55° to 60° by day. Plant in a mixture of 2 parts peat moss, 1 part garden loam and 1 part coarse sand. To each gallon of mix, add 1 tablespoon of bone meal, 1 tablespoon of ground

VINE LILAC
*Hardenbergia violacea*

*For climate zones and frost dates, see maps, pages 146-147.*

limestone and a handful of crushed charcoal. Let the soil dry slightly between thorough waterings. Feed monthly with a balanced fertilizer. If the plant becomes root bound, repot in a slightly larger container. Propagate additional plants from seeds or by rooting cuttings in spring.

**HEART-LEAVED PHILODENDRON** See *Philodendron*
**HEART, PURPLE** See *Setcreasea*
**HEART VINE** See *Ceropegia*
**HEART VINE, BLEEDING** See *Clerodendrum*
**HEARTSEED** See *Cardiospermum*

## HEDERA
*H. canariensis* (Algerian ivy); *H. helix* (English ivy)

Extremely popular as ground covers and as climbers, English and Algerian ivies are among the few evergreen vines that are hardy in northern gardens. These ivies have two stages of growth with distinctly different habits and foliage. In their juvenile stage, their climbing or trailing stems develop small aerial roots that cling tenaciously to any surface; their shiny, leathery leaves are three- to five-lobed. When the ivies reach the tops of their supports, the plants develop stiff, woody stems, become bushy with oval leaves, and produce clusters of small pale green flowers followed by ¼-inch black or purple poisonous berries.

In addition to being longtime favorites as shade-tolerant ground covers and for blanketing masonry walls, English and Algerian ivies can be trained into espaliers and topiaries, displayed in window boxes or planted in garden tubs as specimens. Indoors, they may be grown as hanging plants, trellis climbers or topiaries.

Algerian ivy is distinctive for its wine-red twigs and stems. The large leaves, 5 to 7 inches across, are bright green in summer but turn bronze-green in winter. The variegated Algerian ivy has gray-green leaves edged with blotches of creamy white. Both varieties are hardy in Zones 8-10.

English ivy was brought from Europe by early colonists but has become a wild plant in many parts of the United States. Growing up to 100 feet tall, its dark green 2- to 4-inch leaves are a familiar sight. There are more than 60 named varieties of English ivy with lobed, round or heart-shaped leaves that have smooth, wavy, ruffled or curled edges. Three of the hardiest varieties are Baltica, Bulgaria and 238th Street, named for the location of a churchyard in New York City where it was found. Baltica, hardy in Zones 4-10, has white-veined leaves 1 to 2 inches across and of the three is the most tolerant of sun. Bulgaria, hardy in Zones 5-10, is notably drought-resistant; it has large leaves 4 to 5 inches wide. The variety called 238th Street, hardy in Zones 5-10, has 1½-inch heart-shaped leaves veined in yellow. The adult stage of 238th Street is unusual in that it continues to produce trailing shoots of juvenile growth.

HOW TO GROW. Outdoors, plant Algerian ivy and English ivy in partial to full shade. Both need shade particularly in Zones 4-7 where winters are cold, because ivy in full sun tends to winter-burn. Plant in well-drained garden loam enriched with peat moss, compost or leaf mold. Set the plants out in spring, placing English ivy 12 inches apart and Algerian ivy 18 inches apart. Put plants intended for wall cover as close to the wall as possible. Prune new plants to 6 inches and feed with 10-10-10 fertilizer. Mulch during the summer for weed control. Fertilize established ivy plants only if the leaves begin to turn yellow. Water ivy deeply during periods of drought. Prune ivy annually in the spring to maintain the desired size and shape; remove straggly growth at any time. If an ivy ground cover becomes thin or has bare patches,

VARIEGATED ALGERIAN IVY
*Hedera canariensis* 'Variegata'

shear it close to the ground in early spring to rejuvenate it, or peg a long branch over the bare spot until it takes root.

Indoors, grow Algerian and English ivies in full sun, bright indirect light, or with moderate artificial light for 14 to 16 hours a day. Temperatures of 50° to 55° at night and 68° to 72° during the day, with humidity of 30 to 40 per cent, are best. Grow in a packaged potting soil. Do not fertilize newly potted plants for six months; feed established ivies once a month with a house-plant fertilizer diluted to half the strength recommended on the label. Repot crowded plants at any time. Propagate additional ivy plants by rooting stem cuttings in moist sand or vermiculite.

HELXINE See *Soleirolia*
HENRY HONEYSUCKLE See *Lonicera*
HERALD'S-TRUMPET See *Beaumontia*

## HIBBERTIA
*H. scandens* (Guinea gold vine, snake vine)

Many-branched and bearing dense evergreen foliage, the sometimes twining, sometimes trailing stems of the Guinea gold vine grow 10 to 30 feet long. The dark green leaves of this perennial are oval and 1 to 3 inches long, shiny on top and silken-haired underneath. They are attached to the stems by winged stalks. At the ends of the branches, bright yellow five-petaled flowers 2 inches wide bloom in summer; they are vivid against the dark foliage but have a somewhat unpleasant odor. The rapid growth of the Guinea gold vine makes it useful as a screen on a fence or trellis or as a ground cover. It also makes a handsome specimen plant. It is hardy in Zones 9 and 10 and will withstand light frost.

HOW TO GROW. The Guinea gold vine grows best in a warm, sheltered spot in partial shade, though it will tolerate full sun. Plant in a moist well-drained soil to which leaf mold, compost or peat moss has been added. Prune annually in early spring to thin the branches and to maintain a manageable size of 15 to 20 feet. Guinea gold vine is sometimes infested by thrips. Propagate new plants from stem cuttings.

HONEYSUCKLE See *Lonicera*
HONEYSUCKLE, CAPE See *Tecomaria*
HONEYSUCKLE, CORAL See *Lonicera*
HONEYSUCKLE, EVERBLOOMING See *Lonicera*
HONEYSUCKLE, GIANT BURMESE See *Lonicera*
HONEYSUCKLE, GOLDFLAME See *Lonicera*
HONEYSUCKLE, HALL'S See *Lonicera*
HONEYSUCKLE, HENRY See *Lonicera*
HONEYSUCKLE, TRUMPET See *Lonicera*
HONEYSUCKLE, WOODBINE See *Lonicera*
HOP See *Humulus*
HORSEHEAD PHILODENDRON See *Philodendron*

## HOYA
*H. carnosa* (wax plant); *H. carnosa* 'Compacta' (compact wax plant); *H. carnosa* 'Variegata' (variegated wax plant)

Succulent young stems of wax plants, which grow woody with age, put out rootlets that attach to supports around which the vines twine. Outdoors, they are perennials growing 8 to 15 feet long as trellis climbers or ground cover. Indoors, the slow-growing plants are trained on trellises 2 to 4 feet high or displayed in hanging containers.

The leaves of the wax plant, 2 to 4 inches long, are dark green, thick and leathery. The leaves of the variegated wax plant have red-tinged edges and borders of pale yellow-white around blue-green centers. The compact wax plant's leaves are spotted with silver, contorted, twisted and folded. During

*For climate zones and frost dates, see maps, pages 146-147.*

ENGLISH IVY
*Hedera helix*

GUINEA GOLD VINE
*Hibbertia scandens*

WAX PLANT
*Hoya carnosa*

COMMON HOP
*Humulus lupulus*

summer and early fall, plants produce symmetrical clusters of waxy flowers, fragrant star-shaped blooms that are pink-white with crimson centers. Lasting for several weeks, the flowers are borne each year on the same short spurs, so these should not be removed. Wax plants are hardy outdoors in Zone 10, planted in partial shade.

HOW TO GROW. Indoors, wax plants grow best with at least four hours of direct sun but they will also grow in bright indirect or curtain-filtered sunlight. Maintain temperatures of 60° to 65° at night and 70° or higher by day, as well as humidity of 40 to 50 per cent. Plant the vines in a mixture of 2 parts packaged potting soil to 1 part sand, with 1 tablespoon of ground limestone and 1 tablespoon of bone meal added to each gallon of the mixture. Keep barely moist during the spring and summer growing period, and use a balanced fertilizer such as 10-10-10 every two months. During winter, let the soil become almost dry and withhold fertilizer. Repot in spring if plants are root bound.

Outdoors, choose a location with wind protection and a light, well-drained soil enriched with leaf mold. Keep it moist in summer and somewhat dry in winter. Feed twice at two-month intervals during active growth with 10-10-10 fertilizer. Mulch with leaf mold in the fall. Pruning is seldom required; when it is necessary, however, it should be done in early spring with care taken to spare the flower spurs.

## HUMULUS

*H. japonicus,* also called *H. scandens* (Japanese hop); *H. lupulus* (common hop)

Hops are rapidly growing, coarse-textured vines that provide dense cover in summer for a trellis or for any unsightly feature in the garden. The Japanese hop is a twining annual that grows 20 to 35 feet in a single season. Its rough bright green leaves are 6 to 8 inches wide and have up to 7 lobes with jagged, toothed margins. Only the female plants produce papery, conelike fruit. The perennial common hop, less widely used as an ornamental, is also grown for the fruit used in brewing beer. Hardy in Zones 3-10, this common hop is a twining vine that grows from underground runners.

HOW TO GROW. Hops grow well in either full sun or partial shade and tolerate a wide range of soil conditions. Growth is best, however, in a moist, humus-rich, light loam that is well drained. The vines withstand drought, hot temperatures and wind. Plant seeds of the Japanese hop after all danger of frost is past; set them 18 inches apart at the base of the vine support. Once established, the plants will reseed themselves. Each fall cut the common hop to the ground. Use a light winter mulch. Propagate additional vines from cuttings of runners planted in the spring.

## HYACINTH BEAN See *Dolichos*
## HYBRID PASSIONFLOWER See *Passiflora*

## HYDRANGEA

*H. anomala petiolaris,* also called *H. petiolaris, H. scandens* (climbing hydrangea)

A large, coarse vine excellent for covering expanses of brick or stone, the climbing hydrangea clings to such surfaces with aerial roots. Growing up to 75 feet tall with lateral branches as much as 3 feet long, this deciduous vine has red, shredding bark on older stems, which adds a colorful accent to the garden in winter after the vine's leaves fall. It is in midsummer, however, that climbing hydrangea is at its best, with shiny dark green foliage and white flower clusters extending from the foliage surface. The 2- to 4-inch oval leaves have finely toothed margins, and the tiny fertile flowers and the 1- to 1½-inch sterile flowers surrounding them form flat clusters 5 inches across. Climbing hydrangeas should not be grown against wooden surfaces that could be damaged by their aerial roots. Hardy in Zones 5-10, the vine withstands wind, cold and seaside conditions. It takes two or three years for climbing hydrangea to become well established; after that it is a rapid grower.

HOW TO GROW. The climbing hydrangea thrives and flowers best in full sun but it also grows well in partial shade. Set it in a well-drained garden soil enriched with organic matter. Although the plant needs evenly moist soil during its first few years, once established it tolerates dry conditions. Mulch young plants in the fall for winter protection. Fertilize older plants each spring, using an all-purpose garden fertilizer. Prune in winter or early spring to maintain the desired size or shape. Pests and diseases are rarely a problem. Climbing hydrangea can be started from seed.

HYPOCYRTA See *Nematanthus*

# I

INCH PLANT, FERNLEAF See *Tripogandra*
INCH PLANT, FLOWERING See *Tradescantia*

## IPOMOEA

*I. alba,* also called *I. bona-nox* and *Calonyction aculeatum* (moonflower); *I. multifida,* also called *Quamoclit sloteri* (cardinal climber); *I. purpurea* and *I. tricolor* (morning glory); *I. quamoclit,* also called *Quamoclit pennata* (cypress vine)

A diverse group of twining vines planted for their fast growth and their bright, shapely flowers, the ipomoea vines rapidly climb stakes, strings, posts, fences, trellises, walls or banks. They are usually grown as annuals outdoors in Zones 3-10 but most of them will reseed themselves and return year after year. They can also be grown indoors, trained on a small trellis or permitted to trail from hanging baskets.

The moonflower's prickly stems can grow up to 40 feet in one season. Oval- to heart-shaped 8-inch leaves surround fragrant white flowers up to 6 inches across. These open at night, from midsummer until frost. In Zones 9 and 10, the moonflower is often a perennial. The hybrid cardinal climber has smooth, 20-foot twining stems with finely divided palm-like leaves; its 2-inch red flowers with white centers bloom from summer to fall.

The morning glory has heart-shaped leaves 5 inches long and flowers that open in the morning but close by noon. Up to 4 inches in diameter, the blue, purple, pink, scarlet, white or multicolored blooms can have single or double rows of petals. The *I. tricolor* variety Early Call may be blue, rose or mixed, Pearly Gates is white, Heavenly Blue a bright sky blue, Scarlet O'Hara a deep red. Morning glories branch from their bases and form dense masses of foliage and flowers. They grow up to 20 feet tall; in some regions they have escaped into the wild and are considered a nuisance. The cypress vine is a parent of the hybrid cardinal climber and closely resembles it, with 20-foot stems and dark green fern-like foliage. The scarlet flowers, 1½ inches long, bloom all summer, opening only in the evening or early morning and never in full sun.

HOW TO GROW. Outdoors, ipomoeas grow in full sun or partial shade; in shade the flowering of all but the cypress vine may be curtailed. Plant in any well-drained soil that is not so rich that it produces foliage at the expense of flowers. Shield vines from strong wind, which may shred the foliage.

Indoors, ipomoeas grow best if they are given four hours of direct sunlight a day. They need temperatures of 60° to 65°

*For climate zones and frost dates, see maps, pages 146-147.*

CLIMBING HYDRANGEA
*Hydrangea anomala petiolaris*

CARDINAL CLIMBER
*Ipomoea multifida*

MORNING GLORY
*Ipomoea purpurea*

COMMON WHITE JASMINE
*Jasminum officinale*

at night and 70° or higher during the daytime. Plant them in packaged potting soil and keep it barely moist. When the vines are 4 inches tall, fertilize them with a house-plant fertilizer diluted to half the strength recommended on the label; repeat this application at monthly intervals. Most ipomoeas are propagated from seed, but moonflowers may also be grown from cuttings.

ITALIAN BELLFLOWER See *Campanula*
IVY, ALGERIAN See *Hedera*
IVY, ARALIA See *Fatshedera*
IVY, BOSTON See *Parthenocissus*
IVY, DEVIL'S See *Scindapsus*
IVY, ENGLISH See *Hedera*
IVY, GERMAN See *Senecio*
IVY, GRAPE See *Cissus*
IVY, MARINE See *Cissus*
IVY, PARLOR See *Senecio*
IVY, SWEDISH See *Plectranthus*
IVY, TREE See *Fatshedera*
IVY GERANIUM See *Pelargonium*
IVY TREEBINE See *Cissus*

# J

JACKMAN CLEMATIS See *Clematis*
JAPANESE CLIMBING FERN See *Lygodium*
JAPANESE CREEPER See *Parthenocissus*
JAPANESE HOP See *Humulus*
JAPANESE WISTERIA See *Wisteria*
JASMINE, ANGELWING See *Jasminum*
JASMINE, ARABIAN See *Jasminum*
JASMINE, CAROLINA See *Gelsemium*
JASMINE, CHILEAN See *Mandevilla*
JASMINE, COMMON WHITE See *Jasminum*
JASMINE, CONFEDERATE See *Jasminum*
JASMINE, CONFEDERATE STAR See *Trachelospermum*
JASMINE, MADAGASCAR See *Stephanotis*
JASMINE, POET'S See *Jasminum*
JASMINE, SCENTED STAR See *Jasminum*
JASMINE, SPANISH See *Jasminum*
JASMINE, YELLOW STAR See *Trachelospermum*
JASMINE NIGHTSHADE See *Solanum*

## JASMINUM

*J. floridum; J. multiflorum* (scented star jasmine); *J. nitidum* (angelwing jasmine, Confederate jasmine); *J. officinale* (common white jasmine, poet's jasmine, Spanish jasmine); *J. polyanthum; J. sambac* (Arabian jasmine)

A single jasmine vine can perfume an entire room or garden with the sweet fragrance of its white, yellow or pink blooms. The narrow trumpet-shaped flowers are borne in clusters. *J. floridum,* angelwing jasmine and common white jasmine may be deciduous or evergreen depending on the warmth of the climate. Scented star jasmine, *J. polyanthum* and Arabian jasmine are evergreen. Sprawling vines, jasmines have twining young shoots but grow more attractively when they are tied and trained to garden structures or trellises. In frost-free areas, jasmines can be allowed to ramble as ground covers. They also can be grown as house plants or in a greenhouse.

*J. floridum,* a weak-stemmed shrub, grows 3 feet tall with glossy green leaves each divided into three 1½-inch leaflets. Its clusters of 1-inch yellow flowers appear during the summer and occasionally at other times of the year. Good as a ground cover, the scented star jasmine has hairy stems up to 20 to 30 feet long and 1-inch white flowers that are set among dull green, 2-inch leaves with downy undersides. Angelwing jasmine grows 10 to 20 feet; its shiny dark green leaves, which are 3 inches long, form an attractive evergreen backdrop for the purple flower buds that open into 1½-inch white flowers.

The common white jasmine is a semiclimbing shrub up to 30 feet tall; each glossy leaf has five to seven 2½-inch leaflets. From summer through fall the plant bears 1-inch white flowers that are among the most fragrant of all jasmines. *J. polyanthum* climbs to 20 feet; each of its leaves is formed of five to seven leathery leaflets up to 3 inches long. Blooming from early spring to late fall, its small ¾-inch flowers are pink on the outside, white on the inside. Climbing to a height of 6 feet or more, the Arabian jasmine has dark green leaves 3 inches long; from early spring to late autumn it bears very fragrant flowers that open white, then turn purple as they age.

*J. floridum* and common white jasmine are hardy in Zones 7-10; scented star jasmine and Arabian jasmine are hardy only in Zone 10; angelwing jasmine is hardy in Zones 9-10; *J. polyanthum* is hardy in Zones 9-10. The common white jasmine and the Arabian jasmine are particularly recommended for growing in pots.

HOW TO GROW. Outdoors, plant jasmines in full sun or partial shade. They grow best in a well-drained, light soil enriched with leaf mold, peat moss or compost. From spring through fall, fertilize monthly with a balanced fertilizer such as 10-10-10. Tie the stems to supports and keep the soil evenly moist through the growing season. Prune after flowering to keep the plants thinned and shaped. Provide winter protection in Zones 7-8.

Indoors, jasmines need at least four hours of direct sunlight daily or 14 to 16 hours of strong artificial light. Arabian jasmine needs night temperatures of 60° to 65° and day temperatures of 72° or higher. Grow the other jasmines with night temperatures of 50° to 55° and day temperatures of 68° to 72°. Plant in a mixture of equal parts potting soil, peat moss and coarse sand, adding 1 tablespoon each of bone meal and ground limestone to every gallon of mixture. Keep the soil mixture moist but do not let it become soggy. Fertilize monthly during the growing season with a house-plant fertilizer diluted to half the strength recommended on the label. Propagate additional jasmine plants from seed or by rooting cuttings in moist vermiculite.

JAVA VELVET PLANT See *Gynura*
JENNIE, CREEPING See *Lysimachia*

# K

KANGAROO TREEBINE See *Cissus*
KIWI BERRY See *Actinidia*
KOLOMIKTA ACTINIDIA See *Actinidia*
KOWHAI, RED See *Clianthus*
KUDZU VINE See *Pueraria*

# L

LACE-FLOWER VINE See *Episcia*
LACE VINE, SILVER See *Polygonum*

LANTANA
*L. montevidensis,* also called *L. delicatissima* and *L. sellowiana* (trailing lantana)

When trailing lantana blooms in summer, its arching, 3- to 4-foot stems are lined with dainty inch-wide clusters of rose to lavender flowers. In frost-free areas of Zones 9 and 10, the fast-growing evergreen trailing lantana can be grown out-

ARABIAN JASMINE
*Jasminum sambac*

TRAILING LANTANA
*Lantana montevidensis*

*For climate zones and frost dates, see maps, pages 146-147.*

**CHILEAN BELLFLOWER**
*Lapageria rosea*

**PERENNIAL PEA**
*Lathyrus latifolius*

doors, where it may become 18 to 24 inches high; the plants can be tied to stakes for upright growth, or they can be allowed to ramble as a spectacular ground cover that will take root wherever its pungent 1-inch leaves touch the soil. In areas that are less mild, trailing lantana is usually treated as a hanging-container plant for display indoors or out, or it is planted in the garden as an annual.

HOW TO GROW. Indoors, trailing lantana grows best in at least four hours of full sun or under 12 to 14 hours of bright artificial light daily. Night temperatures of 55° to 60° and day temperatures of 68° or higher are ideal. Plant in commercial packaged potting soil. Let the soil dry slightly between thorough waterings and feed every two weeks with house-plant fertilizer diluted to half the strength recommended on the label. Pinch back the tips during the growing season to encourage a compact shape and profuse flowering. Propagate additional plants at any time from stem cuttings rooted in moist vermiculite.

Outdoors, trailing lantana thrives in full sun in any well-drained soil, although it flowers most abundantly in soil enriched with compost. Plants tolerate dryness but grow best if the soil is kept moist. Each fall or early spring cut back any scraggly branches. If trailing lantana is cut to the ground it will grow back quickly during the spring and summer. Lantana is usually started from cuttings because plants grown from seed are very slow to bloom. Start new outdoor plants from cuttings taken in the early fall; set the young plants outdoors the following spring.

## LAPAGERIA

*L. rosea* (Chilean bellflower, Chile-bells)

Throughout summer and fall in frost-free gardens the bell-shaped blooms of the Chilean national flower are borne on thin wiry stems. A woody evergreen vine twining to about 15 feet, the Chilean bellflower is an open-growing plant with pointed, leathery leaves 2 to 3 inches long. Its pendulous waxy flowers, 3 to 4 inches long and 2 inches wide, appear singly or in clusters of two or three, their overlapping red petals spotted white on the inside. The flowers can be cut for bouquets. Chilean bellflower is attractive on trellises, cascading over walls or from containers and trailing on the ground. It is hardy only in Zone 10, doing best in areas with cool, moist air. It is not tolerant of wind or extreme heat or cold.

HOW TO GROW. Chilean bellflower thrives in partial shade and must be protected from direct sun, especially in summer. Grow it in rich, well-drained sandy soil with humus added and maintain constant, even moisture. Mulch in the fall with coarse, chunky peat moss. Fertilize in fall, spring and again in midsummer with an all-purpose garden fertilizer. Prune in early spring only to shape, maintain size or remove dead branches. Indoors, Chilean bellflower requires the controlled conditions of a cool, shaded greenhouse with night temperatures of 45° to 50° and day temperatures of 55° to 60°. Aphids sometimes infest Chilean bellflower. Propagate additional plants from seeds or from stem cuttings.

## LATHYRUS

*L. japonicus* (beach pea, maritime pea); *L. latifolius* (perennial pea); *L. odoratus* (sweet pea)

A profusion of delicately hued flowers and the alacrity with which the vining stems form a screen on fences or other structures make these ornamental peas outstanding additions to the garden. Given slight support, the vines climb by means of branched tendrils; left unsupported, the beach and perennial peas may be used as ground covers.

The beach pea, a perennial, is hardy in Zones 5-10. Its 2-

foot trailing stems, with leaves composed of up to a dozen 2-inch leaflets, bear spikes of 6 to 10 purple flowers all summer. A vigorous climber, the perennial pea is hardy in Zones 4-10; it has 4-inch blue-green leaves that grow in pairs along stems that may reach 9 feet in length. Clusters of 1½-inch white, rose or magenta flowers bloom through the summer and fall on 12-inch stems. They make long-lasting cut flowers for bouquets. Sweet pea, an annual, is prized for showy and fragrant flowers, which appear from early through late summer in colors that range from blue and lavender through salmon and red. Sweet peas grow rapidly up to 6 feet, with pairs of light-green 2-inch oval leaflets.

HOW TO GROW. Ornamental peas should be started as early as possible to get the benefit of their blooms before hot weather sets in. They will do best in well-prepared soil that is kept cool and moist. The beach pea, which grows naturally along lakeshores and seashores, can be started by sowing seeds in moist sand. This plant needs full sun. Perennial peas will tolerate partial shade but bloom best in full sun. Plant them in early spring, 18 to 24 inches apart and 2 inches deep, in any well-drained soil. Feed plants in the spring with bone meal and remove faded flowers to extend the blooming season. Cut plants to the ground in the fall.

Not an easy plant to cultivate, the sweet pea needs full sun, a long growing season, and cool, moist, humus-rich soil that is neutral or slightly alkaline. In southern parts of the country, plant sweet peas in fall for late winter blooms; in northern zones, especially where summers are hot and dry, prepare the soil in the fall and start the seeds indoors in early spring, or sow directly in the soil when danger of frost is past. Prepare a trench 1 foot wide and 2 feet deep, and fill it with a mixture of two parts compost, two parts loam and one part sand. Soak seeds overnight and dust them with a nitrogen-fixing powder available at garden-supply stores; sow them 18 inches apart and 8 to 10 inches deep, covering the seeds with 2 inches of soil. As the plants grow, gradually pull soil around them until the trench is filled. This leads to deeper roots in a cooler soil. When plants are 4 inches tall, pinch growing tips to encourage side branching, and provide netting, trellis or chicken wire for support. Encourage more blooms by removing spent flowers.

LAUREL-LEAVED CLOCK VINE See *Thunbergia*
LEADWORT See *Plumbago*
LEATHERLEAF PHILODENDRON See *Philodendron*
LESSER BOUGAINVILLEA See *Bougainvillea*
LILAC, VINE See *Hardenbergia*
LIPSTICK PLANT See *Aeschynanthus*
LOESENER BITTERSWEET See *Celastrus*

## LONICERA

*L. heckrottii* (goldflame honeysuckle, everblooming honeysuckle); *L. henryi* (Henry honeysuckle); *L. hildebrandiana* (giant Burmese honeysuckle); *L. japonica* 'Halliana' (Hall's honeysuckle); *L. periclymenum* (woodbine honeysuckle); *L. sempervirens* (trumpet honeysuckle, coral honeysuckle)

Generally hardy and fast growing, honeysuckles need very little care yet produce foliage, flowers and fruit in abundance. Indeed, some species become invasive without careful control. The tubular flowers are borne in pairs, clusters or whorls; often very fragrant, they may be red, orange, coral, yellow or white. In autumn, their berries provide food for birds. The woody, twining stems of most honeysuckles need sturdy supports such as strong trellises, arbors, pergolas, walls and fences. Left prostrate, the plants are also used as ground covers and to control erosion on banks.

*For climate zones and frost dates, see maps, pages 146-147.*

GIANT BURMESE HONEYSUCKLE
*Lonicera hildebrandiana*

WOODBINE HONEYSUCKLE
*Lonicera periclymenum*

**TRUMPET HONEYSUCKLE**
*Lonicera sempervirens*

**MATRIMONY VINE**
*Lycium halimifolium*

Goldflame honeysuckle, a hybrid of uncertain origin, is hardy in Zones 5-10. One of the most commonly planted honeysuckles because of its restrained growth, it has leaves 2 inches long. Spikes of 2-inch flowers, red-to-coral on the outside and yellow on the inside, bloom throughout the summer. A vigorous but not invasive grower, Henry honeysuckle is often chosen over the more rampant Hall's honeysuckle. Its slender stems, with dark green heart-shaped leaves, may reach 15 feet in length. Yellowish or red-purple flowers appear in pairs through the summer and are followed by black berries. Henry honeysuckle is hardy in Zones 5-10. It is evergreen except in the northernmost parts of Zone 5.

The giant Burmese honeysuckle is hardy only in Zones 9 and 10 where its outsized growth creates a lush tropical effect. Ropelike stems up to 80 feet long bear dark, shiny 3- to 6-inch leaves, while pairs of fragrant flowers up to 7 inches long open white and turn deep orange with age. Plants bloom in spring and summer.

The ubiquitous Hall's honeysuckle has become a weedy annoyance in some parts of the eastern United States. It rapidly produces a dense tangle of slender stems that may grow as much as 15 feet in a single season and that root wherever they touch the soil. Evergreen in mild climates, its leaves turn bronze in cold areas before dropping in the late fall. The fragrant white flowers bloom all summer, changing to yellow as they age. Hall's honeysuckle is best used as a ground cover where it cannot invade other areas. The woodbine honeysuckle is similar in appearance to Hall's honeysuckle with small dark green leaves, but its restrained growth is more easily controlled. The unopened flower buds are a reddish purple. The open flowers are a creamy yellow inside and yellow to purple outside. Both vines are hardy in Zones 5-10. Trumpet honeysuckle is another rampant grower useful as a ground cover; it is hardy in Zones 4-10. With stems that may grow to 50 feet, it presents a straggly appearance. The scentless 2-inch-long coral or red flowers bloom throughout the summer and into fall. Red berries develop in the fall.

HOW TO GROW. Most honeysuckles will grow in both full sun and partial shade. They grow best in a rich well-drained garden soil. Hall's and trumpet honeysuckles will tolerate drought; all the others need evenly moist soil. The giant Burmese honeysuckle needs protection from the wind. Set plants out in spring or fall, 3 feet apart on banks and 6 feet apart on level ground. Honeysuckles rarely need fertilizing unless they are planted in poor soil; feed them with a balanced fertilizer such as 10-10-10.

Prune honeysuckle vines when flowering ends to maintain the desired size and shape. Some of the old stems should be removed each year to encourage new growth from the base. Propagate additional plants from stem cuttings rooted in moist sand or vermiculite.

**LOVE-IN-A-PUFF** See *Cardiospermum*
**LOW'S CREEPER** See *Parthenocissus*

## LYCIUM

*L. halimifolium* (matrimony vine)

With spiny, arching branches up to 10 feet long, matrimony vine grows less like a vine than a rambling shrub, making it useful as a ground cover, an informal screen or a blanket over a retaining wall. Able to spread even in poor soil, it can overwhelm a garden if it is not kept under control; its branches take root wherever they touch the soil. The glossy gray-green leaves of matrimony vine are deciduous. Pale purple flowers ½ inch long bloom singly or in clusters along the branches in the summer and are followed by long-lasting red to orange berries in the autumn. The vine is wind resistant and hardy throughout Zones 3-10.

HOW TO GROW. Matrimony vine grows best in full sun and in any well-drained soil. Tie branches to supports to achieve upright growth. Prune in spring, thinning to limit size and remove suckers. Propagate by seeds, cuttings or suckers.

## LYGODIUM
*L. japonicum* (Japanese climbing fern)

Delicate pale green fronds grow along the wiry stems of the Japanese climbing fern. This tropical plant is grown mainly as a house plant; it needs only a light trellis, wire, nylon filament or bamboo stick for support. Japanese climbing fern has fronds 4 to 8 inches long that are papery and finely divided. The fertile fronds, which bear spores, have more leaflets than the sterile fronds and thus a more feathery appearance. The stems of the Japanese climbing fern reach 8 to 10 feet in length. Hardy in Zones 7-10, it is grown outdoors as a landscape plant in the southeastern United States.

HOW TO GROW. Indoors, Japanese climbing fern grows best in bright to very bright indirect or curtain-filtered sunlight. Provide temperatures of 50° to 60° at night and 70° to 80° by day, with humidity of 40 to 60 per cent. Plant in equal parts of peat moss, packaged potting soil and coarse sand, with 1 tablespoon of bone meal added to each gallon of the mixture. Keep the soil evenly moist and fertilize the plant twice during the growing season, using fish emulsion diluted to half the strength recommended on the label.

Outdoors, Japanese climbing fern should be planted in intermittent shade. It does best when it is grown in moist, well-drained, slightly acid soil. Each spring cut off old fronds before the new growth emerges. Additional plants can be propagated from spores or by division.

## LYSIMACHIA
*L. nummularia* (moneywort, creeping Jennie)

A creeping vine used in aquariums, wet soils and along pool edges, moneywort can also be grown in hanging containers and window boxes. Round, bright green leaves up to an inch across appear in closely spaced pairs along the stems. From late spring to early fall, bright yellow cup-shaped flowers, an inch or less across, are borne in leaf joints. Moneywort is a perennial with leaves that remain green until early winter, even in cold areas. The plant is hardy in Zones 2-10.

Stems grow flat along the ground, rooting as they grow. They readily spread to the point of being invasive, especially in lawns, but they will serve as a ground cover under trees where grass will not grow.

HOW TO GROW. Indoors, moneywort will grow in full sun or curtain-filtered light. Plant it in equal parts of packaged potting soil, peat moss and coarse sand; add 1 tablespoon each of bone meal and ground limestone to every gallon of the mixture. Keep the soil evenly moist. Feed plants every three months with a balanced fertilizer such as 10-10-10. Moneywort will also grow in water up to 2 inches deep.

Outdoors, grow the plant in either sun or shade in humus-enriched soil that remains constantly moist. Set plants 9 to 18 inches apart. Propagate by division or cuttings.

# M
MADAGASCAR JASMINE See *Stephanotis*
MADAME GALEN TRUMPET CREEPER See *Campsis*

## MANDEVILLA
*M. laxa*, also called *M. suaveolens* (Chilean jasmine); *M. splendens*, also called *Dipladenia splendens*

*For climate zones and frost dates, see maps, pages 146-147.*

JAPANESE CLIMBING FERN
*Lygodium japonicum*

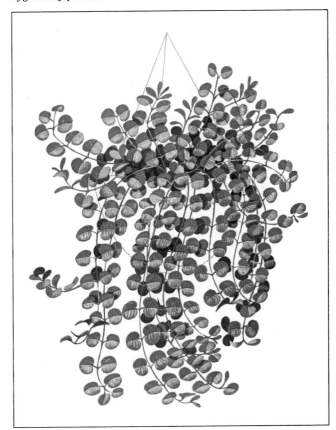

MONEYWORT
*Lysimachia nummularia*

*Mandevilla splendens*

Quantities of fragrant flowers compensate for sparse foliage and for the care mandevillas require. Opening during the day and closing at night, the flowers are produced in early summer and again in early fall, even when plants are young. As house plants, mandevillas can be kept pruned to about 3 feet long. Outdoors in frost-free areas, they can be trained to grow on pergolas, arches or pillars. Chilean jasmine is deciduous; *M. splendens* is evergreen. Both species are hardy in Zones 9 and 10.

Throughout the summer, the Chilean jasmine produces trumpet-shaped white flowers 2 inches across. Its rapidly growing wiry stems may climb 15 or 20 feet. Since this vine loses its lower leaves, other densely growing vines should be planted around its base. The narrow heart-shaped leaves, 3 to 6 inches long, are thin and dark green with gray-green undersides. Long, unsightly seed pods develop in fall if faded flowers are not removed. *M. splendens* has narrow, pointed leaves 3 to 8 inches long. The trumpet-shaped flowers, 2 to 4 inches across, are pale pink when they open, with rose-pink eyes. As the flowers age, their color deepens to rose. The stems of *M. splendens* reach 10 to 15 feet in length.

HOW TO GROW. Indoors, mandevillas need curtain-filtered or bright indirect sunlight. Provide night temperatures of 60° to 65° and day temperatures above 70°. Plant in a mixture of equal parts peat moss, packaged potting mix and builder's sand. Keep the mixture evenly moist during the growing season and let it dry slightly when plants are resting. In spring and summer, feed every two weeks with a fertilizer high in phosphorus such as 10-20-10.

Outdoors, grow mandevillas in partial shade. They need rich, well-drained sandy soil with humus added, and they should be mulched in the fall with leaf mold or compost. When flowering is over, remove spent blooms and prune vines to maintain shape and size or to promote bushiness. Propagate from stem cuttings taken in early spring and rooted in moist sand or vermiculite.

## MANETTIA

*M. inflata,* also called *M. bicolor* (Brazilian firecracker)

While still very young, Brazilian firecracker blooms freely all year. A fast-growing twining tropical vine, it has waxy narrow-tubed flowers ¾ inch long that are scarlet tipped with yellow. Oval 2-inch leaves densely cover thin stems that can grow 4 to 6 feet long. An evergreen, Brazilian firecracker can be grown in a pot and trained up a lightweight trellis or allowed to spill over the sides of the container. Outdoors, it can be grown in Zone 10.

HOW TO GROW. Brazilian firecracker grows best in curtain-filtered or indirect sunlight or in 12 to 14 hours a day of medium artificial light. Maintain night temperatures of 55° to 60° and day temperatures of 68° to 72°. Plant in packaged potting soil. Keep the soil barely moist and fertilize every two weeks during active growth with a flowering-house-plant fertilizer diluted to half the strength recommended on the label. During dormancy, withhold fertilizer and let the soil dry out slightly between waterings. Pinch off growing tips and prune back stems to keep plants the size and shape desired. Since the roots of this plant should not be crowded, transfer it to a larger pot before the soil ball is filled with roots. Outdoors, plant the Brazilian firecracker in partial shade and protect it from wind. Set it in rich, moist, well-drained sandy soil. Propagate in early spring from root divisions or stem cuttings started in moist sand or vermiculite.

BRAZILIAN FIRECRACKER
*Manettia inflata*

**MARINE IVY** See *Cissus*
**MARITIME PEA** See *Lathyrus*

MATRIMONY VINE See *Lycium*
MAURANDIA (MAURANDYA) See *Asarina*
MAYPOP See *Passiflora*
MEMORIAL ROSE See *Rosa*

## MENISPERMUM
*M. canadense* (moonseed)

The dense foliage of moonseed can be used to cover raw banks, rocks and walls, but because it spreads by means of long underground runners, it can become an invasive annoyance unless it is kept under close control. One of the few vines that will flourish in moist shade, it needs a support to climb. Twining to 15 feet high, the thin branches bear ivy-like leaves 4 to 8 inches across. Inconspicuous greenish-white flowers bloom all summer, followed by small black fruit with crescent-shaped seeds. Fruit and seeds are poisonous. This perennial remains evergreen in warm areas but will die back to the ground in cool regions. It is hardy in Zones 5-10.

HOW TO GROW. Moonseed grows in either sun or shade. It grows best in rich, moist garden soil, but it also tolerates very wet, poor soil and needs no protection from the wind. Plant it away from cultivated areas. If it invades a garden, moonseed can be eradicated only by using a weed killer. Prune regularly to control its size. Propagate from seeds, stem cuttings or root divisions started in moist sand or vermiculite.

MEXICAN BREADFRUIT See *Monstera*
MEXICAN CREEPER See *Antigonon*
MEXICAN FLAME VINE See *Senecio*
MONEYWORT See *Lysimachia*

## MONSTERA
*M. deliciosa*, also called *Philodendron pertusum* (monstera, Swiss cheese plant, ceriman, Mexican breadfruit)

In Central American jungles, evergreen monsteras have leaves 3 feet long and almost as broad on wrist-sized stems up to 30 feet long; their edible cone-shaped fruits are 8 inches long. But monsteras seldom bear fruit indoors; they are grown as house plants for their height—6 feet or more—and their dark green foliage. The circular leaves, which feel like soft, polished leather, grow 8 to 12 inches or more in length. The deeply slit mature leaves have holes along the midline, prompting one popular name, Swiss cheese plant.

Monsteras are climbers; they need tree-fern poles or other rough supports to which their cordlike aerial roots can attach themselves. Some of these roots hang down and may push into the soil of the pot, helping to nourish and support the plant. Monsteras may be grown outdoors in Zone 10.

HOW TO GROW. Monsteras adapt to a variety of conditions but grow best in bright indirect or curtain-filtered sunlight. Direct sun will burn the leaves, but too little light will deter leaf splitting and cause smaller leaf size. Night temperatures of 65° to 70° and day temperatures of 75° to 85° are ideal. Plants will tolerate temperatures below 60° but will not produce new growth. Keep monsteras out of drafts and away from heat sources. Provide humidity of 50 per cent or more and spray the plants often. Wash the leaves once a month.

Plant monsteras in a commercial packaged potting mix. A 6- to 8-inch pot will support a plant 3 feet tall, but split leaves will not appear on new growth unless a larger container is provided. Keep the soil barely moist at all times. Delay fertilizing newly potted plants for four to six months; feed established plants twice a year, in early spring and early summer, with a general-purpose fertilizer such as 5-10-5. The plant is generally pest-free. Repot crowded plants at any season; propagate from stem cuttings.

*For climate zones and frost dates, see maps, pages 146-147.*

**MOONSEED**
*Menispermum canadense*

**MONSTERA**
*Monstera deliciosa*

**GOLDFISH PLANT**
*Nematanthus wettsteinii*

**BOWER PLANT**
*Pandorea jasminoides*

MOONFLOWER See *Ipomoea*
MOONSEED See *Menispermum*
MORNING GLORY See *Ipomoea*
MOSAIC PLANT See *Fittonia*
MUSCADINE GRAPE See *Vitis*
MYRTLE, CREEPING See *Vinca*

# N

NASTURTIUM See *Tropaeolum*

## NEMATANTHUS

*N. gregarius,* also called *N. radicans, Hypocyrta radicans; N. wettsteinii,* also called *Hypocyrta wettsteinii* (both called goldfish plant)

Brightly colored tubular flowers with small closed pouches bloom profusely along the slender stems of goldfish plants. The branching stems set with opposite pairs of glossy oval green leaves grow upright at first, then droop; they reach lengths of 1 or 2 feet. In summer *N. gregarius* has 1-inch orange flowers tipped with yellow growing among 1½-inch leaves. *N. wettsteinii* bears leaves and flowers both less than 1 inch long; the many blooms scattered among the thick green leaves are bright red or orange tipped with yellow. Under ideal greenhouse conditions it may bloom year round, but more commonly it blooms in summer and fall. Both goldfish plants are house plants.

HOW TO GROW. The goldfish plant grows in bright indirect sunlight or 14 to 16 hours of low to medium artificial light a day most of the year. In winter while the flower buds are developing, increase the light. Provide temperatures of 65° to 70° at night and 75° to 80° by day. Use a humidity tray to keep humidity as close to 60 per cent as possible. Plant in packaged potting soil. Keep the soil moist but not soggy. Use tepid water; cold water can cause circular marks on the leaves. Feed established plants every two weeks during the growing season with any standard house-plant fertilizer diluted to half the recommended strength. In late fall and winter, when both species are semidormant, do not fertilize, and water sparingly. If plants become too large or straggly, cut them back after they flower to encourage compact growth. Occasional pinching will force the stems to branch. Repot overcrowded plants in late winter. Goldfish plants may be infested by green flies. Propagate additional plants by rooting cuttings of stem tips in moist vermiculite, sand or perlite.

NEPHTHYTIS See *Syngonium*
NIGHTSHADE See *Solanum*

# O

OAK, FLOWERING See *Chorizema*
ORANGE STREPTOSOLEN See *Streptosolen*
ORCHID, VANILLA See *Vanilla*
ORCHID VINE See *Stigmaphyllon*
ORIENTAL BITTERSWEET See *Celastrus*
ORIENTAL CLEMATIS See *Clematis*

# P

PALAY RUBBER VINE See *Cryptostegia*

## PANDOREA

*P. jasminoides* (bower plant); *P. pandorana* (wonga-wonga vine)

The fast-growing evergreen pandoreas, with twining stems that may reach 30 feet in height, make ornamental coverings for fences, accents on arbors or ground covers. Their bright glossy leaves are made up of three to nine oval leaflets 1 to 3 inches long. Trumpet-shaped flowers bloom from midsummer into fall, followed by winged seed pods. The bower vine may have scant foliage, especially if neglected, but its clusters of 1½- to 2-inch-long flowers, white with pink throats, are plentiful. The wonga-wonga vine has luxuriant, dense foliage but inconspicuous ¾-inch flowers that are yellowish white with throats spotted or streaked with purple. The bower plant is hardy in Zones 9 and 10; the wonga-wonga vine only in Zone 10.

HOW TO GROW. Both vines grow well in full sun or partial shade, in moist, deep, well-drained soil enriched with organic matter. Plant young pandoreas in locations where they will be protected from the wind. Water during dry periods to keep the soil constantly moist. Prune in early spring to control the size and shape of the plants and to remove dead branches. Feed annually with a general-purpose garden fertilizer. If aphids attack, control them with insecticide. Propagate from seeds or cuttings of new stem growth.

PAPER FLOWER See *Bougainvillea*
PARADISE FLOWER See *Solanum*
PARLOR IVY See *Senecio*
PARROT'S BILL See *Clianthus*

## PARTHENOCISSUS

*P. henryana* (silver-vein creeper); *P. quinquefolia* (Virginia creeper, woodbine); *P. quinquefolia* 'Engelmannii' (Engelmann creeper); *P. quinquefolia* 'Saint-Paulii' (St. Paul's creeper); *P. tricuspidata* (Boston ivy, Japanese creeper); *P. tricuspidata* 'Lowii' (Low's creeper); *P. tricuspidata* 'Veitchii' (Veitch's creeper)

Climbing by twisting tendrils often tipped with adhesive discs, these handsome species and varieties of parthenocissus grow into colorful blankets or accents for rough walls, arches and arbors. The plants also may be used as a ground cover, rooting as they spread to form a carpet up to 1 foot high. In autumn the vines bear clusters of shiny dark blue berries, while the leaves turn fiery colors before dropping, to expose a delicate tracery of woody stems.

The slow-growing silver-vein creeper is at its best as a ground cover. Its five-leaflet leaves, each leaflet 1½ to 3 inches long, unfolds scarlet, matures to dark green veined with white with purple undersides, and turns scarlet again in the fall. It can grow 20 feet tall if given wires or strings to cling to. Planting it in partial shade will bring out its vivid coloring; sunlight may bleach out the markings. Silver-vein creeper is hardy in Zones 8-10.

The vigorous, fast-growing, high-climbing Virginia creeper has five-leaflet leaves, each leaflet measuring 2 to 6 inches long, while the thick, leathery leaves of Engelmann creeper are smaller and grow more densely. St. Paul's creeper, with small leaves that are hairy when young, clings better to stone and rough surfaces than the other two. Virginia creeper and its varieties are hardy in Zones 3-10; the varieties have a denser habit of growth than the species. All turn vivid scarlet in the autumn.

Fast-growing Boston ivy has lustrous three-lobed leaves that grow up to 8 inches long and turn yellow, orange or scarlet in autumn. This vine is one of the best for clinging to brick or stone and withstands both city pollution and seashore conditions. It grows up to 60 feet tall. The deeply lobed leaves of Low's creeper are ¾ to 1½ inches long; they are purplish when they open, mature to apple green, then change to red in the fall. It does not cling as tenaciously as the species. Veitch's creeper grows oval or three-lobed leaves no more than 1 to 2 inches across; they are also purplish

VIRGINIA CREEPER
*Parthenocissus quinquefolia*

BOSTON IVY
*Parthenocissus tricuspidata*

*For climate zones and frost dates, see maps, pages 146-147.*

**BLUE PASSIONFLOWER**
*Passiflora caerulea*

**RED PASSIONFLOWER**
*Passiflora coccinea*

when young. Small-leaved varieties provide a more delicate display but are less vigorous than the species. Boston ivy and its varieties are hardy in Zones 4-10.

HOW TO GROW. Parthenocissus vines grow in sun or partial shade; silver-vein creeper will develop more foliage color in the shade. Parthenocissus vines tolerate most soils, even those that are dry, but a deep, rich, moist, well-drained loam is best. In early spring or fall, set plants 3 to 4 feet apart near the support on which they will grow. Young climbers will generally need to be guided to their supports. Prune the vines in early spring to restrain or direct the growth of climbers or to induce branching of plants that are used as a ground cover. The vines are susceptible to leaf hoppers, Japanese beetles and mildew; Boston ivy is subject to leaf-scale infestation. As necessary, treat the plants with insecticide or fungicide. Propagate additional plants from cuttings taken in the spring.

## PASSIFLORA

*P. alato-caerulea,* also called *P. pfordtii* (hybrid passionflower); *P. caerulea* (blue passionflower); *P. coccinea* (red passionflower, red granadilla); *P. edulis* (purple granadilla); *P. incarnata* (wild passionflower, maypop); *P. jamesonii; P. quadrangularis* (giant granadilla); *P. racemosa,* also called *P. princeps* (all called passionflower)

Bearing spectacular flowers, passionflowers make striking house plants when trained on supports. Outdoors in warm climates, the tendril-bearing vines grow 20 feet or more and provide an eye-catching cover for a fence or trellis. The open petals and sepals of the flower frame a crown fringed with filaments that in turn enclose a column bearing the reproductive parts. The flowers appear from late spring to early fall, depending on the species. In the tropics some species bear edible fruit, but they seldom develop in temperate climates.

The hybrid passionflower has three-lobed leaves and bears purple, blue, pink and white 4-inch flowers. Blue passionflower, which grows rampantly unless regularly pruned, can be used as a ground cover; the blue, white, purple and pink 3- to 4-inch flowers have a dark crown surrounded by paler petals and sepals and the leaves have five to nine lobes. Red passionflower bears scarlet flowers 3 to 5 inches wide, the vivid petals and sepals encircling a purple, pink and white crown; leaves are oval. The purple granadilla, with 2- to 2½-inch white and purple flowers, has three-lobed leaves with toothed edges. The wild passionflower, with 2-inch white or pale lavender flowers, has three-lobed toothed leaves. *P. jamesonii* bears 3- to 4-inch coral flowers among glossy, spiny-toothed leaves with three deep-cut lobes. The fragrant giant granadilla has white, pink and purple flowers up to 3 inches wide and oval leaves. *P. racemosa* has deep red petals and sepals and a purple crown banded in white; its leaves may be lobed or unlobed.

HOW TO GROW. As house plants, passionflowers grow best with four hours or more of direct sunlight a day and night temperatures of 55° to 65° and day temperatures of 68° or higher. Plant in commercial potting soil and provide a climbing support. Keep the soil evenly moist. Feed the vine every two weeks with an all-purpose fertilizer applied at half the strength recommended on the label. When growth slows in the fall, stop fertilizing and let the soil dry slightly between waterings until new growth starts. In January cut the plants back to 6 inches to force new growth.

Outdoors, passionflowers are hardy in Zones 7-10. Red passionflower, blue passionflower, hybrid passionflower and wild passionflower lose their leaves in colder regions, but they are evergreen farther south; the other species are evergreen. Plant them in full sun near a support. They will grow best in a deep, moist, well-drained sandy loam that has been enriched with compost or leaf mold. Prune the vines heavily in fall or early spring to remove deadwood and to control rampant growth. Propagate additional plants from cuttings 4 to 6 inches long, taken at any time during active growth. Germination of seed is slow and uncertain.

PASSIONFLOWER See *Passiflora*
PASSION VINE, PURPLE See *Gynura*
PEA, AUSTRALIAN FLAME See *Chorizema*
PEA, BEACH See *Lathyrus*
PEA, DESERT See *Clianthus*
PEA, GLORY See *Clianthus*
PEA, MARITIME See *Lathyrus*
PEA, PERENNIAL See *Lathyrus*
PEA, SWEET See *Lathyrus*

## PELARGONIUM

*P. peltatum* (ivy geranium)

The trailing stems of the ivy geranium grow up to 4 feet long, bearing ivy-shaped, shiny, succulent leaves and 2- to 3-inch clusters of pink, red, lavender or white flowers. They bloom continuously from spring to late summer. Vigorous plants for window boxes or hanging pots or other containers, ivy geraniums are also used as a flowering perennial ground cover in frost-free areas. The stems root as they rapidly cover the ground with dense, shrubby mounds of foliage, each 3 to 5 feet across.

HOW TO GROW. Indoors, the plants need at least four hours of direct sunlight a day. Temperatures of 45° to 55° at night and 68° to 72° by day are ideal, although night temperatures as high as 65° will be tolerated. Grow ivy geraniums in a packaged potting mixture and let the soil become moderately dry between thorough waterings. Dry, yellow or dropping lower leaves indicate too much water, temperatures that are too high or lack of nutrients. Fertilize the plants every two weeks from spring through autumn and feed once a month in winter with a house-plant fertilizer applied at half the strength recommended on the label. Ivy geraniums thrive when roots are somewhat crowded, but move plants to larger pots before they become root bound. Potted plants can be brought into bloom indoors in northern areas, then moved outdoors for the summer.

Outdoors, ivy geraniums are hardy only in Zones 9 and 10. Plant them in sun and light, well-drained soil enriched with organic matter. Apply a mulch of leaf mold in fall and feed with an all-purpose garden fertilizer in spring. Keep the soil moderately dry to stimulate blooming. Start plants at any time, spacing them 12 to 18 inches apart. Pinch tips back once or twice in spring to encourage branching. Prune established plants hard in early spring to prevent legginess and woody growth. Remove dead flowers to prolong the blooming season. Control aphids with insecticide. Propagate at any time from stem cuttings, but allow the juicy cut ends to dry before inserting them in moist sand and root.

PEPPER See *Piper*
PERIWINKLE See *Vinca*
PERENNIAL PEA See *Lathyrus*

## PHASEOLUS

*P. coccineus,* also called *P. multiflorus* (scarlet runner bean)

A display of flaming red flowers that lasts throughout the summer distinguishes the scarlet runner bean. This tender perennial vine, often grown as an annual in the north, will

GIANT GRANADILLA
*Passiflora quadrangularis*

IVY GERANIUM
*Pelargonium peltatum*

*For climate zones and frost dates, see maps, pages 146-147.*

SCARLET RUNNER BEAN
*Phaseolus coccineus*

SPEARHEAD PHILODENDRON
*Philodendron hastatum*

climb 10 to 20 feet by means of twining stems. For upright growth, young plants need early guidance and must be tied to a pole or other support until they are well established. Leaves 3 to 5 inches long, each composed of three green broadly oval leaflets, form a dense yet delicate backdrop for profuse sprays of pealike flowers. These are followed by pods up to a foot long; left on the vine, the pods turn black mottled with purple. Scarlet runner beans will quickly and brilliantly cover fences, trellises and other garden structures. Scarlet runner bean is hardy in Zones 9 and 10.

HOW TO GROW. Plant seeds outdoors in early spring, 2 inches deep in a sunny place sheltered from wind. Scarlet runner beans grow best in rich, moist well-drained loam that has been cultivated 12 inches deep and enriched with organic matter. After the seeds germinate, water when necessary to keep the foliage from turning yellow. The plants are relatively free of pest and disease damage.

PHILODENDRON
*P. erubescens* (red-leaved philodendron); *P. guttiferum* (leatherleaf philodendron); *P. hastatum* (spearhead philodendron); *P. oxycardium,* also called *P. cordatum, P. scandens* (heart-leaved philodendron); *P. panduraeforme,* also called *P. bipennifolium* (fiddle-leaved philodendron, horsehead philodendron); *P. squamiferum* (anchorleaf philodendron)

Philodendrons have earned their place on lists of all-time-favorite house plants because they survive in dim corners, grow even when neglected, and offer a great choice of foliage types. Young philodendrons often have leaves quite different from those they put forth at maturity. Philodendrons usually are trained on or tied to upright slabs of bark or poles of tree-fern fiber, into which they can sink their tough, cordlike aerial roots. Unsupported, the plants will creep along the ground or cascade from hanging containers. Those given upright supports develop much larger leaves than those left to creep or trail.

Philodendron foliage offers an almost unlimited variety of size, shape, texture and color. The 10-inch-long arrow-shaped leaves of the red-leaved philodendron are glossy dark green with a coppery sheen; their undersides are burgundy. Slow-growing leatherleaf philodendron bears 7-inch pointed dark green leaves on stocky stems. Spearhead philodendron's 8- to 12-inch leaves are dark green and sometimes have raised veins when mature.

Heart-leaved philodendron is the most commonly grown species, with heart-shaped green leaves that are ordinarily 2 to 4 inches long but may grow to 12 inches. Fiddle-leaved philodendron has overlapping leaves 5 to 8 inches long that are a dark olive-green. Anchorleaf philodendron climbs by twisting its hairy stems around a support; its glossy leaves, up to 10 inches long, have five lobes. Philodendrons are hardy outdoors in Zone 10.

HOW TO GROW. Although philodendrons will survive with very little light, they grow best when they are given bright indirect or curtain-filtered sunlight or 14 to 16 hours a day of medium artificial light. Maintain night temperatures of 65° to 70° and day temperatures of 75° to 85°. These plants thrive when the humidity ranges between 40 and 60 per cent; frequent mistings or setting pots on a humidity tray will help to maintain a high moisture level.

Plant philodendrons in a packaged general-purpose potting soil and keep the soil barely moist. Wait four to six months before fertilizing newly purchased or potted plants; then fertilize every three or four months with any house-plant fertilizer diluted to half the strength recommended on the label if slow growth is desired. For faster growth apply the fertilizer full strength. Heart-leaved philodendron may be grown in a water-filled container; add a few drops of liquid fertilizer monthly. Wash the leaves occasionally with warm, soapy water to discourage pests and remove dust.

Philodendrons grow best if they are somewhat root bound, but if a plant becomes too crowded in its container it can be repotted at any season. No pruning is necessary, except to remove any diseased or damaged leaves. Philodendrons are sometimes infested by mealy bugs. Propagate additional plants by rooting stem cuttings in water or moist vermiculite.

PHILODENDRON See also *Monstera*

### PILEA

*P. depressa* (creeping pilea)

Creeping pilea roots at each leaf joint, and can be grown either as a house plant or as an evergreen ground cover outdoors in Zone 10. Easy to grow, this succulent has trailing stems lined with tiny leaves that are slightly cupped. This vine is grown in dish gardens, terrariums and as an edging for greenhouse benches as well as in pots.

HOW TO GROW. Grow creeping pilea indoors in curtain-filtered or indirect sunlight or in moderate artificial light for 10 to 12 hours daily. Plant in commercial packaged potting soil and keep the medium evenly moist at all times. Night temperatures of 65° to 70°, day temperatures of 75° to 85° and humidity of 30 to 40 per cent are ideal. Wait six months before fertilizing newly potted plants; fertilize established plants monthly with a house-plant fertilizer diluted to half the strength recommended on the label. Creeping pileas grow best when they are slightly root bound; when replanting, use a pot that is only slightly larger than the previous one. Pinch the plants frequently to prevent straggly growth. Outdoors, grow creeping pilea in shade in any well-drained garden soil. Propagate additional plants by rooting stem cuttings in moist vermiculite or by dividing mature plants.

PINK-ANEMONE CLEMATIS See *Clematis*
PIPE VINE See *Aristolochia*

### PIPER

*P. crocatum* (saffron pepper); *P. nigrum,* also called *P. aromaticum* (black pepper); *P. ornatum* (Celebes pepper, climbing pepper)

By climbing up a stake or other support, any of these pepper vines will grow 3 to 5 feet tall in a warm, humid atmosphere. They also do well in hanging containers, with their stems cascading over the edges. The saffron pepper has pink-veined olive-green leaves 4 to 6 inches long; the undersides are a deep purple. The slow-growing black pepper, a woody vine that climbs by aerial roots, has broadly oval leaves 5 to 7 inches long that are unevenly heart shaped and look like shiny blackish-green leather. Outdoors, inconspicuous flowers borne on spikes 3 to 6 inches long produce ¼-inch green berries that turn red, then black. The dried whole berries are ground to make black pepper; the outer shell is removed to produce white pepper. The plant bears no fruit when it is grown indoors.

Celebes pepper, a twining ornamental climber, has heart-shaped, waxy dark green leaves on reddish stems; the leaves are 5 inches long and 4 inches wide. Their upper surfaces are patterned at first with pink markings that turn white as the leaves age. The undersides are pale green.

HOW TO GROW. Pepper plants grow outdoors in Zone 10. Indoors, they grow best in north-facing windows or in bright indirect or curtain-filtered sunlight. They also do well in

**HEART-LEAVED PHILODENDRON**
*Philodendron oxycardium*

**CREEPING PILEA**
*Pilea depressa*

*For climate zones and frost dates, see maps, pages 146-147.*

**SAFFRON PEPPER**
*Piper crocatum*

medium artificial light 14 to 16 hours daily. Keep night temperatures between 65° and 70° and day temperatures between 75° and 85°; maintain humidity between 40 and 60 per cent. Plant the vines in an all-purpose potting mixture. Keep this mix barely moist at all times. Freshly potted or young pepper plants should not be fertilized for three or four months; fertilize established vines every one to two months with a fertilizer such as 5-10-5 diluted to half the strength that is recommended on the label. Repot overcrowded plants in early spring. Pepper plants are sometimes subject to infestation by spider mites. Propagate additional plants from seeds or stem cuttings.

## PLECTRANTHUS

*P. australis* (Swedish ivy)

An Australian plant, Swedish ivy received its name from the country where it was first grown indoors. This trailing vine has waxy leaves, 1 to 2 inches wide, with scalloped edges. Swedish ivy's pendant stems grow 1½ to 2 feet long, so thickly that they form a living curtain. When the plant is grown under artificial light, tiny white flowers tinged with lavender appear in small spikes.

HOW TO GROW. Swedish ivy grows best in bright indirect sunlight or with 12 to 14 hours of low to medium artificial light daily. Plant it in packaged potting soil and keep it moist but not soggy. Do not feed newly potted plants for three months; feed established plants monthly with house-plant fertilizer diluted to half the strength recommended on the label. Swedish ivy grows well at temperatures of 50° to 65° at night, 65° to 75° by day. Repot Swedish ivy when it becomes crowded. Pinch stems to make plants bushier. Propagate by rooting cuttings in moist vermiculite or in water.

## PLUMBAGO

*P. capensis,* also called *P. auriculata* (Cape plumbago, leadwort)

The Cape plumbago is an evergreen semiclimbing shrub that will grow as a vine if trimmed and tied to a trellis, arch or arbor; without heavy support and training it becomes a spreading mound. Its slender, arching stems grow up to 8 feet long, with light-green oblong leaves 1 to 2 inches long. Pale blue 1-inch flowers bloom in phloxlike clusters in summer and early fall; in parts of California they bloom continuously. Fruit is a cluster of burrs. Outdoors or in, Cape plumbago grows rapidly and needs regular shaping. It can be grown as a sizable tub specimen outdoors in Zone 9 and 10.

HOW TO GROW. Indoors, give Cape plumbago bright sunlight, with night temperatures of 45° to 50°, day temperatures of 60° to 70°. Humidity of 40 to 60 per cent is desirable. Plant in well-drained packaged potting mix and keep the soil evenly moist. Feed established plants monthly with house-plant fertilizer diluted to half the strength recommended on the label. In early spring, just before new growth starts, prune severely to thin the plant, remove suckers, increase bushiness and keep the vine a desirable size. After flowering, stop fertilizing. Reduce watering at this time, but never let the soil become completely dry; it is important for the roots to remain moist and cool. The plant can remain in the light. Repot in early spring. Grow new plants from young stem cuttings rooted in moist vermiculite.

Outdoors plumbago grows best in full sun and prefers a light, somewhat dry, sandy soil. Prune the plant heavily in early spring to thin and remove suckers; flowers are produced at the tips of new growth. If plumbago is attacked by aphids or red spider mites, rinse first with warm water; for heavy infestations, spray with an appropriate insecticide.

**SWEDISH IVY**
*Plectranthus australis*

POET'S JASMINE See *Jasminum*

## POLYGONUM

*P. aubertii* (silver fleece vine, silver lace vine, China fleece vine)

With rapid growth and billowing, lacy masses of fragrant flowers, the silver fleece vine can be used as an accent on porches and pergolas, cascading over the top of a wall, or quickly covering a wire fence. Its many-jointed, shrubby, twining stems grow 15 to 30 feet long and are covered with shiny, bright green 1- to 2½-inch leaves that are pale green with red tips when young. In late summer and early fall, dense 6-inch clusters of small, white to greenish-white flowers bloom profusely along the upper part of the branches.

Silver fleece vine tolerates wind, drought and city conditions and is also generally free of pests and diseases. Hardy in Zones 4-8, the vine may die to the ground in severe winters, but its roots usually survive to produce new growth in the spring.

HOW TO GROW. Silver fleece vine grows best in full sun and will tolerate a variety of soils, even those that are dry. Among the fastest growing of vines, it needs careful pruning and training. Tie the branches to strong supports. The plant flowers on new wood and should be drastically cut back and thinned annually in fall or winter. During the growing season, pinch back the tips to increase bushiness. The plant is so vigorous that fertilizer is rarely needed. Propagate from stem cuttings, seeds or division of a mature vine.

PORCELAIN AMPELOPSIS See *Ampelopsis*
POSSUM GRAPE See *Cissus*
POTATO VINE See *Solanum*
POTHOS See *Scindapsus*

## PUERARIA

*P. lobata,* also called *P. hirsuta, P. thunbergiana* (kudzu vine)

When a fast-spreading, durable ground cover, soil binder or filler plant is needed, kudzu is an appropriate choice. But unless pruned regularly the vine can become an invasive menace in warmer climates, engulfing anything within reach; it is known as "the vine that ate the South."

Grown as an annual in Zones 3-6 and as a perennial in Zones 7-10, kudzu vine is a lazy twiner but spreads quickly by underground runners to form a dense mat of deciduous leaves 3 to 6 inches long on slender, hairy stems. Each leaf is composed of three dark green leaflets, smooth on the upper side and hairy underneath. In frost-free regions, 6- to 10-inch spikes of tiny fragrant violet-purple pea-shaped flowers are produced in midsummer on the previous year's growth. These are followed by hairy, flat seed pods up to 4 inches long. Neither flowers nor fruits are particularly ornamental, as they are usually obscured by the leaves.

Trained as a climber, kudzu vine can rapidly cover an unsightly object or provide quick shade in summer. If it is given strong support it may reach up to 60 to 75 feet in the South; in the North it may grow 15 feet or more in a single season. It may die to the ground even in relatively mild southern winters, but its roots produce new growth in spring, at the expense of that year's flowers. Older plants are less likely to die back in winter.

HOW TO GROW. Kudzu vine thrives in full sun or partial shade in any well-drained soil and resists drought and wind damage. Fertilizing is unnecessary. Prune tips in the growing season to keep the plant from becoming woody and rangy; then cut it back severely each fall to keep it under control. In frost-free areas, leave some of the old canes to ensure flowers

CAPE PLUMBAGO
*Plumbago capensis*

SILVER FLEECE VINE
*Polygonum aubertii*

*For climate zones and frost dates, see maps, pages 146-147.*

**KUDZU VINE**
*Pueraria lobata*

**FLAME VINE**
*Pyrostegia venusta*

the following summer. Kudzu vine is seldom bothered by pests. Sow seeds outdoors after the danger of frost is past, or propagate additional plants from stem cuttings or by root division of mature plants.

PURPLE ALLAMANDA See *Cryptostegia*
PURPLE GRANADILLA See *Passiflora*
PURPLE HEART See *Setcreasea*
PURPLE PASSION VINE See *Gynura*
PURPLE VELVET PLANT See *Gynura*
PURPLE WINTER CREEPER See *Euonymus*

### PYROSTEGIA

*P. venusta,* also called *P. ignea, Bignonia venusta* (flame vine)

The tropical flame vine is covered with brilliantly colored tubular flowers twice a year. In hanging clusters of 20 to 30 flowers, each 2 to 3 inches long, the reddish-orange blooms grow thickly in winter, more sparsely in summer. The flowers are followed by seed pods 8 to 12 inches long. Each of the flame vine's shiny evergreen 1- to 2-inch leaves is composed of two or three leaflets. Once it is established, the perennial flame vine rapidly becomes a stout, woody plant, climbing 25 to 40 or sometimes even 70 feet across large expanses of wall by means of adhesive-tipped tendrils. An effective pergola covering, it is often used as a screen plant or as an accent vine. Flame vine is hardy in Zone 10.

HOW TO GROW. Plant flame vine in full sun in a rich, moist, well-drained soil to which leaf mold has been added. The vine can tolerate some exposure to wind but will not grow in dry soil. Since the flame vine's flowers are produced on new growth, prune it heavily each year after the winter flowering to insure continued flowering as well as to shape the plant. Fertilize only if the plant is growing poorly, using an all-purpose garden fertilizer. The flame vine is seldom bothered by pests. Propagate additional plants by rooting stem cuttings in moist sand or vermiculite.

## Q

QUAMOCLIT See *Ipomoea*

## R

RAINBOW WANDERING JEW See *Tradescantia*
RAPHIDOPHORA See *Scindapsus*
RED GRANADILLA See *Passiflora*
RED KOWHAI See *Clianthus*
RED-LEAVED PHILODENDRON See *Philodendron*
RED-NERVED FITTONIA See *Fittonia*
RED PASSIONFLOWER See *Passiflora*
RHYNCHOSPERMUM See *Trachelospermum*
RIVERBANK GRAPE See *Vitis*

### ROSA

*R.* 'America'; *R. banksiae* (Banks' rose, Banksia rose); *R.* 'Blaze'; *R.* 'Climbing Crimson Glory'; *R.* 'Climbing Peace'; *R.* 'Dr. W. Van Fleet'; *R.* 'Don Juan'; *R.* 'Dorothy Perkins'; *R.* 'Golden Showers'; *R.* 'New Dawn'; *R.* 'Piñata'; *R.* 'Rhonda'; *R.* 'Tempo'; *R. wichuraiana* (memorial rose)

Few vining plants provide the spectacular floral displays of climbing and rambling roses. Although these roses use their thorns to cling to surfaces, the weight of their 8- to 20-foot stems will topple them unless their canes are tied to supports. Allowed to trail, rambling varieties can be ground covers, helping to hold the soil in place. Some climbers bloom only once a year while others provide a continuous display of bloom from spring through fall. In a range of colors from white to yellow through pink and red, the flowers have single, semidouble or double layers of petals.

Except for Dr. W. Van Fleet, which blooms only in the spring, the climbers that bear large flowers bloom continuously throughout the warm months. Included in this group of reliable bloomers are Blaze with scarlet flowers; New Dawn, blush pink; America, coral pink; Rhonda, medium pink with coral tones; Tempo, deep red; Piñata, bright yellow edged with orange red; and Dr. W. Van Fleet, pink fading to flesh white. Dark red Don Juan and daffodil-yellow Golden Showers are pillar roses, a subclass of the large-flowered climbers. They have stiff, upright stems and are best grown vertically.

Climbing hybrid tea roses are genetic mutations of bush hybrid tea roses that offer the exquisitely shaped blooms of their parents, though they are not as hardy, and they flower less profusely. Climbing Crimson Glory, a red rose that has a clove fragrance, and Climbing Peace, a yellow rose edged with pink, are both climbing hybrid teas that bloom in the spring and again in fall.

Hardiest of the vining roses, the ramblers are also the slowest growers. They bear their single- or double-petaled flowers in clusters, and they are easily trained to grow on trellises, arbors, fences or pergolas because their stems are so pliable. The light pink Dorothy Perkins belongs in this group as do two Oriental species, the semievergreen white-flowered memorial rose and the semievergreen Banks' rose, which bears yellow or creamy white flowers. The memorial rose is especially satisfactory as a ground cover because its canes readily produce new roots when they are in contact with moist soil. Most climbing roses are hardy in Zones 6-10, but ramblers are hardy as far north as Zone 5.

HOW TO GROW. Roses grow best in full sun or where they receive at least five hours of sun daily. They need adequate air circulation and protection from drying winds. Plant roses in spring, setting them 5 to 8 feet apart. Beds with heavy, well-drained clay soils to which compost has been added are best; ramblers will also grow in sandy soils. Water roses heavily in dry weather. Fertilize annually in the fall by spreading compost, and feed the plants in the spring with a general-purpose garden fertilizer. Do not plant other perennials close to roses, and keep their beds free of dead leaves and weeds to minimize insect and disease problems. Immediate removal of spent flowers helps to lengthen the blooming season. Prune out dead, diseased or old canes in spring immediately after flowering, and shape plants by removing crossing or inward-growing branches. In colder areas, where temperatures drop to around zero, place canes on the ground and mound with soil for winter protection.

ROSARY VINE See *Ceropegia*
ROSE See *Rosa*
ROYAL TRUMPET VINE See *Distictis*
ROYAL VELVET PLANT See *Gynura*
RUBBER VINE, PALAY See *Cryptostegia*
RUNNER BEAN, SCARLET See *Phaseolus*

# S

SAFFRON PEPPER See *Piper*
ST. PAUL'S CREEPER See *Parthenocissus*
SCARLET CLEMATIS See *Clematis*
SCARLET RUNNER BEAN See *Phaseolus*
SCENTED STAR JASMINE See *Jasminum*

## SCINDAPSUS

*S. aureus*, also called *Epipremnum aureum, Pothos aureus* and *Raphidophora aurea* (devil's ivy, pothos, golden pothos)

*For climate zones and frost dates, see maps, pages 146-147.*

*Rosa* 'Golden Showers'

MEMORIAL ROSE
*Rosa wichuraiana*

**DEVIL'S IVY**
*Scindapsus aureus*

Devil's ivy is a climbing vine that clings with aerial roots or is grown trailing from a hanging container. As a house plant, it will grow 6 to 10 feet from a pot. The waxy green and yellow heart-shaped leaves are 2 to 4 inches long when the vine is young and 6 to 12 inches as it matures. Three varieties are Golden Queen with leaves almost entirely yellow, Marble Queen with green leaves extensively marbled with white as they unfold and becoming increasingly green as they age, and Tricolor with medium green leaves splashed cream, yellow and pale green.

HOW TO GROW. Devil's ivy grows best in bright indirect or curtain-filtered sunlight, or under medium artificial light for 12 to 14 hours daily; if there is too little light, leaves tend to lose their markings and revert to solid green. Temperatures of 65° to 70° at night and 75° to 85° by day are best. Grow plants in packaged potting soil mixed with an equal amount of peat moss or shredded sphagnum moss. Allow the potting mixture to dry slightly between thorough waterings. If too moist, the roots will rot. Vines will climb slabs of bark or tree fern, or they may be grown in water with fertilizer added. They are generally pest free.

Wait four to six months before feeding newly purchased or potted plants growing in potting mix. Feed established plants every month or two with a house-plant fertilizer diluted to half the strength recommended on the label. For large plants, repot every second or third year. Pinch back stems to any length. Propagate devil's ivy at any time from stem cuttings rooted in moist sand or vermiculite.

## SEDUM

*S. morganianum* (burro's tail)

A trailing succulent, the burro's tail sedum branches at its base into hanging stems 1½ to 3 feet long. These stems are solidly covered with tear-shaped leaves up to 1 inch long, which are coated with a powdery blue dust called bloom, similar to that on blueberries and plums. The leaves of burro's tail are fragile and break off easily. At the ends of the stems, red flowers bloom in small clusters during the summer, but the plant is notable chiefly for its interesting foliage. Usually grown in hanging containers indoors, burro's tail may also be used outdoors in rock gardens, but the plant is hardy only in Zones 9 and 10.

HOW TO GROW. Burro's tail grows best indoors with four or more hours of direct sun or 12 to 16 hours a day of bright artificial light. From spring through fall, night temperatures should be between 50° and 65°; day temperatures between 68° and 72°. Grow burro's tail in a mixture of equal parts of packaged potting soil and sharp sand, with 1 tablespoon of ground limestone and 1 tablespoon of bone meal added to each gallon of the mix. Water the plant thoroughly from spring through fall, letting the soil become dry to the touch between waterings. Withhold fertilizer from newly potted plants for four to six months; fertilize established plants three times a year—in early spring, late spring and late summer.

Rest the plant in winter, watering it only enough to keep it from shriveling. Since burro's tail is delicate, avoid repotting but increase water and fertilizer for old plants. Propagate by rooting detached leaves in moist sand.

Outdoors, burro's tail will grow in full sun or partial shade. It tolerates almost any soil that is well drained. Plant at any time when the soil can be cultivated, setting plants in a location offering protection from wind and rain.

## SENECIO

*S. confusus* (Mexican flame vine); *S. mikanioides* (German ivy, parlor ivy); *S. scandens* (flame vine)

**BURRO'S TAIL**
*Sedum morganianum*

The rangy stems of the senecios intertwine and take root as they grow, forming a ground cover that is almost constantly dotted with bright daisy-like flowers. If supported, the vines will climb 20 feet or more and often grow over banks, low walls and shrubs. Frost kills the vines to the ground but they grow again from the roots in Zones 9 and 10. As house plants they trail gracefully from hanging containers if the stem ends are pinched back to keep the plants small.

In spring and early summer, Mexican flame vine bears 1½-inch orange-red flowers with yellow centers. German ivy, a fast-growing vine, is valued mainly for its lobed light-green leaves that resemble English ivy's. An inconsistent bloomer, it sometimes bears 1- to 3-inch clusters of yellow flowers, mostly in winter. Flame vine blooms in late summer and fall, with bright yellow flowers ¾ inch wide in loose branching clusters, against long, pointed gray-green leaves.

HOW TO GROW. Indoors, senecios grow best in curtain-filtered summer sun and at least four hours of direct winter sunlight daily. Maintain temperatures of 50° to 60° at night and 65° to 75° by day, with humidity between 40 and 50 per cent. Plant in packaged potting soil kept evenly moist. German ivy may be grown in water alone; add a few drops of liquid fertilizer monthly. Wait to fertilize plants until they are well established—at three or four months—then feed them every two months with house-plant fertilizer diluted to half the strength recommended on the label. Pinch back tips for bushy growth.

Outdoors, the plants grow best in partial shade where they will be protected from the hottest summer sun. Plants grow best in light, moist, well-drained soil to which leaf mold has been added. Set plants 1 foot apart for ground cover, 2 to 3 feet apart when they are to be supported by walls or trellises. Prune annually after the flowers fade. Propagate additional plants from stem cuttings rooted in moist sand or vermiculite.

## SETCREASEA
*S. purpurea*, also called *S. pallida* 'Purple Heart' (purple heart)

Purple heart is a creeper that is often used as a ground cover in Zone 10; elsewhere it is not hardy and must be grown as a house plant. The leaves and flowers are borne on smooth purple stems that may grow a foot or more in length; the pointed leaves, which are 5 to 7 inches long, are purple with fine white hairs. The pink flowers, ½ to ¾ inch wide, are translucent. Purple heart is widely grown indoors either in pots or hanging containers.

HOW TO GROW. Indoors, purple heart grows best in temperatures of 60° to 65° at night and 70° to 75° by day. In direct sun or bright artificial light, the leaves are bright and iridescent; in indirect light the leaves are a dull reddish-green and the plants become leggy. Plant in packaged potting soil and let it become slightly dry between thorough waterings. Wait three to four months to fertilize newly potted or purchased plants; fertilize established plants every two months with a standard house-plant fertilizer. Pinching encourages branching and a fuller shape.

Outdoors, plant purple heart in well-drained sandy garden soil in full sun or partial shade. Space the plants 8 inches apart. Propagate additional plants by rooting stem cuttings in moist sand or vermiculite.

SILVER FLEECE VINE See *Polygonum*
SILVER LACE VINE See *Polygonum*
SILVER-NERVED FITTONIA See *Fittonia*
SILVER-VEIN CREEPER See *Parthenocissus*
SILVER VINE See *Actinidia*

*For climate zones and frost dates, see maps, pages 146-147.*

GERMAN IVY
*Senecio mikanioides*

PURPLE HEART
*Setcreasea purpurea*

**CHALICE VINE**
*Solandra maxima*

**COSTA RICAN NIGHTSHADE**
*Solanum wendlandii*

SKYFLOWER See *Thunbergia*
SMILAX See *Asparagus*
SNAKE VINE See *Hibbertia*

## SOLANDRA

*S. guttata* (goldcup chalice vine, cup-of-gold, trumpet plant);
*S. maxima,* also called *S. hartwegii* and *S. nitida* (both called chalice vine)

Rapidly climbing evergreens, the tropical chalice vines can be held to a height of 15 to 20 feet with regular pruning. In Zones 9 and 10 they grow best in frost-free locations that offer protection from wind. They will not tolerate frost. Both species bear leaves 3 to 6 inches long on thick, woody stems; the leaves of goldcup are hairy, while *S. maxima* has smooth, glossy leaves. Very fragrant trumpet-shaped flowers bloom principally in early spring, though flowers may appear intermittently throughout the rest of the year. Red fruits about 2½ inches in diameter follow the flowers. Goldcup chalice vine bears 9-inch cream-colored blooms with purple splotches; crinkled petal edges fold back around the tops of the cups. Flowers of *S. maxima* are 6 to 9 inches long and are yellow with brownish stripes descending inside the cup from ruffled edges. Chalice vines can be trained on large walls, pergolas or fences or allowed to ramble as a ground cover.

HOW TO GROW. Chalice vines grow best when they are given full sun in cooler coastal areas; give them partial shade in hotter inland locations. Plant them in any moist, well-drained soil. For abundant flowers, do not fertilize the plants, but water them generously during periods of active growth. Chalice vines should be tied firmly to strong supports. During the resting period after flowering, allow the soil to become dry between waterings. Prune annually in late spring to force branching and increase flower production and to control the size of the plant. Propagate additional plants from stem cuttings taken in summer.

## SOLANUM

*S. dulcamara* (bitter nightshade); *S. jasminoides* (jasmine nightshade); *S. wendlandii* (Costa Rican nightshade, potato vine, paradise flower)

Perennial nightshades twine their branching stems around trellises or other supports to form lacy screens of deciduous or evergreen foliage. Their star-shaped flowers are produced in loose clusters that are set off by glossy leaves 1 to 4 inches long. The brightly colored fruits and the juice of wilted leaves are known to be poisonous in some species and are suspect in others.

Bitter nightshade, hardy in Zones 5-10, may climb up to 15 feet high but usually grows prostrate. In warm regions it reseeds so readily and spreads so rapidly by underground runners that some gardeners regard it as a weed. Its flowers, purple with green spots, bloom throughout the summer. Jasmine nightshade grows 10 to 20 feet long. Its 1-inch white flowers are tinged with pale blue; they bloom from midsummer to the first frost. The vine, often evergreen, may lose its leaves during chilly periods but this does not endanger the plant; it is hardy in Zones 9 and 10. The coarse, shrubby Costa Rican nightshade grows up to 50 feet long and is hardy only in Zone 10. It bears clusters of pale lilac-blue 2½-inch flowers in summer and fall.

HOW TO GROW. The nightshades grow best in full sun with a south or west exposure. Plant them in spring in any well-drained soil, placing them close to the supports they are to climb. Prune when new growth appears in spring, removing excess growth and cutting back remaining shoots to encourage thicker branching. Propagate from seeds or cuttings.

## SOLEIROLIA

*S. soleirolii,* also called *Helxine soleirolii* (baby's tears)

Tiny, round leaves only ¼ inch wide line the delicate stems of baby's tears. Used as a creeping evergreen ground cover in Zone 10 and protected areas of Zone 9, it spreads quickly, its stems rooting wherever they touch the soil, to form cushion-like mounds about 3 inches high. In summer, it bears inconspicuous white flowers. As a house plant, baby's tears will spill over the edges of hanging containers, concealing their contours with a dense mat of trailing stems.

HOW TO GROW. Indoors, baby's tears grows best in indirect or curtain-filtered sunlight or under low artificial light for 14 to 16 hours a day. Temperatures of 50° to 55° at night and 65° to 70° by day, with humidity as close to 50 per cent as possible, are ideal. Plant in packaged potting soil and keep it constantly moist but not soggy. Do not fertilize newly potted plants for six months; feed established plants once a month with house-plant fertilizer diluted to half the strength recommended on the label. Outdoors, grow baby's tears in partial shade in rich, well-drained garden soil. Space plants 6 to 12 inches apart, and water them regularly until they become established. Propagate by rooting stem cuttings in moist sand or vermiculite at any time of year.

SPANISH JASMINE See *Jasminum*
SPEARHEAD PHILODENDRON See *Philodendron*
SPRENGER ASPARAGUS See *Asparagus*
STAR JASMINE, CONFEDERATE See *Trachelospermum*
STAR JASMINE, SCENTED See *Jasminum*

## STEPHANOTIS

*S. floribunda* (stephanotis, Madagascar jasmine)

Twining up to 15 feet on a trellis or other support, stephanotis is a slow-growing vine with thick, glossy evergreen leaves. From spring to early fall, the vine produces profuse clusters of waxy, fragrant white flower trumpets, each about 2 inches long. The flowers, long lasting on the vine and when cut, are traditional favorites in bridal bouquets and are used in leis in Hawaii. The fleshy seed pods 6 inches long hang from the vine for two years while they ripen. Stephanotis can be grown outdoors in Zone 10; elsewhere it is grown in a greenhouse or is severely pruned to keep it an appropriate size for a house plant.

HOW TO GROW. Grow stephanotis indoors where it will receive at least four hours of direct sunlight daily, although partial shading from midsummer sun may be needed to prevent the leaves from scorching. For best bloom, stephanotis needs night temperatures of 60° to 65° and day temperatures of 70° or higher. Plant in packaged potting soil. During the spring-through-fall growing season, keep the soil moist but never soggy; good drainage is essential. Fertilize monthly with a house-plant fertilizer diluted to half the strength recommended on the label. During the winter when the plant is dormant, withhold fertilizer and let the soil dry slightly between waterings. Somewhat lower temperatures in winter will not harm the plant. Outdoors, grow stephanotis in partial shade; hot, direct sun may damage the foliage. Plant the vine in well-drained garden soil enriched with leaf mold or compost. Prune in spring to remove weak stems. Stephanotis may be cut back occasionally to encourage new stems. Mealy bugs and scales sometimes attack this plant. Propagate from seeds or from stem cuttings with three or four joints in a moist mixture of one part sand and one part perlite.

## STIGMAPHYLLON

*S. ciliatum* (golden vine, orchid vine, butterfly vine)

*For climate zones and frost dates, see maps, pages 146-147.*

**BABY'S TEARS**
*Soleirolia soleirolii*

**STEPHANOTIS**
*Stephanotis floribunda*

**GOLDEN VINE**
*Stigmaphyllon ciliatum*

**ORANGE STREPTOSOLEN**
*Streptosolen jamesonii*

In a mild climate, the slender, 10- to 20- foot stems of the golden vine will twine around a trellis or fence to create a delicate evergreen specimen or screen. From spring through fall, the vine bears profuse clusters of inch-wide golden flowers resembling small orchids among heart-shaped leaves 2 to 3 inches long. Young leaves have a reddish or coppery tint. Older stems eventually become woody. The plant will survive mild cold in Zones 9 and 10; elsewhere it can be grown in a greenhouse.

HOW TO GROW. Grow the golden vine outdoors in partial shade in a location sheltered from wind. The vine grows best in well-drained soil enriched with compost. The soil should be moist but not soggy. Prune in winter or early spring to remove dead, broken or weak branches and to shape the vine. In a warm greenhouse, plant the golden vine in a soil-filled bench; it does not grow well if its roots are confined in a pot. Give it night temperatures of 60° to 65° and day temperatures of 70° to 85°. Pests do not often infest golden vine. Propagate by taking stem cuttings in fall and rooting them in moist vermiculite heated from underneath to 70°.

## STREPTOSOLEN

*S. jamesonii* (orange streptosolen)

A shrubby vine with leaning 8- to 10-foot stems, orange streptosolen can be trained as a thick evergreen screen by tying its arching stems to a trellis. Or the plant can be left unsupported to sprawl in loose mounds that will form a cover for a steep bank. When grown outdoors in protected areas of Zone 9 and in Zone 10, the vine bears clusters of inch-wide, bright orange-to-red flower trumpets among its prominently ribbed 1½-inch oval leaves in summer and intermittently at other times. It blooms in winter or spring when it is grown indoors in a pot or hanging container placed in a greenhouse or sunny window.

HOW TO GROW. Outdoors, grow orange streptosolen in full sun in any well-drained garden soil enriched with compost. Water thoroughly during dry periods. Severely prune the vine—especially an older one—after it flowers to thin the plant and control its rampant growth. Indoors, grow orange streptosolen where the plant will receive at least four hours of direct sun in winter, bright or curtain-filtered sun in summer. Temperatures of 50° to 55° at night and 68° to 72° by day are ideal for flowering. Plant in any packaged potting soil and keep the soil moist but not soggy. Fertilize monthly with a house-plant fertilizer diluted to half the strength recommended on the label. Pinch back a young plant to encourage bushy growth, or train it to climb a stake or trellis. Prune an older plant lightly after flowers fade to shape it and keep it to a size appropriate for its container. Propagate by rooting stem cuttings in moist vermiculite.

SWEDISH IVY See *Plectranthus*
SWEET AUTUMN CLEMATIS See *Clematis*
SWEET CLOCK VINE See *Thunbergia*
SWEET PEA See *Lathyrus*
SWISS CHEESE PLANT See *Monstera*

## SYNGONIUM

*S. podophyllum* (arrowhead plant, nephthytis); *S. wendlandii*

On both the arrowhead plant and *S. wendlandii,* young and old plants have distinctly different leaves. Juvenile foliage is paper thin and arrow shaped, but adult leaves split into several pointed leaflets and eventually become wide fans of finger-like leaflets. Leaves grow on long stalks that rise from creeping or climbing stems that have fleshy aerial roots. The stems will drape from pots or hanging containers, or they can be pinned with wire to slabs of bark or poles made of tree-fern fiber. The 3-inch juvenile leaves of the arrowhead plant are slightly variegated with white or yellow, while the mature leaves, which grow up to 11 inches wide on 2-foot stems, are a solid green. Both the youthful and mature leaves of *S. wendlandii* are marked with gray or white along their ribs; this vine is smaller than the arrowhead plant, with mature leaves 4 to 6 inches long on 6-inch stems. Both of these vines can be grown outdoors in Zone 10, but they are usually grown as house plants.

HOW TO GROW. Indoors grow either the arrowhead vine or *S. wendlandii* in bright indirect or curtain-filtered sunlight, or with 12 to 14 hours of medium artificial light daily. Night temperatures of 65° to 70° and day temperatures of 75° to 85° are best. Plant in a packaged potting soil and keep the soil barely moist, never soggy. Do not feed newly potted plants for three or four months; fertilize established plants every two months with a house-plant fertilizer diluted to half the amount recommended on the label. Pinch back long stems to encourage branching for bushier plants. Propagate additional plants at any time from stem cuttings rooted in water or in moist sand or vermiculite.

# T

TAHITIAN BRIDAL VEIL See *Tripogandra*

## TECOMARIA
*T. capensis* (Cape honeysuckle)

A tropical evergreen shrub, Cape honeysuckle has flexible stems that may grow 15 to 25 feet long. They can be trained vertically or horizontally to embellish fences or walls. The shiny, dark green compound leaves have five to nine leaflets, each ¾ to 2 inches long. This lacy foliage sets off masses of orange-red or scarlet 2-inch funnel-shaped flowers that bloom in summer and are followed by slender 2-inch seed pods. The variety Aurea has yellow flowers. Cape honeysuckle is hardy in Zones 8 and 9.

HOW TO GROW. Cape honeysuckle grows best in full sun. Plant it in moist but well-drained fertile sandy soil. Water well in dry weather, since it will not tolerate drought. Provide a support of adequate size. Prune annually in spring after flowering has ended to control its rapid growth and spur the development of new branches. The plant will flower on this new growth. Propagate from seeds or stem cuttings rooted in moist sand or vermiculite.

## THUNBERGIA
*T. alata* (black-eyed-Susan vine, clock vine); *T. fragrans* (sweet clock vine); *T. grandiflora* (skyflower, Bengal clock vine); *T. laurifolia* (laurel-leaved clock vine)

Twining, brightly flowered clock vines are tender perennials often grown outdoors as annuals in the north to cover low trellises and walls. The flowers bloom against a backdrop of dense oval or triangular leaves. Black-eyed-Susan vine grows up to 10 feet tall but can be cut back indoors and grown as a trailing plant or trained to a small trellis. It bears many 1- to 2-inch-wide flowers with dark centers and white, buff, yellow or orange petals. Leaves are 1 to 3 inches long. Outdoors the plant is hardy in Zone 10; in colder areas it is grown as an annual.

The sweet clock vine, hardy in Zone 10, bears fragrant flowers 1½ inches wide and triangular 3-inch leaves. Skyflower is hardy in Zones 8-10. It blooms in drooping clusters of 3-inch blue or, rarely, white flowers. Stems growing from 10 to 20 feet have leaves 6 to 8 inches long. The laurel-leaved clock vine has clusters of light-blue flowers with white

*For climate zones and frost dates, see maps, pages 146-147.*

**ARROWHEAD PLANT**
*Syngonium podophyllum*

**CAPE HONEYSUCKLE**
*Tecomaria capensis*

**BLACK-EYED-SUSAN VINE**
*Thunbergia alata*

**STAR JASMINE**
*Trachelospermum jasminoides*

throats. Stems grow from 30 to 50 feet and carry leaves 6 to 8 inches long. The plant is hardy in Zone 10.

HOW TO GROW. Indoors, black-eyed-Susan vines grow best in at least four hours of direct sunlight a day. Night temperatures from 50° to 60° and day temperatures from 68° to 72° are ideal. Plant in a packaged potting soil and keep it moist but not soggy. Fertilize every two weeks during the fall and winter growing season with a house-plant fertilizer diluted to half the strength recommended on the label. Prune after flowering to keep the size of the plant manageable.

In the garden, clock vines grow best in a sunny location where they are protected from strong wind. Plant in moist but well-drained soil to which leaf mold has been added. Tie branches to a lattice or other support for upright growth. Mulch plants during the winter in milder areas, to carry them over. Prune after flowering; cut straggly vines off at the soil level to induce fresh growth. Propagate additional plants from stem cuttings or from seeds sown indoors six weeks before the average date of the last spring frost.

## TRACHELOSPERMUM
*T. asiaticum,* also called *Rhynchospermum asiaticum* (yellow star jasmine); *T. jasminoides* (star jasmine, Confederate star jasmine)

The evergreen star jasmines are prized for their heavily scented clusters of phloxlike flowers, which bloom on twining stems in spring and summer. Growing slowly to 15 feet or more, the delicate stems interweave, forming a dense, neat mat of thick, glossy oval leaves that are pale green when they open and darker as they mature. Yellow star jasmine has leaves 1 to 2 inches long and yellow-white flowers in 2- to 3-inch clusters. It is hardy in Zones 7 and 8. Star jasmine has somewhat pointed leaves 2 to 3 inches long and white wavy-lobed flowers in clusters 2 to 3 inches wide; it is hardy in Zone 9. As house plants, the vines will spill over the edges of hanging containers, or they can be trained on small trellises. Outdoors they frame porches, accent trellises or screen fences and walls. They can also be used as a ground cover.

HOW TO GROW. Indoors, star jasmines grow best in bright indirect or curtain-filtered sunlight except in winter, when they need at least four hours of direct sunlight a day. Night temperatures of 50° to 55° and day temperatures of 68° to 72° are ideal. Plant in packaged potting soil and water thoroughly whenever the soil becomes slightly dry to the touch. Fertilize every two to three months with a standard house-plant fertilizer.

Both star jasmines grow best outdoors in partial shade; they tolerate full sun in cool areas. A moist but well-drained soil to which leaf mold has been added is best. Yellowish leaves indicate the need for fertilizer, which should be applied in spring. Tie stems to a fairly heavy support. Prune after flowering if necessary to restrain growth. If the vine is grown as a ground cover, trim upward-twining stems. Propagate additional plants from stem cuttings.

## TRADESCANTIA
*T. albiflora* 'Laekenensis' (rainbow wandering Jew); *T. blossfeldiana* (flowering inch plant); *T. fluminensis* (wandering Jew); *T. fluminensis* 'Variegata' (variegated wandering Jew); *T. navicularis* (chain plant)

Trailing from hanging pots, tradescantias are easy-to-grow house plants. They are valued chiefly for their foliage, often highly variegated. Rainbow wandering Jew is a variety that has pale green leaves marked with purple and white and tinged with pink. The flowering inch plant has purple stems, covered with white hairs, that trail or grow erect. Alternating along the stems are leaves that are smooth and dark green on the metallic-looking upper surface, purple and downy underneath; they grow up to 4 inches long and 1¾ inches wide. Clusters of tiny purple and pink flowers 1½ inches wide appear from spring through fall.

Wandering Jew is a trailing vine with trailing or erect shiny green stems that may root at leaf joints. Its 1- to 1½-inch leaves, oval with long points, are green with reddish-purple undersides. The variegated wandering Jew has some leaves banded with cream or white; others may be almost entirely green, cream or white. It has white flowers. The chain plant, a small creeping vine, has succulent green leaves only ¾ inch long. Its flowers are rose-purple. It grows more slowly than the other tradescantias.

HOW TO GROW. Tradescantias grow best in bright indirect or curtain-filtered sunlight; strong sun is injurious, but good light is needed for strong foliage color, especially in the variegated types. Tradescantias also do well with 14 to 16 hours per day of medium artificial light, which promotes good leaf color. Temperatures of 50° to 55° at night and 68° to 72° by day are best. The plants withstand dry air if the soil is kept moist, but they grow best with humidity between 30 and 40 per cent. If humidity is high, allow the soil to dry slightly between waterings. Do not overwater. Wandering Jew or variegated wandering Jew may be grown in water with a few drops of liquid fertilizer added every month or so.

Plant tradescantias in a packaged potting mixture. Delay feeding until plants are well established and then fertilize them every other month with a house-plant fertilizer such as 5-10-5 diluted to half the recommended strength. Too much fertilizer may weaken the colors of variegated leaves, while too little may cause older leaves to drop off. Root stem cuttings at any time of year in water or moist vermiculite.

TRAILING LANTANA See *Lantana*
TREE IVY See *Fatshedera*
TREEBINE See *Cissus*

TRIPOGANDRA

*T. multiflora,* also called *Tradescantia multiflora* (Tahitian bridal veil, fernleaf inch plant)

Gracefully trailing stems make Tahitian bridal veil well suited for a hanging container, and its fragrant dainty flowers increase its ornamental value. Blooming in early summer, the white flowers are scattered along the stems, which are tightly packed with dark olive-green leaves 1 to 2 inches long; the undersides of the leaves are purple. This plant was formerly classified as a *Tradescantia,* the genus that includes the wandering Jew, which the Tahitian bridal veil closely resembles. In Zone 10 where this vine is hardy, it is used in window boxes or grown in the sun in rock gardens.

HOW TO GROW. Tahitian bridal veil grows well in bright indirect or curtain-filtered sunlight in summer and direct sunlight in winter, or in 14 to 16 hours a day of medium artificial light. Maintain night temperatures of 50° to 55° and day temperatures of 68° to 72°. Plant the vines in packaged potting soil. Let the soil become moderately dry before watering thoroughly. Feed the plants every one to two months with a house-plant fertilizer diluted to half the strength recommended on the label. Repot crowded plants at any season.

Outdoors, the vines grow well in full sun or partial shade. Plant between October and March in any well-drained soil. Pinch frequently to promote branching and prevent straggly growth. If the plants become heavy, cut some stems back to the soil; new growth will appear. Propagate additional plants from stem cuttings taken at any time.

*For climate zones and frost dates, see maps, pages 146-147.*

VARIEGATED WANDERING JEW
*Tradescantia fluminensis* 'Variegata'

TAHITIAN BRIDAL VEIL
*Tripogandra multiflora*

**COMMON NASTURTIUM**
*Tropaeolum majus*

**VANILLA ORCHID**
*Vanilla planifolia*

## TROPAEOLUM

*T. majus* (common nasturtium); *T. peregrinum* (canary-bird flower, canary nasturtium)

Annual vines that climb 10 feet high with coiling leaf stems, nasturtiums produce gaudy arrays of bright, tartly fragrant flowers among long-stemmed bright green leaves 1½ to 2½ inches wide. Common nasturtiums have single or double 2-inch-wide funnel-like flowers with 1-inch spurs; they may be white, yellow, orange, salmon, pink, scarlet or dark red. The leaves are shield shaped. Canary-bird flowers bear fringed 3-part yellow flowers, 1 inch long, which resemble tiny birds in flight. The leaves are deeply cut into five lobes. The flowers and young leaves of both species are edible, adding a peppery flavor to salads. Both vines grow quickly and may be trained on trellises or posts or allowed to trail from window boxes or over the ground. As house plants, they bloom most of the winter from seed sown in late summer, creating a bright display for hanging containers.

HOW TO GROW. Outdoors, plant nasturtiums in full sun and in infertile, dry, sandy soil. (Rich soil or added fertilizer stimulate foliage production at the expense of flowers.) To lengthen the flowering period, sow seed indoors in peat pots in late winter; then set outdoors, pots and all, after the danger of frost has passed. Otherwise wait until spring and sow the seeds outside where the plants will grow all summer. Nasturtiums should not be transplanted. Space the seeds or plants 4 to 6 inches apart. Water during hot, dry weather to keep the leaves from withering. Pinch off some leaves and remove faded flowers to spur more profuse flowering. Tie young plants to supports to induce climbing.

As house plants, nasturtiums grow best with at least four hours of direct sunlight a day and good ventilation. Night temperatures of 40° to 55° and daytime temperatures of 68° or lower are ideal. Plant them in a packaged potting soil and keep it moist to slightly dry. Feed the plants monthly with a house-plant fertilizer diluted to one fourth the strength recommended on the label. Heavy fertilizing or watering gives lush foliage but fewer flowers. Nasturtiums are subject to infestations of aphids, which cluster under the leaves and buds. Propagate additional plants from seed at any time; soak the seeds overnight before sowing.

TRUMPET CREEPER See *Campsis*
TRUMPET FLOWER, EVENING See *Gelsemium*
TRUMPET HONEYSUCKLE See *Lonicera*
TRUMPET PLANT See *Solandra*
TRUMPET VINE See *Distictis*
TUBEROUS BEGONIA, HANGING See *Begonia*

# V

## VANILLA

*V. planifolia* (vanilla orchid)

A climbing orchid, the vanilla is an intriguing vine to try in a humid greenhouse or plant room—if you have space. It climbs by means of sticky aerial roots, and the fleshy stems may reach lengths of more than 100 feet. A cutting has been known to grow 40 feet in three years. Only very large plants produce flowers and then only under ideal growing conditions. Given these, 2½- to 3-inch greenish-yellow flowers are produced intermittently throughout the year. The flowers, which are borne on 3-inch spikes, last for several days among leathery gray-green leaves 6 to 8 inches long. The vanilla orchid usually requires hand pollination to produce the fragrant 6-inch-long beanlike pods from which seeds are taken to make vanilla extract.

HOW TO GROW. The vanilla orchid grows best in warm,

moist air. Maintain night temperatures of 60° to 65° and day temperatures of 70° to 85°. Provide at least four hours of bright sunlight a day and humidity of 40 to 60 per cent. Plant in a mixture of 2 parts coarse peat moss, 2 parts sandy soil, 1 part perlite and 1 part fine fir bark. Provide a tree-fern slab or other support for climbing. Keep the soil mixture evenly moist all year. Fertilize at every third watering with a balanced fertilizer such as 18-18-18 diluted to half the strength recommended on the label. When the soil begins to deteriorate and drains poorly, replace the top layer, being careful to avoid disturbing the roots. Propagate by stem cuttings, each with three to five leaf nodes.

VANILLA TRUMPET VINE See *Distictis*
VARIEGATED PERIWINKLE See *Vinca*
VARIEGATED WANDERING JEW See *Tradescantia*
VARIEGATED WAX PLANT See *Hoya*
VEITCH'S CREEPER See *Parthenocissus*
VELVET PLANT See *Gynura*
VENEZUELA TREEBINE See *Cissus*

## VINCA

*V. major* (greater periwinkle); *V. major* 'Variegata' (variegated periwinkle); *V. minor* (common periwinkle, creeping myrtle)

Flowering evergreen periwinkles have rooting stems that quickly spread to cover bare ground in sun or shade. Growing up to 5 feet long, periwinkles can also serve as trailing plants for window boxes, outdoor tubs and hanging containers. Greater periwinkle is hardy in Zones 8-10; its stems send out shoots up to 3 or 4 feet long and bear 1- to 3-inch oval leaves. Variegated periwinkle has green leaves with creamy white edges and markings. A perennial in Zones 9 and 10, it is grown as an annual in colder areas. Common periwinkle is hardy in Zones 4-10. Grown often as a ground cover, it has glossy oval leaves up to 2 inches long on shoots that form a mat 6 inches high. In early spring all three vines produce lavender-blue flowers ¾ to 2 inches wide.

HOW TO GROW. Periwinkles grow best in deep moist soil enriched with organic matter but will tolerate poor soil. In Zones 8-10 they thrive in partial to deep shade; in Zones 4-7 they grow well in partial shade or full sun. Set out plants that will be grown as annuals after all danger of frost is past, spacing them 6 inches apart. Periwinkles to be grown as perennials may be planted in spring or fall; space them 6 to 12 inches apart. Mulch new plants to conserve moisture. Pinch back young shoots frequently to encourage bushiness. Large expanses of periwinkle may be sheared occasionally to induce new growth. Once established, periwinkles need little care and are seldom bothered by pests. Propagate by division in the spring or by cuttings at any time.

VINE LILAC See *Hardenbergia*
VIRGINIA CREEPER See *Parthenocissus*

## VITIS

*V. coignetiae* (crimson vine, glory vine); *V. labrusca* (fox grape); *V. riparia* (riverbank grape); *V. rotundifolia* (muscadine grape); *V. vinifera* (European grape); *V.* 'Concord'; *V.* 'Delaware'; *V.* 'Fredonia'

The combination of lush foliage, edible fruit and brilliant autumn foliage color attracts many gardeners to grapevines. These vigorous climbers attach themselves to supports with holdfasts or twining tendrils. When they drop their leaves in autumn, a network of thick, woody stems is exposed. The fruit of some species is better suited for eating, making jelly

COMMON PERIWINKLE
*Vinca minor*

*For climate zones and frost dates, see maps, pages 146-147.*

or making wine than that of others. Since some species are likely to grow better than others in your region, the advice of an agricultural extension agent or local nurseryman may be helpful in selecting the best grapevines for you.

Widely grown for screening and other decorative uses, the crimson vine may be the fastest growing grapevine; it shoots up as much as 50 feet in one season. Its 1-foot heart-shaped leaves with toothed edges turn coppery to red in the fall, but its fruit is neither edible nor ornamental. Fox grape, another good screening vine and a parent of many cultivated grapes, has lobed leaves more than 6 inches wide that are green on top and either pale rust or white on the underside. The edible purple-black thick-skinned fruit is musky and sweet. Both of these species are hardy in Zones 5-9.

The riverbank grape, hardy as far north as Zone 3 and common along streams in New England, has bright glossy leaves, fragrant yellow-green flowers and small, tart, purple-black fruit that makes good jelly. Muscadine grape, hardy to Zone 6, grows up to 90 feet tall with nearly round 5-inch leaves that turn yellow in the fall; its thick-skinned purple fruit is musky. The European grape, grown as a wine grape in California, has large purple fruits and delicately lobed blue-green leaves 3½ to 6 inches wide. Stems grow 45 to 60 feet long and the plant is hardy to the warmer regions of Zone 7. Grape varieties that produce fruit especially good for eating and wine-making include Concord, bearing the thick-skinned black fruit especially popular among home gardeners; Delaware, with bright red juicy fruit; and Fredonia, an early-fruiting variety that bears sweet black grapes.

HOW TO GROW. Grapevines thrive in full sun. Though they will grow in a wide variety of soils, they do best in a moist, well-drained slighty alkaline soil. Fertilizer should not be applied unless the plant is being grown for foliage. In spring, plant at least two vines to assure pollination, spacing them at least 8 feet apart. Tie up young stems to a sturdy arbor, wire or other support. Vines used for screening or decoration should be pruned in fall or spring to restrain their growth. For best fruit production, prune heavily in winter, cutting each shoot back to one or two leaf buds; however, such severe pruning will destroy the vine's ornamental value. Propagate by covering a trailing branch with soil; it will root, forming a new plant that can be severed and transplanted.

VITIS See also *Cissus*

# W

WANDERING JEW See *Tradescantia* and *Zebrina*
WAX PLANT See *Hoya*
WHITE JASMINE, COMMON See *Jasminum*
WHITE ITALIAN BELLFLOWER See *Campanula*
WILD PASSIONFLOWER See *Passiflora*
WINTER CREEPER See *Euonymus*

## WISTERIA
*W. floribunda* (Japanese wisteria); *W. sinensis* (Chinese wisteria)

Delicately hued fragrant flowers in pendulous clusters a foot long or longer festoon wisteria vines for long periods in the spring. Hardy in Zones 3-10, these deciduous vines climb by twining and grow to great lengths. With age, their stems become woody, twisted trunks. The velvety green seed pods that follow the flowers grow up to 7 inches long and cling to the vine through the winter. A strong grower, wisteria needs space and sturdy support. Avoid planting it near young trees; wisteria may encircle and eventually strangle them.

Japanese wisteria twines to heights of 25 to 30 feet. Its

**CRIMSON VINE**
*Vitis coignetiae*

sweetly scented violet flower clusters are 12 to 18 inches long and often bloom in sequence from top to bottom. Each leaf is made up of 13 to 19 leaflets in a wide fan. The variety Alba bears 12-inch clusters of fragrant white flowers; Issai has deep blue 12-inch clusters; Rosea bears pink clusters 18 inches long; and Macrobotrys bears reddish-violet-colored clusters up to 3 feet long. Chinese wisteria is slightly less hardy than Japanese and its flowers are less fragrant. It twines from left to right to heights of 50 feet or more. The blue-to-violet flower clusters, 6 to 12 inches long, bloom all at once before the leaves appear. Each leaf has seven to 13 leaflets. The varieties Alba and Jako have white flowers.

HOW TO GROW. Wisterias grow best in full sun in locations protected from strong wind. They need well-drained garden loam with leaf mold added. Plant pot-grown rather than field-grown vines, since wisterias do not transplant satisfactorily. Set each plant about a foot from its support, tie the young branches to start them in the right direction, keep the plant well watered, and mulch it during the first winter. Young wisterias frequently expend all of their energy in new growth and may not flower for seven or more years. To stimulate flowering, prune the roots by digging an 18- to 24-inch-deep trench in a circle around the main stem; the trench should be spaced one foot from the trunk for each inch of the main stem's diameter. In addition, cut back long new shoots to half their length in summer and again in winter, and fertilize in fall by scattering and scratching in ½ pound of superphosphate for each inch of diameter of the main stem. Prune established plants heavily after they flower and again in winter to promote abundant flowering and to contain rampant growth; trim new shoots back to within six buds from the base of the branch and cut out all weak wood.

WONGA-WONGA VINE See *Pandorea*
WOODBINE See *Parthenocissus*
WOODBINE HONEYSUCKLE See *Lonicera*

# Y

YAM See *Dioscorea*
YELLOW STAR JASMINE See *Trachelospermum*

# Z

ZEBRINA

*Z. pendula* (wandering Jew)

Sometimes used as a ground cover in warm climates, this type of wandering Jew is more commonly grown as a house plant for its ornamental foliage. Its stems will trail from hanging pots and many reach 5 or 6 feet in length if not cut back. The leaves are banded with green and silver on the top surface and are reddish-purple underneath. They grow up to 3 inches long, alternating along the stems. Like the tradescantia it resembles (also called wandering Jew), it is easy to care for and grows rapidly. As a perennial ground cover in Zones 9 and 10, or when grown under artificial light, it bears small clusters of violet flowers, usually in summer.

HOW TO GROW. This wandering Jew grows well in bright indirect or curtain-filtered sunlight; medium artificial light for 14 to 16 hours a day may deepen the colors of the leaves. Temperatures of 65° to 70° at night and 75° to 85° by day are best, with a humidity of 40 to 60 per cent. Plant in packaged potting soil; repot when roots become crowded. Keep the soil evenly moist but not soggy. After the plant has become established, feed every month or two with house-plant fertilizer diluted to half the recommended strength. Pinch off tips to encourage branching and bushiness. Root terminal stem cuttings in water or moist vermiculite.

*For climate zones and frost dates, see maps, pages 146-147.*

**CHINESE WISTERIA**
*Wisteria sinensis*

**WANDERING JEW**
*Zebrina pendula*

# Appendix

## Vines: the right time, the right place

Minimum winter temperatures and the first and last dates of frost have a lot to do with the vine-clad appearance of a garden. The map below, to which the encyclopedia entries are keyed, shows the average low temperatures that can be expected in 10 zones of North America. It will help gardeners to choose vines such as hardy winter creepers, English ivy and Oriental bittersweet that continue to provide outdoor color in the cold winters of Zones 4 and 5. It is always best, however, to check out how these vines behave in your area in the specific place you mean to put them—against a north-facing wall, for instance, or on an arbor—since microclimates and growing conditions may vary within temperature zones.

A glance at the spring frost map and dates on the facing page can similarly alert you to start, before dormancy ends, the hard pruning needed by vines that flower on new growth. It can also tell you when to plant seeds of slow-germinating annual vines, such as nasturtiums, indoors so they will be ready to set out when the ground warms up.

As summer ends and the first autumn frosts draw near, container-grown vines can be tidied up and brought in from the patio or garden to decorate the house through the winter. In fact, many tender vines like the orange streptosolen, hardy outdoors only along the Gulf Coast, can flourish in northern living rooms throughout the year and will brighten windows while the snows swirl outside.

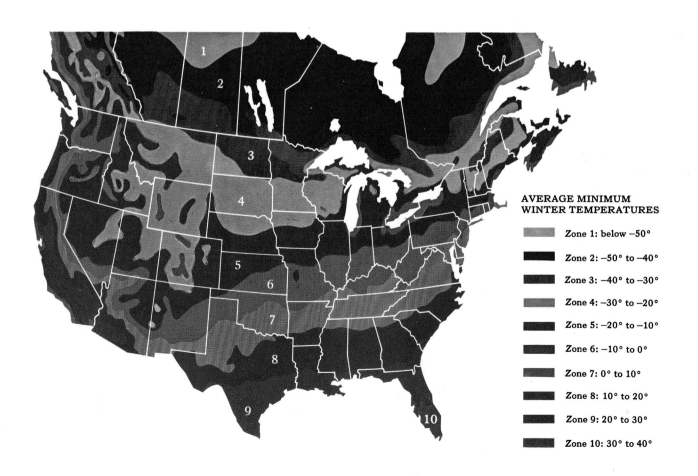

**AVERAGE MINIMUM WINTER TEMPERATURES**

Zone 1: below −50°

Zone 2: −50° to −40°

Zone 3: −40° to −30°

Zone 4: −30° to −20°

Zone 5: −20° to −10°

Zone 6: −10° to 0°

Zone 7: 0° to 10°

Zone 8: 10° to 20°

Zone 9: 20° to 30°

Zone 10: 30° to 40°

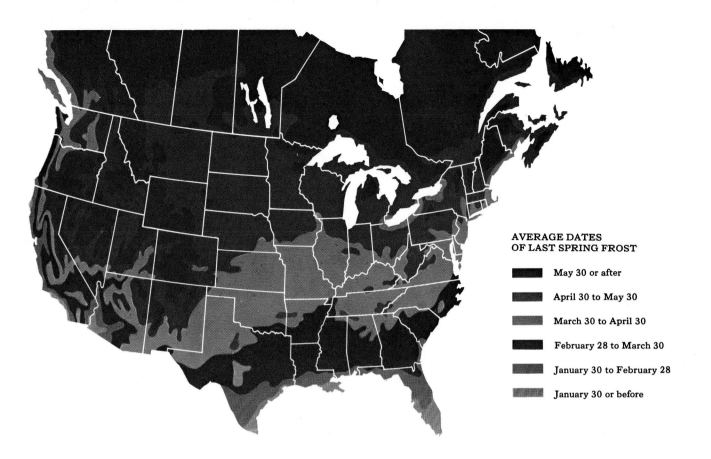

**AVERAGE DATES
OF LAST SPRING FROST**

- May 30 or after
- April 30 to May 30
- March 30 to April 30
- February 28 to March 30
- January 30 to February 28
- January 30 or before

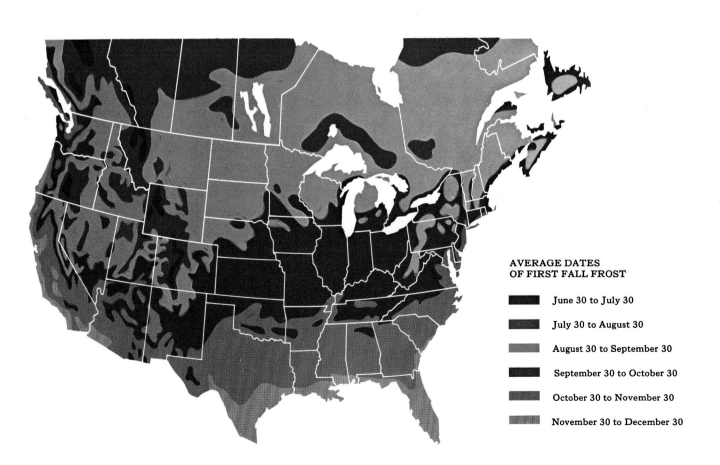

**AVERAGE DATES
OF FIRST FALL FROST**

- June 30 to July 30
- July 30 to August 30
- August 30 to September 30
- September 30 to October 30
- October 30 to November 30
- November 30 to December 30

# Characteristics of 237 vines

| | CLIMBING MEANS | | | | | TRAITS | | | | | | | | GROWTH RATE | | | LIGHT NEEDS | | | USES | | | | |
|---|---|---|---|---|---|---|---|---|---|---|---|---|---|---|---|---|---|---|---|---|---|---|---|---|
| | Leaner | Thorn climber | Weaver | Rooter | Grasper | Evergreen | Deciduous | Annual | Perennial | Flowers | Fruits/berries | Green foliage | Variegated foliage | Fast | Medium | Slow | Bright | Medium | Dim | Ground cover | Shade | Specimen plant | Screen | House plant |
| **ACTINIDIA ARGUTA** (bower actinidia) | | | | | • | | • | | • | • | • | • | | • | • | | | | | • | | • | | |
| **ACTINIDIA CHINENSIS** (Chinese gooseberry) | | | | | • | | • | | • | • | • | • | | • | • | | | | | • | • | • | | |
| **ACTINIDIA KOLOMIKTA** (Kolomikta actinidia) | | | | | • | | • | | • | | | • | • | • | • | | | | | | | • | | |
| **ACTINIDIA POLYGAMA** (silver vine) | | | | | • | | • | | • | | | • | • | • | • | | | | | | | • | | |
| **AESCHYNANTHUS MARMORATUS** (lipstick plant) | • | | | | | • | | | • | • | | | • | • | • | • | • | • | | | | | | • |
| **AESCHYNANTHUS RADICANS** (lipstick plant) | • | | | | | | • | | • | • | | • | | • | • | • | • | • | | | | | | • |
| **AESCHYNANTHUS SPECIOSUS** (lipstick plant) | • | | | | | | • | | • | • | | • | | • | • | • | • | • | | | | | | • |
| **AKEBIA QUINATA** (five-leaf akebia) | | | • | | | • | • | | • | • | | • | | • | | | • | • | | • | • | • | | |
| **ALLAMANDA CATHARTICA** (allamanda) | • | | | | | • | | | • | • | | • | | • | | | • | | | | | • | | |
| **AMPELOPSIS BREVIPEDUNCULATA** (porcelain ampelopsis) | | | | | • | | • | | • | | • | • | | • | | | • | • | | • | • | • | • | |
| **ANTIGONON LEPTOPUS** (coral vine) | | | | | • | • | • | | • | • | | • | | • | | | • | | | | | • | • | |
| **ARISTOLOCHIA DURIOR** (Dutchman's-pipe) | | | • | | | | • | | • | • | | • | | • | | | • | • | | | • | | • | |
| **ARISTOLOCHIA ELEGANS** (calico flower) | | | • | | | • | | | • | • | | • | • | • | | | • | • | | | | | • | |
| **ASARINA BARCLAIANA** (maurandia) | | | • | • | • | • | | • | | • | | • | | • | | | • | | | | | | • | • |
| **ASARINA ERUBESCENS** (creeping gloxinia) | | | • | • | • | • | | • | | • | | • | | • | | | • | | | | | • | • | • |
| **ASPARAGUS ASPARAGOIDES** (smilax asparagus) | • | | | | • | • | | | • | | | • | • | | | • | | | | | | | • | • |
| **ASPARAGUS DENSIFLORUS 'SPRENGERI'** (Sprenger asparagus) | • | | | | | • | | | • | | | • | • | • | • | | | | | | | • | • | • |
| **ASPARAGUS PLUMOSUS** (asparagus fern) | • | | | | • | • | | | • | | | • | | • | | | • | | | | | | • | • |
| **BEAUMONTIA GRANDIFLORA** (herald's-trumpet) | • | | | | • | • | | | • | • | | • | | • | | | • | | | | | • | • | |
| **BEAUMONTIA JERDONIANA** (beaumontia) | • | | | | • | • | | | • | • | | • | | • | | | • | | | | | • | • | |
| **BEGONIA TUBERHYBRIDA 'PENDULA'** (hanging tuberous begonia) | • | | | | | | • | | • | • | | • | | | • | | | • | | | | | | • |
| **BIGNONIA CAPREOLATA** (crossvine) | | | | • | • | • | | • | | • | | • | | • | | | • | • | | • | | • | • | |
| **BOUGAINVILLEA GLABRA** (lesser bougainvillea) | | • | | | | • | | | • | • | | • | | • | | | • | | | | | • | • | |
| **BOUGAINVILLEA SPECTABILIS** (Brazilian bougainvillea) | | • | | | | • | | | • | • | | • | | • | | | • | | | | | • | • | |
| **BOWIEA VOLUBILIS** (climbing onion) | | | | | • | | • | | • | | • | • | | • | • | | • | • | | | | | | • |
| **CAMPANULA ISOPHYLLA** (Italian bellflower) | • | | | | | • | | | • | • | | • | | • | | | • | | | • | | | | • |
| **CAMPANULA ISOPHYLLA 'ALBA'** (white Italian bellflower) | • | | | | | • | | | • | • | | • | | • | | | • | | | • | | | | • |
| **CAMPSIS GRANDIFLORA** (Chinese trumpet creeper) | | | | • | | | • | | • | • | | • | | • | | | • | | | | | • | • | |
| **CAMPSIS RADICANS** (trumpet creeper vine) | | | | • | | | • | | • | • | | • | | • | | | • | | | | | • | • | |
| **CAMPSIS TAGLIABUANA 'MADAME GALEN'** (Madame Galen trumpet creeper) | | | | • | | | • | | • | • | | • | | • | | | • | | | | | • | • | |
| **CARDIOSPERMUM HALICACABUM** (balloon vine) | | | | • | • | • | • | • | | • | • | | • | | | | • | | | | | | • | |
| **CELASTRUS ORBICULATUS** (Oriental bittersweet) | | | | | • | | • | | • | • | • | • | | • | | | • | • | | • | | | • | |
| **CELASTRUS ROSTHORNIANUS** (Loesener bittersweet) | | | | | • | | • | | • | • | • | • | | • | | | • | • | | • | | | • | |
| **CELASTRUS SCANDENS** (American bittersweet) | | | | | • | | • | | • | • | • | • | | • | | | • | • | | • | | | • | |
| **CEROPEGIA WOODII** (rosary vine) | • | | | | | • | | | • | | | • | • | • | • | | • | | | | | | | • |
| **CHORIZEMA CORDATUM** (Australian flame pea) | • | | | | | • | | | • | • | | • | | | • | • | • | | | | | • | • | |
| **CISSUS ANTARCTICA** (kangaroo treebine) | • | | | | • | • | | | • | | • | | • | | | • | | | | • | • | • | • | |
| **CISSUS DISCOLOR** (begonia treebine) | • | | | | • | • | | | • | | | • | • | | | • | | | | • | • | • | • | |
| **CISSUS INCISA** (ivy treebine) | • | | | • | • | • | | | • | | • | | • | | • | | | | • | • | • | • | |
| **CISSUS RHOMBIFOLIA** (grape ivy) | • | | | | • | • | | | • | | | • | | • | | | • | | | | • | • | • | |
| **CLEMATIS 'DUCHESS OF EDINBURGH'** | | | | | • | | • | | • | • | | • | • | • | | • | • | | | | • | • | • | |
| **CLEMATIS 'ERNEST MARKHAM'** | | | | | • | | • | | • | • | | • | • | • | | • | • | | | | • | • | • | |
| **CLEMATIS 'GIPSY QUEEN'** | | | | | • | | • | | • | • | | • | • | • | | • | • | | | | • | • | • | |
| **CLEMATIS 'HAGLEY HYBRID'** | | | | | • | | • | | • | • | | • | • | • | | • | • | | | | • | • | • | |
| **CLEMATIS JACKMANII** (Jackman clematis) | | | | | • | | • | | • | • | | • | • | • | | • | • | | | | • | • | • | |
| **CLEMATIS 'LORD NEVILLE'** | | | | | • | | • | | • | • | | • | • | • | | • | • | | | | • | • | • | |
| **CLEMATIS 'MME. BARON-VEILLARD'** | | | | | • | | • | | • | • | | • | • | • | | • | • | | | | • | • | • | |
| **CLEMATIS MONTANA RUBENS** (pink-anemone clematis) | | | | | • | | • | | • | • | | • | • | • | | • | • | | | | • | • | • | |

148

| | CLIMBING MEANS | | | | | TRAITS | | | | | | | | GROWTH RATE | | | LIGHT NEEDS | | | USES | | | | |
|---|---|---|---|---|---|---|---|---|---|---|---|---|---|---|---|---|---|---|---|---|---|---|---|---|
| | Leaner | Thorn climber | Weaver | Rooter | Grasper | Evergreen | Deciduous | Annual | Perennial | Flowers | Fruits/berries | Green foliage | Variegated foliage | Fast | Medium | Slow | Bright | Medium | Dim | Ground cover | Shade | Specimen plant | Screen | House plant |
| **CLEMATIS 'NELLY MOSER'** | | | | | ● | | ● | | ● | ● | | | | ● | ● | | ● | ● | | | ● | ● | ● | |
| **CLEMATIS ORIENTALIS** (Oriental clematis) | | | | | ● | | ● | | ● | ● | | | | ● | ● | | ● | ● | | | ● | ● | ● | |
| **CLEMATIS PANICULATA** (sweet autumn clematis) | | | | | ● | ● | ● | | ● | ● | ● | | | ● | ● | | ● | ● | | ● | ● | ● | ● | |
| **CLEMATIS 'PRINS HENDRIK'** | | | | | ● | | ● | | ● | ● | | | | ● | ● | | ● | ● | | | ● | ● | ● | |
| **CLEMATIS TANGUTICA** (golden clematis) | | | | | ● | | ● | | ● | ● | ● | | | ● | ● | | ● | ● | | | ● | ● | ● | |
| **CLEMATIS TEXENSIS** (scarlet clematis) | | | | | ● | | ● | | ● | ● | | | | ● | ● | | ● | ● | | | ● | ● | ● | |
| **CLEMATIS VITICELLA** (clematis) | | | | | ● | | ● | | ● | ● | | | | ● | ● | | ● | ● | | | ● | ● | ● | |
| **CLERODENDRUM THOMSONIAE** (bleeding heart vine) | | | | | ● | ● | | | ● | ● | | ● | | | ● | | ● | ● | | | | ● | | ● |
| **CLIANTHUS FORMOSUS** (desert pea) | ● | | | | | ● | | | ● | ● | | | | | ● | | ● | ● | | | | ● | | |
| **CLIANTHUS PUNICEUS** (parrot's bill) | ● | | | | | ● | | | ● | ● | | | | | ● | | ● | ● | | | | ● | | |
| **COBAEA SCANDENS** (cup-and-saucer vine) | | | | | ● | ● | ● | ● | ● | ● | | | | ● | | | ● | | | | | ● | ● | ● |
| **COLUMNEA ALLENII** (columnea) | ● | | ● | | | ● | | | ● | ● | | | | | ● | | ● | | | | | | | ● |
| **COLUMNEA GLORIOSA** (columnea) | ● | | ● | | | ● | | | ● | ● | | | | | ● | | ● | | | | | | | ● |
| **COLUMNEA HIRTA** (columnea) | ● | | ● | | | ● | | | ● | ● | | | | | ● | | ● | | | | | | | ● |
| **COLUMNEA TULAE 'FLAVA'** (columnea) | ● | | ● | | | ● | | | ● | ● | | | | | ● | | ● | | | | | | | ● |
| **CRYPTOSTEGIA GRANDIFLORA** (palay rubber vine) | | | | | ● | ● | | | ● | ● | | ● | | | ● | | ● | | | | | ● | ● | |
| **DIOSCOREA BATATAS** (cinnamon vine) | | | | | ● | ● | ● | | ● | ● | | ● | | ● | | | ● | ● | | | | ● | | |
| **DIOSCOREA BULBIFERA** (air-potato yam) | | | | | ● | ● | ● | | ● | ● | | ● | | ● | | | ● | ● | | | | ● | ● | ● |
| **DISTICTIS LAXIFLORA** (vanilla trumpet vine) | | | | | ● | ● | | | ● | ● | | | | ● | | | ● | ● | | | | | ● | ● |
| **DISTICTIS 'RIVERS'** (royal trumpet vine) | | | | | ● | ● | | | ● | ● | | | | ● | | | ● | ● | | | | | ● | ● |
| **DOLICHOS LABLAB** (hyacinth bean) | | | | | ● | ● | | ● | ● | ● | | | | ● | | | ● | | | | | | ● | ● |
| **EPISCIA CUPREATA** (flame violet) | ● | | ● | | | ● | | | ● | ● | | | ● | | ● | | ● | | | | | | | ● |
| **EPISCIA CUPREATA 'ACAJOU'** (episcia) | ● | | ● | | | ● | | | ● | ● | | | ● | ● | | | ● | | | | | | | ● |
| **EPISCIA DIANTHIFLORA** (lace-flower vine) | ● | | ● | | | ● | | | ● | ● | | ● | | | ● | | ● | | | | | | | ● |
| **EPISCIA LILACINA** (episcia) | ● | | ● | | | ● | | | ● | ● | | ● | ● | | ● | | ● | | | | | | | ● |
| **EPISCIA REPTANS** (flame violet) | ● | | ● | | | ● | | | ● | ● | | ● | ● | | ● | | ● | | | | | | | ● |
| **EUONYMUS FORTUNEI 'COLORATA'** (purple winter creeper) | ● | | | ● | | ● | | | ● | | | ● | ● | | ● | | ● | ● | | ● | | ● | ● | |
| **EUONYMUS FORTUNEI 'MINIMA'** (baby winter creeper) | ● | | | ● | | ● | | | ● | | | ● | ● | | ● | | ● | ● | | ● | | | ● | |
| **EUONYMUS FORTUNEI RADICANS** (common winter creeper) | ● | | | ● | | ● | | | ● | | ● | ● | | | ● | | ● | ● | | ● | | ● | ● | |
| **EUONYMUS FORTUNEI VEGETA** (big-leaf winter creeper) | ● | | | ● | | ● | | | ● | | ● | ● | | | ● | | ● | ● | | ● | | ● | ● | |
| **FATSHEDERA LIZEI** (fatshedera) | ● | | | | | ● | | | ● | | | ● | | ● | ● | | ● | ● | | ● | | | | ● |
| **FICUS PUMILA** (creeping fig) | | | | ● | | ● | | | ● | | | ● | | ● | ● | | ● | ● | | | | | ● | ● |
| **FITTONIA VERSCHAFFELTII** (red-nerved fittonia) | ● | | | | | ● | | | ● | | | | ● | ● | | | ● | | | | | | | ● |
| **FITTONIA VERSCHAFFELTII ARGYRONEURA** (silver-nerved fittonia) | ● | | | | | ● | | | ● | | | | ● | ● | | | ● | | | | | | | ● |
| **GELSEMIUM SEMPERVIRENS** (Carolina jasmine) | | | | ● | ● | ● | | | ● | ● | | ● | | | ● | | ● | ● | | ● | ● | | ● | ● |
| **GYNURA AURANTIACA** (Java velvet plant) | ● | | | | | ● | | | ● | | | | ● | ● | | | ● | | | | | ● | | ● |
| **GYNURA AURANTIACA 'PURPLE PASSION'** (purple passion vine) | ● | | | | | ● | | | ● | | | | ● | ● | | | ● | | | | | ● | | ● |
| **HARDENBERGIA COMPTONIANA** (Compton coral-pea) | | | | | ● | ● | | | ● | ● | | | | | | ● | | ● | | | | ● | ● | ● |
| **HARDENBERGIA VIOLACEA** (vine lilac) | | | | | ● | ● | | | ● | ● | | ● | | | | ● | | ● | | ● | | ● | ● | ● |
| **HEDERA CANARIENSIS** (Algerian ivy) | ● | | | ● | | ● | | | ● | | | ● | ● | ● | | | ● | ● | | ● | | ● | ● | ● |
| **HEDERA CANARIENSIS 'VARIEGATA'** (variegated Algerian ivy) | ● | | | ● | | ● | | | ● | | | | ● | ● | | | ● | ● | | ● | | ● | ● | ● |
| **HEDERA HELIX** (English ivy) | ● | | | ● | | ● | | | ● | | | ● | | ● | | | ● | ● | | ● | | ● | ● | ● |
| **HEDERA HELIX 'BALTICA'** | ● | | | ● | | ● | | | ● | | | ● | | ● | | | ● | ● | | ● | | ● | ● | ● |
| **HEDERA HELIX 'BULGARIA'** | ● | | | ● | | ● | | | ● | | | ● | | ● | | | ● | ● | | ● | | ● | ● | ● |
| **HEDERA HELIX '238TH STREET'** | ● | | | ● | | ● | | | ● | | | | ● | ● | | | ● | ● | | ● | | ● | ● | ● |
| **HIBBERTIA SCANDENS** (Guinea gold vine) | ● | | | | ● | ● | | | ● | ● | | ● | | | ● | | ● | ● | | | | ● | ● | |
| **HOYA CARNOSA** (wax plant) | ● | | ● | | | ● | | | ● | ● | | ● | | | | ● | ● | ● | | | | | | ● |
| **HOYA CARNOSA 'COMPACTA'** (compact wax plant) | ● | | ● | | | ● | | | ● | ● | | | ● | | | ● | ● | ● | | | | | | ● |

| | Leaner | Thorn climber | Weaver | Rooter | Grasper | Evergreen | Deciduous | Annual | Perennial | Flowers | Fruits/berries | Green foliage | Variegated foliage | Fast | Medium | Slow | Bright | Medium | Dim | Ground cover | Shade | Specimen plant | Screen | House plant |
|---|---|---|---|---|---|---|---|---|---|---|---|---|---|---|---|---|---|---|---|---|---|---|---|---|
| HOYA CARNOSA 'VARIEGATA' (variegated wax plant) | | | ● | | | ● | | | ● | ● | | | ● | | ● | | ● | ● | | | | ● | | ● |
| HUMULUS JAPONICUS (Japanese hop) | | | | ● | | | ● | ● | | | | ● | | ● | | | ● | ● | | | ● | | ● | |
| HUMULUS LUPULUS (common hop) | | | | ● | ● | ● | | ● | | | ● | ● | | ● | | | ● | ● | | | ● | | ● | |
| HYDRANGEA ANOMALA PETIOLARIS (climbing hydrangea) | | | | ● | | | ● | | ● | ● | | ● | | ● | | | ● | ● | | | ● | | ● | |
| IPOMOEA ALBA (moonflower) | | | ● | | | ● | ● | ● | ● | | | ● | | ● | | | ● | ● | | ● | | ● | ● | ● |
| IPOMOEA MULTIFIDA (cardinal climber) | | | ● | | | ● | ● | ● | ● | | | ● | | ● | | | ● | ● | | ● | | ● | ● | ● |
| IPOMOEA PURPUREA (morning glory) | | | ● | | | ● | ● | ● | ● | | | ● | | ● | | | ● | ● | | ● | | ● | ● | ● |
| IPOMOEA QUAMOCLIT (cypress vine) | | | ● | | | ● | ● | ● | ● | | | ● | | ● | | | ● | ● | | ● | | ● | ● | ● |
| IPOMOEA TRICOLOR (morning glory) | | | ● | | | ● | ● | ● | ● | | | ● | | ● | | | ● | ● | | ● | | ● | ● | ● |
| IPOMOEA TRICOLOR 'EARLY CALL' | | | ● | | | ● | ● | ● | ● | | | ● | | ● | | | ● | ● | | ● | | ● | ● | ● |
| IPOMOEA TRICOLOR 'HEAVENLY BLUE' | | | ● | | | ● | ● | ● | ● | | | ● | | ● | | | ● | ● | | ● | | ● | ● | ● |
| IPOMOEA TRICOLOR 'PEARLY GATES' | | | ● | | | ● | ● | ● | ● | | | ● | | ● | | | ● | ● | | ● | | ● | ● | ● |
| IPOMOEA TRICOLOR 'SCARLET O'HARA' | | | ● | | | ● | ● | ● | ● | | | ● | | ● | | | ● | ● | | ● | | ● | ● | ● |
| JASMINUM FLORIDUM | ● | | | | | ● | ● | | ● | ● | | ● | | ● | ● | | ● | ● | | | | ● | ● | |
| JASMINUM MULTIFLORUM (scented star jasmine) | ● | | | ● | ● | | | | ● | ● | | ● | ● | ● | ● | | ● | ● | | ● | | ● | ● | |
| JASMINUM NITIDUM (angelwing jasmine) | ● | | | | ● | | | | ● | ● | | ● | ● | ● | ● | | ● | ● | | | | ● | ● | |
| JASMINUM OFFICINALE (common white jasmine) | ● | | | ● | ● | ● | | | ● | ● | ● | ● | | ● | ● | | ● | ● | | | | ● | ● | |
| JASMINUM POLYANTHUM | ● | | | | ● | | | | ● | ● | | ● | ● | ● | ● | | ● | ● | | | | ● | ● | |
| JASMINUM SAMBAC (Arabian jasmine) | ● | | | ● | ● | | | | ● | ● | | ● | ● | ● | ● | | ● | ● | | | | ● | ● | |
| LANTANA MONTEVIDENSIS (trailing lantana) | ● | | | | ● | ● | ● | ● | | ● | | ● | | ● | | | ● | | | ● | | ● | | |
| LAPAGERIA ROSEA (Chilean bellflower) | | | | ● | ● | | | | ● | ● | ● | ● | | | ● | | ● | | | | | ● | | ● |
| LATHYRUS JAPONICUS (beach pea) | | | | ● | | | ● | | ● | ● | | ● | | ● | | | ● | | | ● | | ● | | |
| LATHYRUS LATIFOLIUS (perennial pea) | | | | ● | | | ● | | ● | ● | | ● | | ● | ● | | ● | | | ● | | ● | | |
| LATHYRUS ODORATUS (sweet pea) | | | | ● | | | ● | ● | | ● | | ● | | ● | | | ● | | | ● | | ● | | |
| LONICERA HECKROTTII (goldflame honeysuckle) | | | | ● | | | ● | | ● | ● | | ● | | ● | ● | | ● | ● | | ● | | ● | | |
| LONICERA HENRYI (Henry honeysuckle) | | | | ● | ● | ● | | | ● | ● | ● | ● | | ● | ● | | ● | ● | | ● | | ● | | |
| LONICERA HILDEBRANDIANA (giant Burmese honeysuckle) | | | | ● | ● | ● | | | ● | ● | | ● | | ● | ● | | ● | ● | | ● | | ● | | |
| LONICERA JAPONICA 'HALLIANA' (Hall's honeysuckle) | | | | ● | ● | ● | | | ● | ● | | ● | | ● | ● | | ● | ● | | ● | | ● | | |
| LONICERA PERICLYMENUM (woodbine honeysuckle) | | | | ● | | | ● | | ● | ● | ● | ● | | ● | ● | | ● | ● | | ● | | ● | | |
| LONICERA SEMPERVIRENS (trumpet honeysuckle) | | | | ● | ● | ● | | | ● | ● | ● | ● | | ● | ● | | ● | ● | | ● | | ● | | |
| LYCIUM HALIMIFOLIUM (matrimony vine) | ● | | | ● | | | ● | | ● | ● | ● | ● | | ● | ● | | ● | | | | | ● | | |
| LYGODIUM JAPONICUM (Japanese climbing fern) | | | | ● | | | ● | | ● | | | ● | | | ● | | | ● | | ● | ● | ● | | ● |
| LYSIMACHIA NUMMULARIA (moneywort) | ● | | ● | | | ● | | ● | ● | ● | | ● | | ● | ● | | ● | ● | | ● | ● | | ● | ● |
| MANDEVILLA LAXA (Chilean jasmine) | | | | ● | | | ● | | ● | ● | | ● | | ● | | | ● | | | | | ● | | ● |
| MANDEVILLA SPLENDENS | | | | ● | ● | | | | ● | ● | | ● | | ● | | | ● | | | | | ● | | ● |
| MANETTIA INFLATA (Brazilian firecracker) | ● | | | ● | ● | | | | ● | ● | | ● | | ● | | | ● | | | | | ● | | ● |
| MENISPERMUM CANADENSE (moonseed) | | | | ● | | | ● | | ● | ● | ● | ● | | ● | ● | | ● | ● | ● | ● | | | ● | |
| MONSTERA DELICIOSA (monstera) | | | | ● | | ● | | | ● | | | ● | | | ● | | ● | | | | ● | | | ● |
| NEMATANTHUS GREGARIUS (goldfish plant) | ● | | | | | ● | | | ● | ● | | ● | | ● | ● | | ● | | | | | | | ● |
| NEMATANTHUS WETTSTEINII (goldfish plant) | ● | | | | | ● | | | ● | ● | | ● | | | ● | ● | ● | | | | | | | ● |
| PANDOREA JASMINOIDES (bower plant) | | | | ● | ● | | | | ● | ● | ● | ● | | ● | ● | | ● | ● | | ● | | | ● | ● |
| PANDOREA PANDORANA (wonga-wonga vine) | | | | ● | ● | | | | ● | | | ● | ● | ● | ● | | ● | ● | | ● | | | ● | ● |
| PARTHENOCISSUS HENRYANA (silver-vein creeper) | | | ● | ● | | ● | | | ● | | | ● | ● | | ● | | ● | | | ● | ● | | ● | |
| PARTHENOCISSUS QUINQUEFOLIA (Virginia creeper) | | | ● | ● | | ● | | | ● | | ● | ● | ● | ● | | | ● | | | ● | ● | | ● | |
| PARTHENOCISSUS QUINQUEFOLIA 'ENGELMANNII' (Engelmann creeper) | | | ● | ● | | ● | | | ● | | ● | ● | ● | ● | | | ● | | | ● | ● | | ● | |
| PARTHENOCISSUS QUINQUEFOLIA 'SAINT-PAULII' (St. Paul's creeper) | | | ● | ● | | ● | | | ● | | ● | ● | ● | ● | | | ● | | | ● | ● | | ● | |
| PARTHENOCISSUS TRICUSPIDATA (Boston ivy) | | | ● | ● | | ● | | | ● | | ● | ● | ● | ● | | | ● | ● | | ● | ● | | ● | |
| PARTHENOCISSUS TRICUSPIDATA 'LOWII' (Low's creeper) | | | ● | ● | | ● | | | ● | | ● | ● | ● | ● | | | ● | ● | | ● | ● | | ● | |

150

| | CLIMBING MEANS | | | | | TRAITS | | | | | | | | GROWTH RATE | | | LIGHT NEEDS | | | USES | | | | |
|---|---|---|---|---|---|---|---|---|---|---|---|---|---|---|---|---|---|---|---|---|---|---|---|---|
| | Leaner | Thorn climber | Weaver | Rooter | Grasper | Evergreen | Deciduous | Annual | Perennial | Flowers | Fruits/berries | Green foliage | Variegated foliage | Fast | Medium | Slow | Bright | Medium | Dim | Ground cover | Shade | Specimen plant | Screen | House plant |
| **PARTHENOCISSUS TRICUSPIDATA 'VEITCHII'** (Veitch's creeper) | | | | • | • | | • | | • | | • | • | • | • | | | • | • | | • | | • | • | |
| **PASSIFLORA ALATO-CAERULEA** (hybrid passionflower) | | | | • | • | • | • | | • | • | | | | • | | | • | | | | • | • | • | • |
| **PASSIFLORA CAERULEA** (blue passionflower) | | | | • | • | • | • | | • | • | | | | • | | | • | | | | • | • | • | • |
| **PASSIFLORA COCCINEA** (red passionflower) | | | | • | • | • | • | | • | • | | | | • | | | • | | | | • | • | • | • |
| **PASSIFLORA EDULIS** (purple granadilla) | | | | • | • | • | • | | • | • | • | | | • | | | • | | | | | • | • | • |
| **PASSIFLORA INCARNATA** (wild passionflower) | | | | • | • | • | • | | • | • | • | | | • | | | • | | | | | • | • | • |
| **PASSIFLORA JAMESONII** (passionflower) | | | | • | • | • | | | • | • | | | | • | | | • | | | | | • | • | • |
| **PASSIFLORA QUADRANGULARIS** (giant granadilla) | | | | • | • | • | | | • | • | • | | | • | | | • | | | | | • | • | • |
| **PASSIFLORA RACEMOSA** (passionflower) | | | | • | • | • | | | • | • | | | | • | • | | • | | | | | • | | • |
| **PELARGONIUM PELTATUM** (ivy geranium) | • | | • | | | • | | | • | • | | • | | • | | | • | | | • | | • | | • |
| **PHASEOLUS COCCINEUS** (scarlet runner bean) | | | | • | | | • | • | | • | | | | • | | | • | | | | | • | • | • |
| **PHILODENDRON ERUBESCENS** (red-leaved philodendron) | | | | • | | • | | | • | | | | • | • | | | • | • | | | | | | • |
| **PHILODENDRON GUTTIFERUM** (leatherleaf philodendron) | | | | • | | • | | | • | | | • | | | | • | • | • | | | | | | • |
| **PHILODENDRON HASTATUM** (spearhead philodendron) | | | | • | | • | | | • | | | • | | | | | • | • | | | | | | • |
| **PHILODENDRON OXYCARDIUM** (heart-leaved philodendron) | • | | | • | | • | | | • | | | • | | | | | • | • | | | | | | • |
| **PHILODENDRON PANDURAEFORME** (fiddle-leaved philodendron) | | | | • | | • | | | • | | | • | | | | | • | • | | | | | | • |
| **PHILODENDRON SQUAMIFERUM** (anchorleaf philodendron) | | | | • | • | • | | | • | | | • | | | | | • | • | | | | | | • |
| **PILEA DEPRESSA** (creeping pilea) | • | | • | | | • | | | • | | | • | • | • | | | • | | | • | | | | • |
| **PIPER CROCATUM** (saffron pepper) | • | | | • | • | • | | | • | | | • | • | • | • | | • | | | | | | | • |
| **PIPER NIGRUM** (black pepper) | • | | • | | | • | | | • | | | • | | | • | | • | | | | | | | • |
| **PIPER ORNATUM** (Celebes pepper) | • | | | • | • | • | | | • | | | • | • | • | • | | • | | | | | | | • |
| **PLECTRANTHUS AUSTRALIS** (Swedish ivy) | • | | | | | • | | | • | | | • | | | | | • | • | | | | | | • |
| **PLUMBAGO CAPENSIS** (Cape plumbago) | • | | | | | • | | • | • | • | | | | • | | | • | | | | • | • | • | • |
| **POLYGONUM AUBERTII** (silver fleece vine) | | | • | | | | • | | • | • | | | | • | | | • | | | | • | • | • | |
| **PUERARIA LOBATA** (kudzu vine) | | | • | • | • | | | | • | | | • | | • | • | | • | • | | • | • | | • | |
| **PYROSTEGIA VENUSTA** (flame vine) | | | • | | • | • | | | • | • | | | | • | | | • | | | | | • | • | |
| **ROSA 'AMERICA'** | • | • | | | | | • | | • | • | | | | • | • | | • | | | | | • | | |
| **ROSA BANKSIAE** (Banks' rose) | • | | | | | | • | | • | • | | | | • | • | | • | | | | | • | | |
| **ROSA 'BLAZE'** | • | • | | | | • | | | • | • | | | | • | • | | • | | | | | • | | |
| **ROSA 'CLIMBING CRIMSON GLORY'** | • | • | | | | • | | | • | • | | | | • | • | | • | | | | | • | | |
| **ROSA 'CLIMBING PEACE'** | • | • | | | | • | | | • | • | | | | • | • | | • | | | | | • | | |
| **ROSA 'DR. W. VAN FLEET'** | • | • | | | | • | | | • | • | | | | • | • | | • | | | | | • | | |
| **ROSA 'DON JUAN'** | • | • | | | | • | | | • | • | | | | • | • | | • | | | | | • | | |
| **ROSA 'DOROTHY PERKINS'** | • | • | | | | • | | | • | • | | | | • | • | | • | | | • | | • | | |
| **ROSA 'GOLDEN SHOWERS'** | • | | | | | • | | | • | • | | | | • | • | | • | | | | | • | | |
| **ROSA 'NEW DAWN'** | • | • | | | | • | | | • | • | | | | • | • | | • | | | | | • | | |
| **ROSA 'PIÑATA'** | • | • | | | | • | | | • | • | | | | • | • | | • | | | | | • | | |
| **ROSA 'RHONDA'** | • | • | | | | • | | | • | • | | | | • | • | | • | | | | | • | | |
| **ROSA 'TEMPO'** | • | • | | | | • | | | • | • | | | | • | • | | • | | | | | • | | |
| **ROSA WICHURAIANA** (memorial rose) | • | • | • | | • | • | • | | • | • | | | | | • | | • | | | • | | • | | |
| **SCINDAPSUS AUREUS** (devil's ivy) | • | | • | | • | • | | | • | | | | • | • | | | • | • | | | | | | • |
| **SEDUM MORGANIANUM** (burro's tail) | • | | | | | • | | | • | | • | | | • | • | • | • | • | | | | • | | • |
| **SENECIO CONFUSUS** (Mexican flame vine) | | | • | • | • | • | | | • | • | | | | • | • | | • | • | | | | • | | • |
| **SENECIO MIKANIOIDES** (German ivy) | | | • | • | • | • | | | • | | | • | | • | | | • | | | • | | • | | • |
| **SENECIO SCANDENS** (flame vine) | | | • | • | • | • | | | • | | | • | | • | | | • | | | | | • | | • |
| **SETCREASEA PURPUREA** (purple heart) | • | | | | | • | | | • | | | | • | • | • | | • | • | | • | | • | | • |
| **SOLANDRA GUTTATA** (goldcup chalice vine) | • | | | | | • | | | • | • | | • | | • | | | • | • | | | | • | • | |
| **SOLANDRA MAXIMA** (chalice vine) | • | | | | | • | | | • | • | | • | | • | | | • | • | | | | • | • | |

| | CLIMBING MEANS | | | | | TRAITS | | | | | | | | GROWTH RATE | | | LIGHT NEEDS | | | USES | | | | |
|---|---|---|---|---|---|---|---|---|---|---|---|---|---|---|---|---|---|---|---|---|---|---|---|---|
| | Leaner | Thorn climber | Weaver | Rooter | Grasper | Evergreen | Deciduous | Annual | Perennial | Flowers | Fruits/berries | Green foliage | Variegated foliage | Fast | Medium | Slow | Bright | Medium | Dim | Ground cover | Shade | Specimen plant | Screen | House plant |
| SOLANUM DULCAMARA (bitter nightshade) | | | | • | • | • | | | • | • | | • | | • | | | • | | | • | | | • | |
| SOLANUM JASMINOIDES (jasmine nightshade) | | | | • | • | • | | | • | • | | • | | • | | | • | | | | | | • | • |
| SOLANUM WENDLANDII (Costa Rican nightshade) | | | | • | | • | | | • | • | | • | | • | | | • | | | | | | • | • |
| SOLEIROLIA SOLEIROLII (baby's tears) | • | | | | • | • | | | • | | | • | | • | | | • | • | • | • | | | | • |
| STEPHANOTIS FLORIBUNDA (stephanotis) | | | | • | • | • | | | • | • | | • | | | | • | • | • | • | | | • | | • |
| STIGMAPHYLLON CILIATUM (golden vine) | | | | • | • | • | | | • | • | | • | | • | • | | • | | | | | • | • | • |
| STREPTOSOLEN JAMESONII (orange streptosolen) | • | | | | • | • | | | • | • | | • | | • | | | • | | | • | | | • | |
| SYNGONIUM PODOPHYLLUM (arrowhead plant) | • | | | • | • | | | | • | | | • | • | • | | | • | | | | | | • | • |
| SYNGONIUM WENDLANDII | • | | | • | • | | | | • | | | • | • | • | | | • | | | | | | • | • |
| TECOMARIA CAPENSIS (Cape honeysuckle) | • | | | | • | • | | | • | • | | • | | • | | | • | | | • | | • | • | |
| THUNBERGIA ALATA (black-eyed-Susan vine) | • | | | • | • | • | • | • | | • | | • | | • | | | • | | | | | | • | |
| THUNBERGIA FRAGRANS (sweet clock vine) | | | | • | • | • | | | • | • | | • | | • | | | • | | | • | | | • | |
| THUNBERGIA GRANDIFLORA (skyflower) | | | | • | • | • | | | • | • | | • | | • | | | • | | | | | | • | |
| THUNBERGIA LAURIFOLIA (laurel-leaved clock vine) | | | | • | • | • | | | • | • | | • | | • | | | • | | | | | | • | |
| TRACHELOSPERMUM ASIATICUM (yellow star jasmine) | | • | | | • | • | | | • | • | | • | | | • | • | • | • | | • | • | | • | • |
| TRACHELOSPERMUM JASMINOIDES (star jasmine) | | • | | | • | • | | | • | • | | • | | | • | • | • | • | | • | • | | • | • |
| TRADESCANTIA ALBIFLORA 'LAEKENENSIS' (rainbow wandering Jew) | • | | | • | • | | | | • | | | • | • | • | | | • | | | • | | | | • |
| TRADESCANTIA BLOSSFELDIANA (flowering inch plant) | • | | | • | • | | | | • | | | • | • | • | | | • | | | • | | | | • |
| TRADESCANTIA FLUMINENSIS (wandering Jew) | • | | | • | • | | | | • | | • | • | | • | | | • | | | • | | | | • |
| TRADESCANTIA FLUMINENSIS 'VARIEGATA' (variegated wandering Jew) | • | | | • | • | | | | • | | | • | • | • | | | • | | | • | | | | • |
| TRADESCANTIA NAVICULARIS (chain plant) | • | | | • | • | | | | • | | • | • | | • | • | | • | | | • | | | | • |
| TRIPOGANDRA MULTIFLORA (Tahitian bridal veil) | • | | | • | | • | | | • | • | | • | | • | | | • | | | • | | | | • |
| TROPAEOLUM MAJUS (common nasturtium) | | | | • | | • | • | | • | | | • | | • | | | • | | | • | | • | • | • |
| TROPAEOLUM PEREGRINUM (canary-bird flower) | | | | • | | • | • | | • | | | • | | • | | | • | | | • | | • | • | • |
| VANILLA PLANIFOLIA (vanilla orchid) | | | | • | • | | | | • | • | | • | | • | | | • | | | | | | • | • |
| VINCA MAJOR (greater periwinkle) | • | | | • | • | | | | • | | • | • | | • | • | | • | • | | • | | | | • |
| VINCA MAJOR 'VARIEGATA' (variegated periwinkle) | • | | | • | • | • | • | | • | | | • | • | • | | | • | • | | • | | | | • |
| VINCA MINOR (common periwinkle) | • | | | • | • | | | | • | | | • | • | • | | | • | | | • | | | | • |
| VITIS COIGNETIAE (crimson vine) | | | | • | | | • | | • | | • | • | | • | | | • | | | | • | • | • | |
| VITIS 'CONCORD' | | | | • | | | • | | • | | • | • | | • | | | • | | | | • | • | • | |
| VITIS 'DELAWARE' | | | | • | | | • | | • | | • | • | | • | | | • | | | | • | • | • | |
| VITIS 'FREDONIA' | | | | • | | | • | | • | | • | • | | • | | | • | | | | • | • | • | |
| VITIS LABRUSCA (fox grape) | | | | • | | | • | | • | | • | • | | • | | | • | | | | • | • | • | |
| VITIS RIPARIA (riverbank grape) | | | | • | | | • | | • | | • | • | | • | | | • | | | | • | • | • | |
| VITIS ROTUNDIFOLIA (muscadine grape) | | | | • | | | • | | • | | • | • | | • | | | • | | | | • | • | • | |
| VITIS VINIFERA (European grape) | | | | • | | | • | | • | | • | • | | • | | | • | | | | • | • | • | |
| WISTERIA FLORIBUNDA (Japanese wisteria) | | | | • | | | • | • | • | • | | • | | • | | | • | | | | | • | • | |
| WISTERIA FLORIBUNDA 'ALBA' | | | | • | | | • | | • | • | | • | | • | | | • | | | | | • | • | |
| WISTERIA FLORIBUNDA 'ISSAI' | | | | • | | | • | | • | • | | • | | • | | | • | | | | | • | • | |
| WISTERIA FLORIBUNDA 'MACROBOTRYS' | | | | • | | | • | | • | • | • | • | | • | | | • | | | | | • | • | |
| WISTERIA FLORIBUNDA 'ROSEA' | | | | • | | | • | | • | • | • | • | | • | | | • | | | | | • | • | |
| WISTERIA SINENSIS (Chinese wisteria) | | | | • | | | • | | • | • | • | • | | • | | | • | | | | | • | • | |
| WISTERIA SINENSIS 'ALBA' | | | | • | | | • | | • | • | • | • | | • | | | • | | | | | • | • | |
| WISTERIA SINENSIS 'JAKO' | | | | • | | | • | | • | • | • | • | | • | | | • | | | | | • | • | |
| ZEBRINA PENDULA (wandering Jew) | • | | • | | • | | | | • | | | • | • | • | | | • | | | • | | | | • |

# Bibliography

American Home Editors, *American Home Garden Book and Plant Encyclopedia.* M. Evans & Co., 1963.

Atkinson, Dr. Robert E., *Vines in Your Home.* T.F.H. Publications, Inc., 1961.

Ballard, Ernesta D., *Garden in Your House.* Harper & Row, Publishers, 1971.

Bartrum, Douglas, *Climbing Plants.* John Gifford, London, 1968.

Bates, Marston, and Humphrey, Philip S., eds., *The Darwin Reader.* Charles Scribner's Sons, 1956.

Baumgardt, John P., *Hanging Plants for Home, Terrace and Garden.* Simon and Schuster, 1972.

Bean, W. J., *Wall Shrubs and Hardy Climbers.* Putnam, London, 1939.

Blake, Claire, *Greenhouse Gardening for Fun.* William Morrow & Co., Inc., 1967.

Bonnie, Fred, *Flowering Trees, Shrubs, and Vines: A Guide for Home Gardeners.* Galahad Books, 1976.

Brilmayer, Bernice, *All About Vines and Hanging Plants.* Doubleday & Co., Inc., 1962.

Brooklyn Botanic Garden, *Ground Covers and Vines.* BBG, 1978.

Brooklyn Botanic Garden, *Handbook on Vines.* BBG, 1972.

Brooklyn Botanic Garden, *Weed Control in the Home Garden.* BBG, 1975.

Chittenden, Fred J., ed., *The Royal Horticultural Society Dictionary of Gardening,* 2nd ed. Clarendon Press, 1974.

Countryside Books, *Vines and Ivy in Your Home.* A. B. Morse Co., 1976.

Crockett, James U., *Crockett's Indoor Garden.* Little, Brown & Co., 1978.

Darwin, Charles, *On the Movements and Habits of Climbing Plants.* Taylor and Francis, London, 1865.

Davidson, William, and Rochford, T. C., *House Plants, Cacti & Succulents.* Galahad Books, 1976.

Dulles, Marion, *Greenhouse Gardening Around the Year.* The Macmillan Co., 1956.

Elbert, George and Virginie, *Plants that Really Bloom Indoors.* Simon and Schuster, 1974.

Elbert, Virginie F. and George A., *The Miracle Houseplants.* Crown Publishers, Inc., 1976.

Fisk, J., *Success With Clematis.* Thomas Nelson and Sons, Ltd., 1962.

Fitch, Charles M., *The Complete Book of House Plants.* Hawthorn Books, 1972.

Fonty Quer, Pio, *Physiology of Plants.* Harper & Brothers, 1960.

Free, Montague, *All About Houseplants.* Doubleday, 1946.

Genders, Roy, *Covering a Wall: The Culture of Climbing Plants,* 2nd ed. Robert Hale & Co., 1973.

Gothein, Marie Luise, *A History of Garden Art.* J. M. Dent & Sons, Ltd., 1928.

Graf, Alfred Byrd, *Exotic Plant Manual.* Roehrs Co., Inc., 1974.

Graf, Alfred Byrd, *Exotica: Pictorial Cyclopedia of Exotic Plants from Tropical and Near-tropic Regions.* Roehrs Co., Inc., 1973.

Grunert, Christian, *Kletterpflanzen.* J. Neumann, 1961.

Harrison, Richmond E., *Climbers and Trailers.* A. H. & A. W. Reed, London, 1973.

Hay, Roy, and Synge, Patrick M., *The Color Dictionary of Flowers and Plants for Home and Garden.* Crown Publishers, Inc., 1976.

Hessayon, D. G., *Be Your Own House Plant Expert,* 2nd ed. Pan Britannica Industries, Ltd., Waltham Cross, Herts., England, 1976.

Hibberd, Shirley, *The Ivy.* Groombridge & Sons, London, 1872.

Hillier & Sons, Ltd., *Hillier's Manual of Trees & Shrubs.* A. S. Barnes and Co., 1972.

Hottes, Alfred C., *A Little Book of Climbing Plants.* A. T. De La Mare Co., Inc., 1933.

Hottes, Alfred Carl, *Climbers and Ground Covers.* A. T. De La Mare Co., Inc., 1947.

Howard, Frances, *Landscaping With Vines.* The Macmillan Co., 1959.

Jaffe, M. J., "On Heliotropism in Tendrils of *Pisum sativum:* A Response to Infrared Irradiation," *Planta,* Vol. 92, 1970.

Jaffe, M. J., "Physiological Studies on Pea Tendrils," *Physiologia Plantarum.* Societas Physiologiae Plantarum Scandinavica, 1972.

Jenkins, Dorothy, and Wilson, Helen Van Pelt, *House Plants for Every Window.* William Morrow, 1975.

Jenkins, Dorothy H., *Vines for Every Garden.* Doubleday, Doran & Co., Inc., 1937.

Kramer, Jack, *1000 Beautiful House Plants and How to Grow Them.* William Morrow, 1969.

McCollon, William, *Vines and How to Grow Them.* Doubleday, 1911.

Macoboy, Stirling, *What Flower Is That?* Crown Publishers, Inc., 1971.

Markham, Ernest, *The Large and Small Flowered Clematis.* Charles Scribner's Sons, 1935.

Menninger, Edwin A., *Flowering Vines of the World: An Encyclopedia of Climbing Plants.* Hearthside Press, Inc., 1970.

Merchants Publishing Co., *Hanging Plants for Modern Living.* Merchants Publishing Co., 1975.

Meyer, Bernard S., and Anderson, Donald B., *Plant Physiology.* D. Van Nostrand Co., Inc., 1952.

Nehrling, Henry, *The Plant World in Florida.* The Macmillan Co., 1933.

Nevling, Lorin I., Jr., "Some Ways Plants Climb," *Arnoldia,* Vol. 28. The Arnold Arboretum of Harvard University, 1968.

Nicolaisen, Age, *The Pocket Encyclopedia of Indoor Plants in Color.* Macmillan Publishing Co., Inc., 1970.

Oster, Maggie, ed., *The Green Pages.* Ballantine Books, Inc., 1977.

Pearce, S. A., *Climbing and Trailing Plants.* W. H. & L. Collingridge, Ltd., London, 1957.

Perkins, Harold O., *Espaliers and Vines for the Home Gardener.* D. Van Nostrand Co., Inc., 1964.

Perry, Frances, *Flowers of the World.* The Hamlyn Publishing Group, Ltd., 1972.

Perry, Frances, ed., *Simon and Schuster's Complete Guide to Plants and Flowers.* Simon and Schuster, 1974.

Pierot, Suzanne, *The Ivy Book.* Macmillan Publishing Co., Inc., 1974.

Potter, Charles H., *Beneath the Greenhouse Roof.* Criterion Books, 1957.

Powell, Thomas and Betty, *The Avant Gardener.* Houghton Mifflin Co., 1975.

Preston, F. G. *The Greenhouse.* Ward, Lock & Co., Ltd., London, 1964.

Prockter, Noel J., *Climbing and Screening Plants.* Faber & Faber, London, 1973.

Reader's Digest Association, Ltd., *Reader's Digest Encyclopedia of Garden Plants and Flowers,* 3rd ed. RDA, Ltd., 1975.

Reader's Digest Association, *Reader's Digest Illustrated Guide to Gardening.* The Reader's Digest Association, Inc., 1978.

Rockwell, F. F., and Grayson, Esther C., *The Rockwells' Complete Book of Roses.* Doubleday, 1958.

Selsam, Millicent E., *Plants That Move.* William Morrow & Co., 1962.

Staff of the L. H. Bailey Hortorium, Cornell University, *Hortus Third: A Dictionary of Plants Cultivated in the United States and Canada.* Macmillan Publishing Co., Inc., 1976.

Sunset Editors, *Ideas for Hanging Gardens.* Lane Publishing Co., 1974.

Tampion, John, *Dangerous Plants.* Universe Books, 1977.

Taylor, Norman, *The Guide to Garden Shrubs and Trees.* Bonanza Books, 1965.

Taylor, Norman, *Taylor's Gardening Encyclopedia.* Houghton Mifflin Co., 1961.

Van der Spuy, Una, *Gardening with Climbers.* Protea Press

Publishers, 1976.

Vines, Robert A., *Trees, Shrubs and Woody Vines of the Southwest*. University of Texas Press, 1960.

Whittemore, Richard D., *Garden Ideas and Projects*. Doubleday & Co., Inc., 1959.

Wilson, Charles L., *The Gardener's Hint Book*. Jonathan Da-

vid Publishers, Inc., 1978.

Wilson, Helen Van Pelt, *Climbing Roses*. Barrows, 1955.

Wyman, Donald, *Shrubs and Vines for American Gardens*. The Macmillan Co., 1969.

Wyman, Donald, *Wyman's Gardening Encyclopedia*. Macmillan Publishing Co., Inc., 1977.

# Acknowledgments

The index for this book was prepared by Anita R. Beckerman. For their help in the preparation of this book, the editors wish to thank the following: B.C. Designs, Brentwood, Calif.; Betty Bagert, New Orleans, La.; J. Roy W. Barrette, Amen Farm, Brooklin, Me.; Mr. and Mrs. Charles T. Berry Jr., Upperville, Va.; Mary Ann Borch, Department of Botany, Ohio University, Athens, Ohio; Genie Cate, Great Falls Greenhouses, Great Falls, Va.; Stephen Chernesky, indoor landscaper, New York City; Mr. and Mrs. Harry A. Councilor, Alexandria, Va.; John Dodt, New Orleans, La.; Severn C. Doughty, Associate Horticulturist, Louisiana Cooperative Extension Service, Metairie, La.; Dumbarton Oaks, Washington, D.C.; Mrs. Nathaniel Felton, New Orleans, La.; Dyson Flanders, Sea Island Company, Sea Island, Ga.; Mrs. Eleanor St. Mark Flotte, New Orleans, La.; Mrs. Peter Garrett, Seattle, Wash.; Pamela J. Harper, Seaford, Va.; Janet Huseby, San Francisco, Calif.; Dr. Mark J. Jaffe, Professor of Sensory Physiology, Ohio University, Athens, Ohio; Mr. and Mrs. George Kackley, Washington, D.C.; Doris Kaufman, Blue Bell, Pa.; Carlton B. Lees, Senior Vice President, New York Botanical Garden, Bronx, N.Y.; Charles C. Montgomery, Consulting Rosarian, American Rose Society, Washington, D.C.; Lorin L. Nevling Jr., Field Museum of Natural History, Chicago, Ill.; Wolfgang Oehme, Baltimore, Md.; Jeannette and Reese Payton, Alexandria, Va.; James H. Pendleton, chief landscape designer, Good Earth Nursery, Burke, Va.; Peter Raven, Director, Missouri Botanical Garden, St. Louis, Mo.; the Salter family, Chester, Pa.; Col. and Mrs. Wilfred Smith, Alexandria, Va.; Edith Stern, Longue Vue Gardens, New Orleans, La.; James A. Van Sweden, Washington, D.C.; Marshall Westover, Vienna, Va.; Judy Wilder, Beverly Hills, Calif.

# Picture credits

The sources for the illustrations in this book are listed below. Credits from left to right are separated by semicolons, from top to bottom by dashes. Cover: John Neubauer. 4: Michael Young. 6: John Neubauer. 9: Drawing by Geo. Price, © 1939, 1967 The New Yorker Magazine, Inc. 10, 11: Dr. Mark Jaffe, College of Arts and Sciences, Ohio University. 15: Charles R. Belinky, from Photo Researchers, Inc. 16: Pamela Harper. 17: John Neubauer; Pamela Harper—Pamela Harper (2); Guy Burgess. 18: Guy Burgess. 20, 21: Drawings by Kathy Rebeiz. 24: Entheos. 27-37: Drawings by Kathy Rebeiz. 39: John Neubauer. 40: © Jaime Ardiles-Arce. 41: John J. Smith. 42, 43: Richard Jeffery. 44, 45: Tom Tracy; Richard Jeffery. 46: Henry Groskinsky. 47: John Neubauer. 48: Pamela Harper. 49-51: John Neubauer. 52: Richard Jeffery. 54-57: Drawings by Kathy Rebeiz. 59: John Neubauer. 60, 61: John Neubauer; Pamela Harper; Richard Jeffery—John Neubauer (2). 62: Tom Tracy. 65: Drawing by Kathy Rebeiz. 66: John Neubauer. 68-75: Drawings by Kathy Rebeiz. 77, 78: Henry Groskinsky. 79: John Neubauer—Henry Groskinsky (2). 80: Henry Groskinsky. 81: John Neubauer. 82, 83: Henry Groskinsky. 84: Charles Phillips; John Neubauer. 85-87: John Neubauer. 88: Illustration by Eduardo Salgado. 90-145: Artists for encyclopedia illustrations listed in alphabetical order: Adolph E. Brotman, Richard Crist, Susan M. Johnston, Mary Kellner, Gwen Leighton, Trudy Nicholson, Allianora Rosse, Eduardo Salgado. 146, 147: Maps by Adolph E. Brotman.

# Index

160